A Long Journey to Joy

A Long Journey to Joy

◆

A Memoir of a Recovery

Yonah Klem, Ed. D.

iUniverse, Inc.
New York Bloomington

Copyright © 2009 by Yonah Klem, Ed. D.

All rights reserved. No part of this book may be used or reproduced by any means, graphic, electronic, or mechanical, including photocopying, recording, taping or by any information storage retrieval system without the written permission of the publisher except in the case of brief quotations embodied in critical articles and reviews.

iUniverse books may be ordered through booksellers or by contacting:

iUniverse
1663 Liberty Drive
Bloomington, IN 47403
www.iuniverse.com
1-800-Authors (1-800-288-4677)

Because of the dynamic nature of the Internet, any Web addresses or links contained in this book may have changed since publication and may no longer be valid. The views expressed in this work are solely those of the author and do not necessarily reflect the views of the publisher, and the publisher hereby disclaims any responsibility for them.

ISBN: 978-0-595-53084-7 (sc)
ISBN: 978-0-595-63140-7 (ebook)

Printed in the United States of America

iUniverse rev. date: 11/05/2009

Exile contains redemption within itself, as a seed contains the fruit.
The Gerer Rebbe

In Memory of

Ruth Lorraine Fisher
Mollie Opper Klem
Phyllis Carpenter

Contents

PROLOGUE xv

EXILE

Beginning 3

After The War 6

Dancing 10

Adolescence 16

Secrets 20

Boys 23

Failure 26

Being Jewish 28

Writing 31

Music 35

Buddha 36

WANDERING

College 41

Los Angeles 45

University Of Wisconsin 48

Meeting Russell 51

The L-Shaped Room 54

Sonia 58

Russell's Father Dies 62

Pregnant With Jonathan 63

Moving To Naperville 65

Experimental Drugs 69

Jeremy 71

Europe 73

Plan Commission 76

The Jewish Community 77

The First Ten Years Of Marriage 79

Collapse 82

Hospital 86

Home Again 88

Being Slippery 90

Shostakovich 92

Meditation: A Beginning 93

A New Name 94

A Movement Meditation 96

My Father's Heart Attacks 99

Young Man Interrupted 101

Dancing With Francis 103

Palo Alto, California 105

Dancing With Nurit And Ehud 110

Jewish Life 113

Back To Naperville 114

Shame-Based Family 119

Spirituality 122

Exams 124

You Must Kill Pride 127

Judaism And Meditation 129

My Mother And Mother-In-Law 130

DEEPENING

1987 135

James 140

First Memories 142

Working With James 145

I Can't Ask For Help 147

A Major Production 149

Blessings 152

Meditation Interrupted 154

Critic 155

Friends 157

Complete Memories..160

Mikvah: A Pool Of Purification...164

My Mother's Death 166

Kaddish..170

Softening...172

Father Without Mother...173

Something Coming..175

Cutting Off Contact 178

The Big Room 180

Practicing 183

Goals...185

The Party, 1991...187

Expressing More..188

Crying...191

Noticing Change..194

Laughter..195

THE DARK TIME OF THE MOON

In The Middle...199

Teshuvah, Or Return..201

Spiritual Path Expanded 203

Killing Pride Revisited..205

Killing Pride The Jewish Way 207

Mysticism And My Mistakes 208

Chesed 211

Voluntary And Involuntary Suffering 212

Heartbreak 214

Acceptance 217

Jewish Teachings On Acceptance 219

Self-Acceptance 221

What Is Mine Is Mine 223

Passion And Pleasure 224

Jewish Passion 227

Wanting And Needing 229

Choosing Life 231

My Father's Death 236

My Sister And Brother 242

My Parents Are Gone 243

A Story 245

NOT THE END

Changing Paradigms 249

Dancing Ends And Meditation Increases 254

Depression And God 256

    The Vashti Group...257

    Jewish Meditation 258

    Chochmat Halev..264

    Labyrinth 267

WORKS CITED 271

ACKNOWLEDGMENT OF PERMISSION TO QUOTE.........273

ACKNOWLEDGMENTS 275

PROLOGUE

"Why can't you be happy?" my mother would often say, with some amount of concern. "Look on the bright side of things." She, herself, never looked bright and cheery when she said this.

In the years I lived at home, she repeatedly told me there wasn't anything wrong.

But there was something wrong. From a very early age, without thought or design, I had learned to space out and numb myself so I could continue to pretend that I was happy. The toxic fumes of the traumas in my life leaked out anyway, choking me, while my mother insisted it was just post-nasal drip.

Her life's work was attending to my father's happiness, which meant doing her best to keep discord of any kind away from him. My troubles didn't fit into her plan.

I tried to avoid my mother's exhortations to happiness; they were too painful for me. When she gave her little pep talks, I disappeared into an interior "someplace else." I never responded to her at these times; I think she assumed my silence meant I agreed with her.

I spent most of my life trying to avoid disturbing my parents with my personal melodrama while trying to look present and accounted for. I cultivated the arts of indirection, denial, and obfuscation (big words were part of my strategy). I buried what I was covering up so well that the sources of my distress were completely hidden, even from myself. It helped to keep things quiet at home, at least in my corner.

As I found ways to heal during the three decades after I left home, I learned that most of my struggles and suffering were the result of mistaken beliefs. I mistakenly thought that I was flawed beyond repair and beyond even God's forgiveness. I also mistakenly thought that I was entirely in charge of my parents' lives and happiness.

A Jewish mystic is intent on forming a deep attachment to God. I think this attachment is something I desired for a long time before I had words to describe it, before I knew there was such a thing as a Jewish mystic. However, my spiritual and psychological mistakes ensured my separation from God and from other people in my life until I learned to correct them.

I am presenting my story so that others with similar struggles and suffering might learn and take hope from my experience, as I learned and took hope from those who came before me. With this book, the gifts I received in the process of my own healing can now be sent back into the world for those who need them. The most astonishing gift was my discovery of how beautiful this life actually is.

But how can I tell this tale after a lifetime of perfecting the art of arranging my words so they never told the most important story, a drama of betrayal, incest, and sexual abuse with an unexpected ending? The pages that follow contain the answer to this question.

My earliest recollection is of an event that occurred when I was about two. During the last months of World War II, my father was stationed in Texas, where he was in training to be a bomber navigator. My mother and I lived near his army base in a compound of small apartments in one-story buildings that all opened onto a large, dusty yard.

One afternoon, my parents and I and several other adults went on an outing to a nearby river. The river was very shallow, and I remember wading in it while the adults visited. I was old enough to know the word for river and to appreciate its remarkable shallowness. Even in the middle the water only came up to my ankles. I recall feeling rather bold and aware that no one told me to stop or came to get me.

At some point I saw the horses—three, perhaps four, riderless horses cantering up to the opposite shore. One was very dark brown, one much lighter, and the others some intermediate color. They paused. They looked around. They dipped their heads and drank. And I watched amazed. I watched and forgot about the adults. I saw how very big the horses were, but I forgot (I have always recalled the scene in this way) how very small I was. I watched until they finished drinking, and they walked off.

This sequence of images remained vivid throughout my life. It is only in recent years that I realized the scene with the horses was a moment of wonder and awareness that I was part of something infinitely more than my small self.

It must not have been long afterwards that the war was over and we all moved back to Chicago to my grandparents' apartment. It was there that the bad things began for which I had no vocabulary. It was there that I refined the art of putting aside the wild sensations in my body, along with the confusion and the fear. I hid them all so my distress would not disturb me and I would not disturb my mother. I "forgot" what happened to me. But I never forgot the horses or the perfect moment when I stood in a shallow river.

EXILE

BEGINNING

I was born at Edgewater Hospital on the north side of Chicago the morning after an intense January snowstorm, in the middle of World War II. I was named Toby after my father's mother's mother. My mother told me they chose that name because it could work for either a boy or a girl. I was planned for and wanted as the first grandchild on my mother's side and the second on my father's.

Both of my grandfathers immigrated to the United States to avoid being drafted into the Russian Army, whose agents often kidnapped Jewish boys for twenty-five-year tours of duty. My mother's mother came to America when she was thirteen to work and to bring her family out of the poverty of their small Eastern European village. My father's mother refused to talk about why she left or what she left behind, except to say that her family wasn't poor.

My parents met at a Halloween party when she was fifteen and he was sixteen. Both of my mother's parents were tailors, so her Little Bo Peep costume must have been fabulous. I don't remember the description of my father's costume. After first meeting my father, my mother continued to date other boys, but my father wanted only her. They married five years later on Halloween weekend of 1939. I've seen the short 16mm film someone took of their wedding. Both of them were beautiful, especially my mother in a slender, silky dress, holding lilies-of-the-valley among the other blossoms of her wedding bouquet.

My parents' first big financial decision was to get a piano. I came several years later. The piano was important to my mother. She was talented enough to have been a professional musician, but I never knew her to perform for anyone except herself. When she wasn't having trouble with a piece and berating herself, when she just played, she was wonderful. I remember at age seven or eight lying on the living room couch as the sound of Chopin magically filled the room. At such moments she was oblivious of me, and yet those times seemed intimate and precious.

The standard infant-care wisdom when I was born called for inflexibly scheduled feedings. My mother later told me that she would often stand outside of my room, weeping, as she watched me cry and call out with hunger, crying until I gave up because it wasn't time to be fed. In another story, I heard about her boiling oatmeal water for my formula and hand washing my baby clothes. She worked hard at motherhood.

For as long as I can remember during my childhood, a fleeting look of worry sometimes flashed across my mother's face when she looked at me. What had I done? Growing up, I was sure the look was due to something about me. I was in my fifties before I understood that she was afraid of me. Perhaps I disturbed her image of a happy, harmonious family; perhaps her fear was about something else I'll never know. The last time I saw her conscious before she died, in a moment when we were alone, I began to speak to her. She looked up at me, tightened her eyes, and frowned a bit. The look had never changed.

My father was drafted the summer after I was born, when he was twenty-six. Most of the time after that, my mother and I lived with her parents, Libby and Sol, and her younger sister, Sarah, in a three-bedroom apartment on Rockwell Street on Chicago's north side.

Sometime after my father became a lieutenant in the Army Air Corps we were able to live closer to his bases: once in Georgia, once in a hotel on the ocean in Florida, and once in a small apartment in Texas. Though we lived nearby, he had to stay with his unit on base and not with us.

The day before my father's unit was to ship out to Europe, he came down with impetigo. He was quarantined for a week, during which the war in Europe ended. Sometime in the middle of May 1945, when I wasn't quite two and a half, he came home, wanting to be loved by his two girls, one of whom wasn't quite sure who he was.

When I was near fifty, I remembered this time and wrote in my journal with the voice of a young child:

Mommy says I have to be a good daughter and love my daddy. But he squeezes too hard. He's scared and nervous underneath. I don't like it when he holds me. He gets upset when I want him to stop. He says I have to love him. I don't like him. He asks Mommy what is the matter with me. I don't think he likes me, either. He hurts me sometimes when he squeezes too hard. He pulls my hair. He says he likes my curls, so he plays with my hair and pulls it. I try to push his hands away, and he gets unhappy, and he feels bad, and I can feel his bad feeling all over. I want to cry, but then there will be more of his bad feeling. He is still tangled in my hair. It hurts where he is still pulling it. Maybe he doesn't know it hurts. There is so much bad feeling coming from him. I am scared of all this feeling. I don't want to cry. I don't know how to make him stop. I don't like the bad feeling. I need someone to help me. My mommy looks at us and talks to daddy and tries to make his bad feeling go away. She tells me that daddy is just playing, that I should be with him and love him because he is my daddy. Now, I am all full of bad feeling. He puts me down. I want to go away.

Did this really happen exactly as I wrote it? I have no way to know, but it is entirely consistent with the atmosphere in our household: my father telling me how a good daughter should be with her daddy; his doing what he wanted, no matter how inappropriate or painful; his letting me know how hurt he was if I squirmed or complained; and my mother always placating him or telling me that he was actually playful and loving and I should be having fun.

AFTER THE WAR

In the immediate aftermath of the war, everyone in my mother's family lived (at least for a while) in the Rockwell Street apartment: my teenaged aunt Sarah, my uncle Abe and aunt Deb and their two sons (before they permanently moved to Los Angeles), my grandparents, my father, my mother, my baby sister, Judi (who was born in January 1946), and me. Other people, who were not members of the family, came and stayed briefly.

There were times, perhaps when the bedrooms were unusually crowded, when I slept in the dining room on some chairs pushed together. I have always had a vivid and visual memory of lying awake in the dining room one particular night when I wasn't yet three. I watched the stormy shadows of the trees outside the window silently jerk back and forth, aware of being dry and warm and terrified at the same time. What was missing for almost fifty more years was who else was in the room, and what he was doing there, and why I was so frightened.

In the spring after I was four, my family finally moved into our own apartment on the third floor of a building that had been built by my father's parents at 4815 N. Bernard Street, about a mile west of Rockwell Street. The dark brick building had a single, six-room apartment on each floor and a tiny, three-room apartment in the basement that opened into the vestibule.

When my grandparents built the building in 1923, the original Swedish community of Albany Park still had occasional small farms nearby with chickens and goats. In 1947 the neighborhood was entirely urban. The Bernard Street building sat along an alley that separated the commercial properties along Lawrence Avenue, just to the south, from the residential areas to the north. Directly across the alley were the National Bank of Albany Park and an empty lot next to it. Down the length of the block were much older houses, some dating to the earliest days of the neighborhood. At the north end of the block was a large apartment complex on one side of the street and Temple Beth Israel on the other.

By the time we moved to Bernard Street, the neighborhood had become overwhelmingly Jewish as the great west-side Jewish community had emptied out into the south and north sides of Chicago after World War II. It was the sort of place where many of the public schools were closed for all of the major Jewish holidays because there were too few non-Jewish children to justify the expense of keeping the buildings open and staffed. It didn't matter how observant anyone was—almost everyone in the neighborhood was Jewish.

My family was on the nonobservant side of the spectrum. All of my grandparents may have been Orthodox by default in the old country, but they left their Orthodoxy behind when they stepped off the boat. The only Jewish holiday we celebrated was Passover, the great telling of my tribe's trek to freedom. The telling was always short and the feast lavish. We never had a Christmas tree, but our Hanukah presents were wrapped in paper with Santas and wreaths and were usually delivered the morning of December 25.

The September before I turned five, I started Sunday school at Temple Beth Israel at the end of the block. For the ten years I went to religious school, the curriculum was a boring mix of Bible stories and information about the Jewish holidays that my family mostly didn't celebrate.

Was God in the mix? I don't remember, but I doubt it. I don't recall God on the syllabus at Sunday school. No one in my family talked about God, although I do recall one exception when I was about ten.

I was standing in our kitchen, facing the big window that looked out onto the rooftops and crowns of the trees all the way to the end of the block, staring hard at the big yellow-brick apartment building there, probably trying to blunt the effects of my mother's anger with me in that moment. I no longer have any idea what she was scolding me about. I wasn't a very difficult or willful child, more likely to lie or be sneaky in my rebellious moments than confrontational.

That day, with exasperation she assured me that God was watching and knew what a bad girl I was. I don't know if she believed what she said. I remember this because it was such a strange thing to say.

My father lived most of his life in his father's building from the time it was built, when he was five, until it came down in the early 1970s to make way for a parking lot for the new Albany Park Bank building. All the years that I lived there, the Bernard Street building was a family building: my father's parents, Anna and Tom, on the first floor; my father's sister, Sophie, and her family on the second; and us on top. Various other families rented the tiny basement apartment over the years.

Family members kept their distance despite the physical proximity. After my mother died, I asked my aunt about her impressions of my mother. The two couples had lived on Bernard Street, and later in a two-flat about a half-mile further north, almost their entire adult lives. When I was growing up, they got together several times a week for a visit over coffee and cake at the end of a day. Nevertheless, my aunt replied that she didn't really know my mother, which I found astonishing.

My father worked at least forty-eight hour, six-day weeks in the hardware store his father owned near the corner of Belmont and Cicero. As I entered adolescence, I heard him telling my mother about his frustration that my grandfather never let him try anything new that might improve their business. This must have been true because, by the time I was fifteen, the store could no longer support two families. My father found a job as a clerk in another hardware store, and my mother went to work as a secretary.

My mother tried to be a model housewife in her ironed housedresses, although she didn't wear high heels as housewives did in the advertising of the day. I imagine we could have stepped out of a TV commercial as the five of us—my brother was born in 1949—piled into our Chevy for a Sunday afternoon drive. We looked good, which I think was the main goal.

My mother worked hard to make us all look good by being a perfect mother. She stayed up late to get all of the ironing done; she cooked and cleaned; she made sure her hair was combed before going out to shop; and she reminded us frequently what an effort she was putting forth on our behalf. Her measure of success was whether or not we looked happy.

Preparing meals was a big part of her idea of perfection. She was a good cook, who had learned her skills from her mother. She made many of her mother's dishes, including meatloaf extended with oats and vegetables, brisket smothered with onions and carrots and prunes, desserts with every dinner, and occasionally a breakfast concoction of oatmeal mixed with eggs that had sometimes made her throw up when she was a schoolgirl. My brother and sister and I didn't like the oatmeal either, but we ate it to avoid her attempts to make us feel guilty for ruining her day by complaining. I think she also learned from her mother that her job was to do what she thought was best for the family whether they liked it or not.

My mother baked cakes and cookies from the *Old Settlement Cookbook* and often decorated them with fanciful frosting designs. She made fancy, multilayered Jell-O molds, especially for the themed birthday parties she threw. Martha Stewart would have approved.

We children were expected to enjoy what she made. If we didn't, my mother frowned and appeared to sink a little, looking as if we had deliberately wounded her.

This persisted long after we left home. My sister, my husband, Russell, and I all stopped eating red meat in our thirties. The three of us often told her that we preferred not to have meat when we came to visit. Even so, she would continue to serve her beautiful brisket. We might take a bite or two to be polite and then say, "No thank you." My mother invariably looked surprised and dismayed. After all, she had spent a great deal of effort making this wonderful meal just for us. How could we not want to eat it? The message was on her face, but she was silent as she continued to serve out the meal. I tried to ignore her and the nauseating mix of anger and guilt stirring around in my stomach.

Money always seemed tight. My mother checked her receipts carefully to make sure every penny was well spent. There was enough money for necessities, but not for luxuries. Opera, theater, and the ballet were considered necessities. My parents bought season tickets to the ballet and the opera. When I was old enough I went to the ballet regularly, too. We sat in or near the very last row at the top of the highest balcony of the Civic Opera House, but we were there.

In the early years of grade school, at the beginning of each school year, my mother took me shopping in the big department stores downtown. She always wore a smart hat, gloves, and high-heeled shoes, and I'm sure I was similarly dressed up. We took the El and went to Wieboldt's, in the center of the State Street shopping district. It wasn't as expensive as Marshall Fields to the north or as cheap as Sears and Goldblatt's to the south. We ate lunch in a restaurant before the adventure was over and we returned home with our packages. These were great events, times when I had her happy and with me for the whole afternoon.

When we children were young, my mother took parenthood classes. I still have some of her old books from them. I suspect she didn't find the answers she was seeking. She likely didn't know what she was looking for, only that something was missing. She continually berated herself and implored us to do as she said and not as she did.

I have only sketchy memories of most of my grade-school years. I recall some small amount of pride when we filled our wagons full of newspapers for the paper drive during the Korean War, although I was never certain where all the paper was going or why. We got our first television on my sister's fifth birthday, one week after I turned eight, and watched Hopalong Cassidy and Captain Video regularly after school. On Sunday evenings, my mother often made a light supper, which she served in the living room so we could watch *The Ed Sullivan Show*. I remember the duck-and-cover drills we did during grade school and watching films of atomic-bomb tests. I couldn't really imagine the horror we were being prepared for.

School was a place where the rules were clear, and I did well. Grades were straightforward and unambiguous. They clearly said whether or not I was doing things right, which I liked.

DANCING

My most vivid childhood memories are of dancing. As a very little girl I loved to dance around the Rockwell Street apartment. Perhaps my mother accompanied me on the piano, or perhaps I danced to a little tune in my head. My mother and grandmother liked my twirling and leaping. They called me a little dancer and noted that my aunt Sarah was a dancer, too, although she had only danced when she was in college. I had to wait to become a real dancer until I turned seven in January 1950, when I was finally old enough for lessons at Edna L. McRae's ballet studio.

For my first lesson, my mother and I took the El downtown and then walked over to the Fine Arts Building at 410 S. Michigan. We entered through a rough-hewn arch surrounded by ornate stonework into a building that had not changed much since the late nineteenth century when it was built. Lining one long wall of the lobby was a bank of elevators that were decorated with elaborate metal work and manned by operators.

We took an elevator to the third floor, and then walked a short distance to the right, past the marble stairway, to the small studio where the youngest beginners were taught. It seemed to be a very large room to me then, perhaps partly because of the enormous windows that overlooked Michigan Avenue, Grant Park, and the lake beyond. I was very excited.

The class of seven-year-old girls was taught by Miss McRae's assistant, Miss D'vrey, a young woman with dark, thick hair neatly pulled back into a bun. She wore a long, black, swirly skirt over a black leotard. The other girls had been taking class for four months already. Most of them knew how to place their feet and arms in first or fifth position; they knew about pointing their toes for *battement tendu* and *ronde de jambe*; and they knew some of the other names for the steps. I vividly recall how hard I tried to remember everything and how impossible it was to keep up with so many new things. I was eager enough not to be dissuaded by my frustration.

Miss D'vrey was gentle and patient. I went back week after week and in time caught up with the rest of the class. These were glorious days, when just my mother and I would set out on the El on Saturday mornings, leaving my father at work and my brother and sister with their cousins on the second floor. The mothers were expected to attend the classes, take notes, and assist the children in practicing.

The year I turned nine, I was ready to take class with Miss McRae, herself, in the main studio on the fifth floor. Shortly after that, Miss McRae banished the mothers from class, insisting that we were all old enough to come downtown by ourselves and take our own notes. And so we did. My mother rode down with me several times to teach me what to look for and what to do. The first time I went downtown by myself I felt a little nervous and grown up all at once. I panicked momentarily when I got off the train one stop too soon, but quickly recognized where I was, and went on my way. After that first time, I never got lost again. In time I became as well acquainted with downtown, especially the eastern side of it, as I was with my own neighborhood.

In the middle of that year, we were sent to Kling's Theatrical Shoe Company for our first pair of pointe shoes. Kling's workshop and showroom were on the third or fourth floor of an old building on Wabash near the Palmer House Hotel, a few blocks north of the Fine Arts Building. When the elevator doors opened, the store, fully visible through a plate glass window, was directly opposite. It was a serious place where the most serious dancers in the city went to get their shoes. The walls were a faded, pale color. They looked like they had been last painted when the building was built. What mattered more to me was that they were covered with dozens of signed photographs from dancers who had bought their shoes from Mr. Kling.

Pointe shoes are never comfortable. They have a hard tip and are fitted small for the purpose of helping the dancer balance as she works to achieve an illusion of weightlessness while standing and maneuvering in unnatural positions with grace and agility. The dancer's toes are slightly protected from the hard surface of the end of the shoe by stuffing the end with cotton wool. To learn to dance *en pointe*, which was the dream of most of the nine-year-olds at the studio including me, was to learn masochism. At first I didn't like the awkwardness and pain of either walking or dancing in such strange shoes, but I loved the idea of learning to dance like the ballerinas I'd seen. I already knew something about ignoring pain, so for me this was just another pain to disregard. I enjoyed my increasing skill.

The main studio was a large rectangular room, with floor-to-ceiling mirrors almost entirely down one length. Opposite the mirrors was a row of tall windows that faced the well of the building. Double rows of barres where we did our technique exercises were attached to the wall surface between the windows. Mr. Heinze, the accompanist, sat at the piano in one corner of the far wall. The floor was unvarnished wood, which Miss McRae dampened with a large watering can to reduce the slipperiness.

Although she never spoke of a professional career, I always assumed that Miss McRae had once been a dancer in a ballet company. There was a large photograph of her, posed *en pointe* in a mid-length gauzy costume out of *Giselle*, that hung just beyond the reception area, where the small hallway turned toward the dressing rooms and the studio beyond. She took it as her responsibility to turn out professional dancers, and she wasn't interested in students who didn't have enough ambition or talent. Although I didn't have much more ambition than to keep up with my studio friends, I must have had enough talent to keep her interested in my progress.

At the end of each year, Miss McRae sat with my mother and me, and eventually just me, announcing what classes I would be expected to take in the fall. My mother was cowed by her and always said yes. I was informed, not consulted, but I didn't object either.

In many ways Miss McRae's studio was one of my favorite places to be because that was where most of my friends were. This was also a world away from my family—a world that increasingly belonged to me. My father paid for my lessons without comment, although it must have been a substantial amount by the end.

In the last two years at Miss McRae's studio, when I was twelve and thirteen, I was finally in the advanced classes, along with my friends. On Mondays and Thursdays after school, and on Saturdays, I took ballet, pointe, tap, and character classes.

Miss McRae never put on recitals. Several times a year, students in her advanced ballet and pointe classes learned a piece of classical choreography, which each of us, in turn, performed for her and the rest of the class. My mother helped me prepare for these events by renting space with a piano in a nearby park field house where I could practice with her playing the music. I was diligent in this work, because I would be dancing in front of a very critical audience. This was, however, about the only time I practiced. Some resentful part of me refused to be as ambitious for myself as Miss McRae was.

As part of this process, Miss McRae taught us how to mark up our music and explain to the pianist just how we wanted it played. When it was our turn to perform for the class, we each had to explain to Mr. Heinze our preferences, just as we had been taught. After we danced for the class, Miss McRae critiqued the performance. This was all to prepare us for going to auditions.

We also performed in plays, in the annual Nutcracker performances at the Opera House, and for conventions as soon as we were accomplished and old enough to do so. The dancers in high school joined the union and got paid for their work. We younger girls practiced so we would be ready when the older girls moved on. Between classes and the rehearsals afterwards, I danced about fifteen hours a week.

Because rehearsals lasted until nine on the weeknights, my father came downtown after he closed up the store to pick me up. I offered to have him drive a few of the other girls home, which he generously agreed to do. He was a very handsome, charming man who loved the attention. I felt very pleased to sit in the front seat next to him as he ferried my friends all over the north side of the city.

Most of my studio friends were Catholic-school girls. There was plenty of talk in the dressing room about the nuns and their austerities and strictness. I had seen nuns, who in those days still wore medieval habits, but knew nothing about them beyond what I heard in the dressing room. None of the girls seemed to like them, and yet, I found the idea of the nuns fascinating. I imagined they lived a protected, safe life, which seemed very attractive. I gave no thought to why I might want to live a protected safe life. Christianity and its theology held no interest for me, but the nuns did. I often thought that if Judaism had nuns, I would want to be one.

On Saturdays, there was a break in the advanced classes so Miss McRae could teach a younger class. This was time for a run down to the lobby to buy candy and soft drinks from the Fine Arts Theater candy stand. One day, properly dressed with a light robe over my practice clothes, I went downstairs, picked out the candy I wanted, and then discovered that I didn't have enough money with me.

A woman, about the age of my mother, stood nearby waiting to make her purchase. She offered me a dime to pay for the candy.

"I can't take it because it isn't right to take money from strangers," I said. *Or to talk to them either*, I thought.

She urged me to take it anyway.

"You won't be able to repay me," she said, "but you can give a dime to someone else who needs it along the way."

That sounded all right. I can't remember the candy, but I never forgot her words. Today I think of her as my first spiritual teacher.

Miss McRae was harsh and demanding, and she was often mean and bitter. She was generally so critical of my dancing that I thought I had no talent at all. She was equally hard with all of us. She yelled at us when we were clumsy or forgot the combination we were doing, called us names, and threw us out of class because our hair bows weren't ironed. Once in a moment of frustration during the summer term, she smacked a girl's sunburned shoulder.

No one ever cried or said anything that might increase her wrath. I learned to ignore her tone, at least up to a point.

My friends from the studio, who were more important to me than my school friends, balanced her criticism and ill temper. I rarely felt happier in those two years than in the crowded dressing room with clothes thrown around or shoved into our personal boxes on the high shelf, all of us smelly with sweat and the very cheap cologne which we applied liberally to cool off in the warmer weather.

At age twelve, we younger students started performing in small amateur theatrical productions. My first performance was in *The Forest Prince*, a children's play put on by the Chicago Park District on April 29 and 30, 1955. Students from McRae's studio provided the ballet interludes.

In addition to learning the dance numbers, in preparation for our first performance we were taken into Miss McRae's private room for lessons in how to apply stage makeup. She also informed us how we were to dress, coming and going: high-heeled shoes, nylon stockings, white gloves, and hats. My father was appalled when told that I would have to get shoes with high (or at least higher) heels when I was so young. When my mother explained to him that this was all in the service of demonstrating that we were proper ladies he relented. I was just very happy to get so dressed up.

The day of the first performance my mother fixed my hair in a proper ballet bun, I dressed in my new shoes and dress, white gloves and a spring hat, and my father drove us to the field house. We dancers brought our own makeup in our dance bags (along with our tights and shiny new pointe shoes), and put on our lipstick and rouge and eyeliner by ourselves. We wore tutus that Miss McRae brought and sparkly ornaments in our hair. When we finally got on stage for our part, I was very excited and competent until the very last moment, when I started to move into the center of the stage instead of off stage as planned. I quickly shifted direction and the dance was over. It was a minor mistake, and no one complained about it later. The excitement didn't wear off nor did the makeup come off until after my family celebrated my performance debut with ice cream afterwards, and we finally went home. The second day, I danced without mistakes and performing was even more fun.

In September 1956, in what was to be my last year with Miss McRae, I sprained my ankle in gym class at school. The sprain was bad enough that I couldn't dance for about a month. As soon as I was able to make it downtown, I was expected to go to every class and rehearsal and to observe and take notes. When I finally joined the class, I was also expected to know exactly what was going on, to fit in seamlessly.

At the first rehearsal I participated in, I got several steps reversed. Miss McRae angrily asked me why I did that. I should have kept my mouth shut. Instead, I muttered something about guessing that I got into a habit. Then she became enraged, even more so than was usual for her, screaming and yelling about my stupidity and incompetence. I was stunned with her rage and her words. I imagine I was hardly breathing. I imagine the rest of the group, standing around this scene, silently watching, as stunned as I was. I don't really know what they were doing, as I tried very hard not to notice them watching my humiliation. I was sure I was as awful as she said. I didn't cry. No one ever cried when she yelled and scolded.

A few days later, I rode the El to the studio, terrified about what to expect. I never considered not going back. I don't recall discussing the matter with my parents. Miss McRae approached me as I entered the studio with what was probably an apology of sorts. I'd never known her to apologize to me or to anyone else. It was too late. I didn't have the courage to quit right then, but I did at the end of the next year's summer session.

I went back briefly a few years later, to try again. Miss McRae invited me in the first day, but she was back to scolding me the second. I went a few more times and then gave up with her for good.

Almost fifty years later, I went back to the Fine Arts Building to check out how accurate my memories about the place actually were. The hall adjacent to the door of what had been Miss McRae's studio held a big plate-glass window. Through the glass I could see that the entire dance studio space had been gutted: all of the interior walls were gone, except for the walls at the far end that enclosed a small washroom. Everything was gone: the wooden floor, on which we had stretched and leapt and turned; the mirrors, in which we scrutinized our straining bodies or glanced at someone else hoping they remembered the combination we had forgotten; the benches where observers sat; the dressing rooms. Everything was gone except the washroom and the outer walls and windows of the perimeter. It all looked dusty and deserted, as if the demolition had taken place a long time ago and no one had been inside since.

As I stared through the window I wondered about this gutted space, cleared of all its memory markers. The past in this place was completely done, finished, over. *Now it is ready for something new,* I thought, *as I am, too.*

ADOLESCENCE

During my early teenage years, I liked the idea of life without Edna McRae in it. One of the first things I did was to have my hair cut in a fashionably short style. As a dancer I needed long enough hair to pull back into a bun to keep it off my face. When I wasn't dancing, my hair tended to be a messy mass of thick waves. Now my hair could be short like the other girls at school.

Because I spent so much time at the studio, I had been moving into adolescence with almost no time for just hanging out after school. No one else I knew was as involved in after-school lessons and activities as I was. The modern practice of over scheduling students was almost unknown in the 1950s. My dance and school worlds were completely separate, with friends in both but without intimate friends in either. I was aware that I had no real close friends, but I was busy enough with school and studio not to be bothered by this.

At first, with more time available, I often felt awkward with the other girls even though I'd known some of them since kindergarten. Now, for the first time in years, I could go to Saturday afternoon birthday parties, or just walk up and down Lawrence Avenue after school the same way teenagers cruise the shopping malls of America today. To be in a small group giggling our way down the street past the delicatessen and the butcher and the clothing shops was a delicious kind of pleasure.

In Chicago at that time, grade schools were K-8, with semesters beginning in September and January. I left Miss McRae's studio after the summer session in the middle of eighth grade, so I had one more semester to go before graduating from grade school in January 1957. The graduating class was at the top of the status hill at school. There was a rising sense of excitement as we approached going to high school. I luxuriated in my new free time. Some of the awkwardness eased as I spent more time doing what the other kids had been doing all along. It was a happy time.

For the winter graduation ceremony, I wore a short-sleeved, light colored dress with a full, bouffant skirt in the style of the time. The boys wore white, long-sleeved shirts, dark blue pants and dark shoes. We all wore our school color ribbons, dark blue and white, pinned on the left side of our dress or shirt.

Ninety-nine of us sat on the stage of the auditorium with the principal. For reasons unknown to me, I had been chosen to give the class speech. I was nervous but pleased and relaxed enough to joke around with some of the other students as I waited through the program until I was to give my speech. From my dance performance experiences I was accustomed to being in front of large audiences. I practiced until I was confident about knowing all my lines, and it went well. After the graduation my mother produced a beautiful cookies and cake reception in our apartment for my relatives and a few friends. Then it was done.

High school started the following Monday.

Roosevelt High School was overwhelmingly Jewish. Most of the non-Jews were from working class families who lived south of Montrose Avenue. The south-of-Montrose boys wore their straight hair combed back in what was called a duck-tail, the hair from each side meeting ideally in a straight line down the back of their heads. Even with pomade, duck-tails took some doing to keep in place, so the boys often had a comb in hand as they attended to their hair. They also wore tighter pants and shirts than the Jewish boys did (no jeans were allowed in those days except when performing hard chores). The south-of-Montrose girls wore tight skirts topped with tight sweaters and generally a lot of makeup. It seemed they all smoked and drank (so I heard), and they seemed slightly dangerous.

In truth, I'm sure not all of the south-of-Montrose kids looked as sexy and rebellious as the ones I remember, nor were all of the Jewish kids so prim and proper. I doubt that the non-Jewish kids actually got into trouble any more than we did. However, they could have been from a foreign country; the two groups had nothing to do with each other. Most of the Jewish students came from homes where education was highly valued. Most of them went to college, but not all. I don't remember any of the south-of-Montrose kids in the honors classes I took, but that may be a faulty memory; they were more likely to be found in home-economics or shop classes.

There were Jewish social clubs in high school, separate ones for girls and boys, high-school versions of sororities and fraternities. The girls clubs were primarily a venue to talk about who was popular and who was dating whom, to compare clothes, and to organize parties with boys clubs. I caught on quickly that social status required being in a social club, so I was delighted when, soon after my freshman semester began, I was asked to join one of the clubs.

After a few months of meetings and parties, a sizeable group of the girls in the club I belonged to suddenly quit and started another club. It was clear enough to those of us left behind that we were not wanted. Today, I would say we were not cool enough. It was obvious to me that I was flawed in some way I couldn't define.

I remember crying bitterly to my mother as she ironed. She listened sympathetically but didn't say much. It was so unfair. It was so mean. It was so permanent.

I don't remember what the other girls did, those who had been left behind as I was. None of them were actually friends I could (or would) talk to about something as painful as this. I think we drifted away from each other, defeated. Or maybe it was just I who took this event as evidence that I was irredeemably unacceptable.

Beginning in the early fall of 1957, in the middle of my freshman year, I became very depressed. I read about teenagers having a rough time with all of the changes in their lives, but I was sure no one else felt as awful as I did. I put on a lively enough act in front of people at school and a suitably happy face at home around my parents, but it was more and more of an effort.

It was around this time that I began thinking of suicide, not so much in the sense of having a plan or doing anything suicidal, but more just wishing I were dead. Social life was daunting and very discouraging. I couldn't keep my moodiness hidden all the time at home, and my mother took it as a personal affront. My father sometimes joined her in scolding me for my self-centeredness. I was not actually a danger to myself because I didn't act on any of my thoughts, but in quiet hours, sitting alone in my bedroom with the door shut, I thought more and more about dying.

I paid a lot of attention to what "normal" girls (or at least the popular ones) were doing. I was careful about the kinds of clothes I wore, but it often seemed that my outfits just didn't look as good or as fashionable as theirs. The popular girls seemed to spend a lot of time giggling and talking about boys and clothes and parties. None of them took school as seriously as I did, nor were they interested in music or ballet or reading as I was. We actually had very little in common, but they seemed so comfortable with themselves, at ease and happy. That's what I wanted.

At any perception of danger of being humiliated I fled into my interior "someplace else" like a gopher into her hole at the first hint of a hawk overhead. The move was fast and unconscious. It may have protected me from the pain of feeling excluded, but it also made me withdrawn and unapproachable. That only added to the "evidence" that I was unacceptable. The idea of dying grew steadily more attractive.

Two classmates became real friends. One was Bonnie, who was twelve when she and her mother moved into a tiny apartment across the street from my bedroom window. She was a serious pianist with many more friends than

I. We often spent time in her apartment or mine talking in a comfortable way about our lives and music. Sometimes we were joined by Evie, a flamboyant girl with a mass of red hair even curlier than mine. Then, the three of us talked about boys and kissing and making out. It was all hypothetical to me, if not to them, but I cherished the chance to at least be in on the conversation.

At the beginning of my first semester in high school, I joined the orchestra and band, and I started learning how to play the flute. In time, I learned to play well enough to be in the concert orchestra and band. I loved playing for football games and rallies, when our fingers froze in the damp autumn winds and our throats grew raw from cheering. We musicians were a crowd of our own, an alternative to the intense social posturing of the clubs and cliques that wasn't working very well for any of us.

In my junior year, the three first-chair flutes, of which I was one, were to play a major role in a Sousa march in the spring concert. I was assigned to play the famous piccolo part. We got matching white dresses with sailor collars, practiced hard, and were a great success.

Several years later, Betsy, the youngest of the trio, committed suicide, taking pills in a motel room in Hyde Park, far from our neighborhood. She was the first person I knew to do what I thought about all the time. I was intrigued about how she got herself to do it more than I was sorry for her.

SECRETS

Toward the end of my freshman year in high school, when I was almost fifteen, I had a genital infection so painful I could barely walk. My mother took me to see Dr. Lash, a gynecologist. Everyone in the waiting room looked at us, peeking up from their magazines from time to time. I couldn't imagine what was so interesting. No one smiled or said anything. Did my mother tell me what was going to happen in the examination room? I don't think so. Somehow, I knew how to lie still and not complain.

Dr. Lash was as unfriendly as the women in the waiting room. He said the infection must have come from sitting on public toilet seats. I didn't tell him that I never sat on public toilet seats. My mother always said they were too unsanitary.

He applied gentian violet, a purple liquid, to the infected area and sent me on my way. I wondered why everyone looked so disapproving, and why I had become so infected, but didn't ask my mother, nor did she speculate out loud.

The answer to that question stayed out of sight a very long time.

I had headaches every day, which I never told anyone about, although they did not subside and disappear until after I married. Years later, I told my therapist that I never had headaches.

"Really?" he asked. Then I remembered that I always had a headache. Today, I think they had to do with trying to keep dreadful secrets from myself so I could keep my distress from disturbing my family. Not disturbing them was the most important thing of all.

I increasingly felt disconnected from my body. We only lived about a block and a half from Roosevelt High School. On the walk to school I often marveled that I could feel my feet on the sidewalk and maybe the breeze on my face, but I could not feel the rest of my body. It was a curious thing not to feel any part of my trunk or upper legs or arms, but I was too numbed out to wonder why.

From the time I was about fifteen, I frequently sat in my room with the door shut and daydreamed about being kidnapped by some men who kept me asleep, and who sometimes allowed me to get up to eat a little something and then put me back to sleep again. At other times of the day, I often replayed the daydream. It felt compelling.

I learned decades later that the daydream had the outlines of truth to it. At least a few times I was taken, if not exactly kidnapped, to a place where a group of men used me. Instead of sleeping I think I expanded my old strategy of hiding in my "someplace else" to the point at which I was as detached from what was happening to my body as it was possible to be.

Just as in deep sleep, I managed to either not notice or remember some things at all, or to sequester some of them so they were completely out of sight until a safer time. In some cases, my memories were not exactly completely out of sight, although I didn't know that at the time. I had strong and strange responses to certain things, which only added to the sense of being crazy. A certain shade of pale green, popular then in institutional and industrial settings—very similar to recent billboards for a popular strong mint—invariably made me anxious and slightly nauseous.

Riding in a car in a slight drizzle with the windshield wipers off so that the drops lingered a bit before they finally slid off, made my skin feel creepy. Certain large men, especially if they resembled Rod Steiger, the actor who played Judd in the movie *Oklahoma*, terrified me.

There was a terrible disparity between what was going on inside of me and my efforts to look untroubled.

My attempts to at least not look unhappy were not always successful. Sometimes I would try to tell my mother how unhappy I was.

"I don't have friends," I said.

"You have plenty of friends," she responded in a helpful tone of voice.

"I'm not pretty enough,"

"Of course you are. You're very pretty," she said with a serious look on her face that made me wonder if she was lying.

"I'm just so unhappy. I don't know why I'm unhappy," I said, slumping in my chair.

"Well, just snap out of it. Stop moping around and look on the bright side of things," she said with her mouth in a slight frown, as she tried to sound encouraging.

"I can't," I would say, slumping even further.

If I kept this up, eventually she stopped trying to convince me that I was wrong and she started to collapse.

"Perhaps I've done something wrong," she said talking to herself as much as to me. "I try so hard to be a good mother. I don't know how to help you."

On and on she went about her real and imagined failings.

Finally, I said, "No, you are a good mother. There's nothing wrong with me. I'm just a little moody today. You haven't done anything wrong."

She would lighten a little, and that conversation would finally be over and done. It was not long before I stopped talking to her about anything that really mattered to me.

Sometimes only rounded shoulders and a despondent voice signaled her collapse. Occasionally, she would start to cry, apparently in grief for her failings. Once, in a similar moment with my brother, Sol, who was trying to talk to her about some deep distress in his life, she literally fell against a wall and sobbed.

I wanted to confide in her; I wanted her help. I could barely tolerate her responses on the occasions when I went to her for help. I tried, not always successfully, to avoid subjects that would upset her.

BOYS

By the end of freshman year, most of the girls seemed to be dating, so I thought I should be dating, although I had no prospects.

I had crushes on boys who barely knew I was around. One was a boy I'd known for most of grade school. He had a tough edge to him, and sometimes I fantasized him pushing me around. We often ended up in groups of boys and girls who went to the movies at the same time—these outings were not planned enough to say we went together. He never paid more attention to me than anyone else. Other boys were very attractive and smart, so I thought, but I barely talked to them.

I joined B'nai Brith Girls, a Jewish girls organization, and briefly dated a boy from AZA, a Jewish group for high-school age boys. He took me to my first dance. My mother tried to tell me that the dress I picked out was really too old for me, but in my eagerness to look sophisticated I insisted on buying it all the same. It was a strapless, gauzy thing that surely required much more of a bosom than I possessed. We went to a fancy place on Michigan Avenue for dinner. I ordered the cheapest thing on the menu for fear that anything else would bankrupt my date. I think I spent the entire evening in a serious attempt to have a wonderful time, but I was probably too intense and not much fun. I didn't get asked out again.

Looking for boys, I joined a Junior Achievement group in another neighborhood, near my grandmother on Rockwell Street. The Junior Achievement movement was an attempt to teach teenagers about business. Our group's adult advisor decided we should manufacture wooden skirt hangers and sell them.

There were in fact more boys than girls in this group. I was far more interested in them than our business project. One of them invited me to a Halloween party with his friends. My mother made me a tall, black witch's hat and costume complete with a small broom. On the way home from a date that had been pleasant enough, he said, "You're Jewish, aren't you?"

"It doesn't have to matter," I said naively.

He didn't say anything, but visibly backed away from me a little. He was polite the rest of the evening and the rest of the time I knew him, but he never called or asked me out again.

I decided I didn't want to spend time doing something I didn't care about with people who were so unlike me, and quit the group.

I joined the Science Club at Roosevelt High School in my sophomore year, when I was fifteen, with a small interest in science but a bigger interest in the fact that the boys far outnumbered the girls. Here, at least, were people with whom I had something in common.

I met Stanley there, a shy, hesitant fellow. He was tall and football-player husky, dark and handsome. He hadn't gone to the same grade school as I, so I knew nothing about him or his family. I thought he was very attractive, and he didn't seem to be going with anyone.

When we started to date I became obsessed with not losing him. I thought about him, it seemed, all of the time. I reviewed every instance he didn't seem to be interested in me every which way I could, to try to be sure I was doing whatever was necessary to keep him.

Did I love him or even like him?

He was attractive and attracted to me, and that was enough. It seemed very important to have a boy friend, and he was my first. It is not an overstatement to say I was terrified of losing him.

In our junior year, we went to our Homecoming dance, held in the school gym. This was a crowded affair with couples from all the grades doing their best to look and behave like the beautiful teens on Dick Clark's *American Bandstand* that we all watched after school. Dick would ask one of the dancers how he liked the last song. The answer was inevitably, "Well, it had a good melody and a really good beat for dancing."

At our Homecoming dance the girls wore dresses and flat shoes, and the boys wore sport jackets. The lights were low, the decorations lent color to every corner, and the rock 'n roll was loud and raucous, except, of course, for the slow dancing songs. Everyone had a class in social dancing as part of eighth-grade gym class, so we all could at least do the jitterbug and foxtrot. Stanley and I were no show offs, but we held each other close during the slow songs.

As we sat on the sidelines talking between dances he started to tell me how much he liked me.

"Does that mean we're going steady?" I asked, overjoyed at the prospect.

As I recall now, he had an unsettled look on his face, as if I'd stumped him with my question. I had my heart set on going steady and ignored (but didn't forget) the look on his face. He didn't say no.

After we had dated for a while, we ended each date making out. We kissed. I know he touched me but I don't remember feeling much. Stanley's hands always stayed on top of my clothes. I don't remember touching him more than holding his hand or hugging or kissing him, lips closed and not too hard. I don't know why he wasn't more sexually aggressive. Perhaps he sensed how reluctant I was. I never said stop. He never asked for more. I never got aroused. I wasn't interested in sex with him or anyone else, but I knew that people my age were supposed to be interested in sex. I was always glad when we stopped whatever we were doing.

FAILURE

My sister Judi was three years younger than I, but it seemed that she moved into her adolescence not long after I did. She was taller and rounder, especially compared to my flat-chested, skinny frame. Judi had lots of friends and dated much earlier than I had. Sometimes at night, when we were in bed in the room we shared, she would tell me about her sexual experimentation, at a time when I could barely get beyond a chaste kiss. It was a one-way conversation. I was jealous of her confidence and her social successes.

She also had a quick tongue and a fast mind. If we got into an argument about something, it seemed she could outwit me every time, so I assumed she was smarter than I was. I hated her for having attributes that I coveted.

Every area of my life seemed to reinforce how inadequate I felt. I started counting the days until I would turn twenty, as if leaving my teens would change my mood.

I mentioned wishing I were older to my father. He said, "You don't want to wish your life away."

That sounded as if it should be wise, but I did want to wish it away.

I think I wished someone would notice and rescue me, but I was good at putting on a happy face and never said anything to anyone. As far as I could tell, no one noticed except my mother from time to time, who told me to snap out of it.

It seemed to me that I was a great disappointment to my mother, although she never exactly said so. That changed one day during the summer I was fifteen. We were in her bedroom talking about something that didn't seem important to me then—I've never remembered what it was. I do remember sitting on the edge of her bed. She was standing, facing me with her back to her bureau; the window was on her right with its brightly lit view of the neighborhood rooftops making a contrast to the darkness in her room.

The topic we were talking about shifted.

"When you decide to watch television, does it ever occur to you to come and see if I need help?" she said in a flat voice. "When you're propped up in your bed reading, why aren't you helping with the laundry? Why don't you ever consider what I need if you have some free time? You never seem to think about anybody but yourself."

Then with deep sadness and resignation in her voice she said, "You are the most selfish, self-centered person I've ever known. I really don't think you will ever change."

I listened, stunned and silent. It was true that I wasn't very helpful around the house unless I was asked. It was also just as true that she rarely asked for help but apparently thought I should just intuit her need.

Her statement that she thought me hopeless devastated me. She had finally put words to her worried looks. It was true that I was a failure as a human being—she said so. As I recall, that was the end of the conversation. I stood up and walked out of her room, down the hall to mine. She stayed where she was, looking sad and silent. I went into my room, closed the door, sat down on the bench by the desk, and thought about dying.

BEING JEWISH

By the ninth and tenth grades of religious school we finally began to talk about subjects that were more interesting to me, like ethics and philosophy. I wanted something more from my teachers but didn't have the courage or the vocabulary to ask, and they didn't deliver. Today, I can say I was hungry then for a spiritual connection, but Reform Jews of the time had excised spirituality out of their curriculum in favor of rationality and logic.

From seventh grade on, our religious school met on Saturday mornings, so we attended the Saturday morning services each week as part of our program. While I was still taking dance class, I had to leave early each week in order to get downtown in time for my tap class.

Our Rabbi, Ernst Lorge, was a stern German intellectual, who frequently admonished us students to be quiet during services and pay attention to the liturgy in the *Union Prayerbook*. No one ever taught us how to pay attention to the liturgy, how to pray, what it meant to pray, and just what was the nature of this deity who seemed to be approachable only with language that was difficult to decipher, even in English. My parents only came to services for the High Holidays, and they never talked about praying. Our religious school teachers primarily taught about the holidays, Jewish history, and Jewish values, not the liturgy or theology.

For my late spring confirmation, the summer I was fifteen, I wore new black patent-leather shoes and a beautiful, flowery dress with stiff crinolines beneath. We girls carried enormous bouquets of peonies. The whole class stood for the entire service. I hoped for nothing less than a divine revelation. The only profound realization at the end was how much my feet hurt. My family celebrated this milestone with a party, inviting everyone in the building and some other relatives. My mother loved to throw parties and "make people happy." My parents and I never talked about what this event might mean to me, my opinions not being relevant to the business of creating a wonderful party.

In the fall, as I watched the congregation from my seat in the High Holiday choir, I noticed people falling asleep during the services. I was deeply disappointed by the hypocrisy of people who professed allegiance to religion but didn't seem to find it important enough to stay awake.

I yearned for something no one else ever talked about, not my family nor my friends nor my teachers. I'd heard the words of the liturgy each week for several years. I yearned for these words to be true, but I doubted that they were.

The God of the liturgy I grew up with was said to be loving and compassionate. I couldn't reconcile that with the constant pain in my life, the reasons for which were incomprehensible.

The God of the liturgy was said to be forgiving. But my mother said I was hopeless. She was the one I had to live with.

The God of the liturgy was said to be steadfast—The Rock of Ages—no matter what. Little in my life was trustworthy. My father was needy one day and arrogant the next, shifting moods and opinions. My mother could support me in dealing with my teenage troubles one moment and be angry with me because I was troubled in the next. The rules shifted without warning, and I was expected to keep up without having been informed about the changes.

The God of the liturgy seemed to be a bad joke. Full of adolescent self-righteousness and some amount of despair, I concluded that religion was a farce. I joined the ranks of what I considered to be right-thinking people and became an atheist, so I thought.

However, I come from a tribe of God wrestlers—that is what the word "Israel" means. In the years that followed, I struggled with my ambivalence and anger at the tradition I thought I had left. I thought about religion and God often; got into debates about whether God exists with anyone interested in talking about it; and felt abandoned when I chose to stay away from High Holiday services.

I got married in the Temple because that was what was expected, and I had no better ideas anyway. After I married, I went to the synagogue that my husband's family attended for the High Holidays. I wanted to be there, but I felt like a hypocrite.

In my early twenties, I came across Max Dimont's book, *Jews, God, and History*. Reading it was a revelation. Dimont was excited about Judaism and Jewish values. Some of the history I knew from Sunday school, but Dimont also described a history of Jewish ideas. I discovered that many of them were familiar and very much what I believed, especially the strong sense of social justice. He also wrote about the long evolution of how Jews understand God as being in history and beyond history—compassionate and just. Dimont's story was much more vivid and rich than anything I had been taught.

For the first time I could see the possibilities of myself in the Jewish world. And yet, if God was a player in history, where was God in my history? God was called a savior and rescuer. So, why hadn't God solved the mysteries of my depression or rescued me from my suffering as I'd asked for so many times? Was I so hopeless and unforgivable that God had given up on me, too?

WRITING

In my late teens I was exposed more and more to poetry and classical literature in the accelerated English classes I took. I got the idea from somewhere that poets were sensitive, suffering artists. Since I was suffering, I embraced writing poetry. This was one place I could express myself without my parents telling me that what I thought and felt wasn't true, that I was just too self-centered, that my thoughts and feelings were more than they could bear.

> I wrote cheerful drivel:
> *I am a dreamer, listen to my dreams*
> *About faraway places and untold schemes.* (1958)
>
> I wrote about my emptiness and despair:
> *I died*
>   *somewhere*
>   *back there*
>   *anywhere.*
>
> *And me*
>   *got lost*
>   *in a*
>   *breeze.*
>
> *Now all*
>   *that's left*
>   *is an*
>   *empty shell*
>
> *Full of nothing.* (1962)
>
> I wrote about the front I put on and what was under it:

Blood seething, quietly, little noise. Only empty-full glare from deadened eyes. Careless sauntering—only a front for very slow pace. Racing, racing.

Blood seething, quietly, little noise. Smile. Pass a word. Pass another. Screaming, confusion, lots of noise. Hate, love, same thing. Out, out. Which way, no way. Chaos. (1962)

I wrote about hiding:
It was like I was hiding in a cloud:
I could see out, but no one could see in.
It was like being an observer from another world.
Passing silently and unnoticed, and watching. (1962)

There were other writings that were on loosely collected pieces of whatever paper happened to be handy at the time. I wrote about enormous, gray, uninhabited cities; empty warehouses; typewriters without paper; merging shadows around great corners; lit street lamps on dark streets with no traffic. I wrote about a sloping hill in the desert; blinding sun at noontime; an empty shack incapable of providing refuge from incessant dry heat.

I wrote about punishment for unnamed crimes and about faceless interrogators who only asked me who I was:

Why do all the judges point their fingers accusingly at me?
Why do they scream out my crimes so that I cannot hear them?
Why don't I stand up and tell them they are wrong?
Could it be they are right?
(No, I cannot tolerate that thought.)
But, if they are wrong why do they scream so?
And why don't I say something? (1962)

When I read Kafka the first time, I thought he had it right.

I wrote stories about people trying to scream but not making any noise. I wrote page after page in the most obtuse, pedantic style imaginable, a kind of caricature of nineteenth- century German philosophers (about whom I actually knew very little). I wrote grandly obscure sentences about Man's pitiful position on the planet and equally obscure essays on such topics as "My Apparent Apathy to Politics and Social Reform," "Reflections on Several Discussions," and "Hate."

Many of these contained unreadable sentences, sterile in the way I observed that some intellectuals wrote. There was obviously much on my mind because I wrote page after page, but the heart of the matter was almost always hidden.

There were so many inner arguments, so many endless pep talks and exhortations to just "snap out of it," with equal measures of self-pity and disgust, as in this rant:

ugliness, stupidness, littleness, puny
hide your messy head in a cardboard box
don't try for answers, don't try for questions
fool, idiot, thinking you're so smart
fumble around, create your mess
then run to cry over spilt milk.

Why keep trying? If you stop long enough to realize how very low down you stand, you will go crazy with self-pity. (1962)

A few times I wrote out brief scenes that seemed like parts of a nightmare:

He follows me; day and night he follows me… Sometimes I see him; fear swells within my soul. When his eyes meet mine I tremble in my shoes. Fear must be his pastime. (1959)

Another scene, completely out of context with the surrounding sentences, I now know sketched the story I was trying to wish away.

First I wrote: *The cool wind teases the sun as they race together over the fields.*

Then I drew a line across the page under the sentence and started again:

He grabbed her fiercely and with much anger, and forced her to the floor. She landed heavily on her knees. Surprise and pain produced a cry. Silence came on demand from his eyes. Darkness, but for a single bulb swinging from the ceiling.

Then, beneath these words, I was off on another topic altogether, slipping into obfuscation as if the preceding words had never happened.

From time to time there were miracles of insight about wholeness and holiness. I never speculated in those early days about where those insights came from or why they did not inform my life. As a young adult, my writing was an attempt to speak with my mouth closed, to give the appearance of communicating without revealing anything.

From early adolescence on, I thought about suicide every day. I wrote suicide notes and left them around the house. No one ever mentioned seeing them.

I thought about it mostly at night, when the distractions of the day had disappeared. I imagined using one of my mother's knives. To get to the kitchen I had to go past my parent's bedroom. I thought a lot about the possibility they might wake up and confront me about why I was up and about. A worse possibility was that they might find me, knife in hand, and tell me there wasn't anything wrong, nothing for me to feel so distraught about, and then send me back to bed. I never really thought it through and never made the attempt.

Once I tried to smother myself in my pillow, a more silent method than walking to the kitchen. It turned out to be impossible, and I cried myself to sleep instead.

MUSIC

My parents had a small collection of LPs, mostly opera, along with some recordings of symphonies and musical theater. I was especially fond of Stravinsky, particularly the *Firebird Suite* near the end before the triumphant finale. For a few minutes, a solo horn plays an ethereal melody above violins that sound like the wings of a dozen large, elegant birds flying into the distance. The horn sang to my loneliness and consoled me in a way I couldn't describe in words. I listened to it again and again when the apartment was empty.

BUDDHA

When I was sixteen, I took a class in public speaking. One of the projects was to write the eulogy of a famous figure in history, and I chose the Buddha. I spent long hours at the main library downtown on Michigan Avenue. The room where books were requisitioned was enormous, with two-storey-tall windows facing Michigan Avenue and the park across the street. After spending a great deal of time preparing my list of books from the card catalogue, I handed in the list and settled in for the wait for the books to be found, gathered, and returned to the desk.

The ones I got were all by and for scholars, written in English with copious quotations in Sanskrit. I could barely make sense of the arcane mystical concepts. However, I noticed the part about a release from suffering. This was the first time I encountered such an idea, and a door opened a tiny crack.

Perhaps suicide isn't the only option, I thought.

A short time later, I read Herman Hesse's *Siddhartha*. At the time I was a big fan of science fiction, and Hesse's rendition of a spiritual quest in ancient India could very well have taken place in another galaxy. Here were details about how one might attain a kind of serenity I couldn't actually imagine. What strange details they were: solitude, meditation, and asceticism that seemed to be punitive.

Hesse's vision of the Buddhist path to enlightenment was far more accessible than the scholarly books I had confronted a years before. His ideas both excited and distressed me. Release from fear and worry was very attractive, but what would this release cost me and could I do what was required? I was excited enough to go to every bookstore in downtown Chicago and buy every copy of the book I could find. I sent one to almost all of the important people in my life. That list included my aunt and uncle in California, but not my parents, who I didn't think would understand.

I was perplexed however. In Hesse's story it appeared that the way to serenity involved leaving everything and everyone behind. Although I was dying where I was, I couldn't imagine leaving. I was much too lonely in my current self-imposed solitude to find the idea of spiritual solitude attractive. By harassing myself endlessly about how I didn't measure up, I was self-punishing in invisible ways that took me farther from enlightenment, not closer. I couldn't understand what Hesse said about nonattachment—the suggestion that one limit the passionate experience of life—when I felt disconnected almost all the time. How could I give up what I didn't have?

And then there was meditation. This I understood as sitting quietly and stilling the mind. It didn't take much stillness for my shame to show itself. A true mystic cultivates greater and greater consciousness. I cultivated the distractions of frenzy and sleep, which were the ultimate in living unconsciously.

A true mystic, as I understand now, strives to surrender to life as it is in all of its wild wonder. Unaware of these principles as a young adult, I felt trapped as if my life were an unending endurance trial, which I wasn't sure I could endure.

I didn't know about the idea of "yet," that perhaps I wasn't ready yet to embark on the spiritual journey *Siddhartha* describes, but I might be one day. I longed for the golden city across a canyon that I had no idea how to cross. But at least it was there. If someone else had found a way to get there, it must be possible. The idea of possibility kept me going.

In my early twenties, I wrote: *Sometimes I feel so certain that I am on the right track— pieces settle gently into their proper places, the wind softly sings a little tune that begs me to follow, and the laughter of Infinity lightly tickles me and reassures me that the goal I seek is the real thing.*

Around the same time, before I left home, I wrote this about my parents and myself: *I could submit to them and compromise myself to them. It would not be a willing undertaking on my part and maybe not even conscious. It would be an attempt to avoid their hurt-filled faces as I stab them over and over by just being me.*

I believed that if I put what I needed or wanted ahead of what my parents wanted, I would be abandoned; that if I spoke my truth about how I felt or what I experienced, I would not be heard or, worse, would be told that I was wrong or, worst of all, it would literally kill or injure them; that I should love the false life that I hated; that my feelings were wrong; that I should feel good when I felt despair; and that there was something deeply flawed in me that I could not feel the way I should. I led more than a double life. I learned very early that it was vital never to look unhappy or troubled. In time, my façade was constructed well enough. No one in my family caught on, not that they tried. None of my friends knew me very well. I trusted no one.

I had placed myself in exile.

WANDERING

COLLEGE

In mid-January 1961, I graduated from Roosevelt High School (named after Teddy), and in less than a week, started college at Roosevelt University (named after Franklin Delano), with no particular major in mind. The university was in the old Auditorium Hotel building, a Louis Sullivan masterpiece on Michigan Avenue, adjacent to the Fine Arts Building where I had danced years before. I paid my own way to school with savings and earnings, but they were insufficient to live away from home.

Part of freshman orientation involved taking a personality or mental-health inventory. A few days after the testing, a counselor called me into her office. When I entered, she was seated facing the door, behind a large, old, wooden desk. She was at least a generation older than I and looked formidable. She motioned for me to have a seat.

"You gave some troubling responses on the screening test you did last week," she said. "We thought it might be best if you came in for some counseling."

She asked questions. My answers were brief and noncommittal; inside, I panicked and barely heard anything she said. My mumbled responses did not reassure her that I didn't need her services. All I remember were her opening lines and something about returning the next week. Embarrassed about being found out, I never went back.

Stanley, my boyfriend from high school, also attended Roosevelt University. One day in 1962, we took a long walk in Grant Park across the street from school. It was early spring, when the snow was gone and the air was mild, but the grasses and flowerbeds in the park had only barely begun to disturb the detritus of the prior fall. As we walked south toward the Field Museum, Stanley said simply, "Will you marry me?"

"Yes," I said.

He looked relieved and happy. He pulled a small box out of his pocket and gave it to me. Inside was a beautiful, simple diamond in a white-gold setting. I smiled and tried to look as happy as he did as I put it on.

"I think we should wait for a few years, until after we've graduated," I said, silently thinking that two years seemed too soon.

We talked about what it might be like to be married and live together. He told me that he liked to change his towels every day.

"I'm sure that would be fine," I answered, but I thought, *I don't think my having to do all that laundry will be fine at all.*

I knew how to speak up about where to go out to eat or which movie to see, but not about anything I cared about.

I don't know what else I said because I was too busy thinking that if it didn't work out, I could get a divorce. I didn't know anyone who had gotten a divorce. It was very uncommon in those days. I didn't tell him about my reservations. I hid from him, too.

Later, when I was alone, I finally realized that thinking about divorce immediately after getting engaged was a very bad sign. I liked the idea of getting married, but the more I thought about marrying Stanley the less I thought it could work. I was increasingly aware that, while I thought Stanley was kind and he didn't push me, I didn't know him very well. In the years we dated, I put too much energy into worrying about what I thought would please him to actually pay much attention to who he really was.

He didn't know me either, as I never talked to him about what really concerned me or how depressed I was. I continually lied to him about what I thought and felt, just as I did with my parents. I always told him I felt fine, no matter what the truth was.

In the days that followed our engagement, I tried very hard to ignore how trapped I felt, but in time, I couldn't. I told my parents about feeling uncertain, and they agreed that it was better not to marry if that's how I felt. Three weeks after our engagement, I returned his ring. We had no classes in common, and it was years before I saw him again.

Breaking my engagement was the most assertive thing I'd ever done. Being honest in that way started an avalanche of anxiety. I decided to actually try therapy and went to a new counselor at Roosevelt.

During the first session, the counselor asked what my family was like.

"My family is nearly perfect," I said. "I grew up in a peaceful, affectionate household."

He looked skeptical and said, "Oh?" His question was like a bulldozer smashing through the brightly painted front of my house to reveal the rotted garbage that filled the interior.

Feeling like I was losing control of myself, I nevertheless went back for another session. In our second session he asked more questions about my family. I avoided saying how bad I felt. At the end of the hour, he told me he was moving and that he would help me find someone else to work with.

I don't remember what I replied. I felt raw and abandoned, more lost than before. I decided to give up on counseling altogether.

I wrote bizarre letters to my aunt Deb and uncle Abe in Los Angeles, whom, I trusted more than any other relatives (my aunt recently returned them to me). I wrote too many words and images just trying to say, I'm drowning. In one I wrote:

Dear Luboffs,
This has been a week of lovely and unusual noises. For instance, I just heard thunder for the first time in months. What a great sound, full of life and power, and, best of all, the sound of spring pushing the winter aside.

There are important sounds, too: like the sounds of anguish and grief and despair and unhappiness. These are sounds that cry loudly and make you sit with tense breath.

Let's not forget the sounds of running—the most important of all. It takes the form of an angry stomach, complaining... Or the sound of quiet people sitting and screaming towards insanity.
Stop and listen and see if I'm not right.
Love, Toby

Their responses were compassionate and encouraging: they didn't scold me or criticize me for being strange or unpleasant, or complain that I was just being melodramatic. I provided no details, so there wasn't much they could say; but the mere fact that they didn't try to convince me that I had an overactive imagination was comfort enough.

As spring finally took hold, I attached myself to a boy in my anthropology class. We were studying tribal social structure and mores with a teacher who had taught the course so often he was no longer interested in what he was teaching. The subject matter was actually interesting to me, but in the turmoil that followed breaking my engagement with Stanley, I didn't care much what I was studying. I was, however, very interested in the fact that Michael gave me amphetamines that he stole from his physician father. I loved being wired and sort of numb all at once.

We never actually dated. Instead we took a few walks or sat in Grant Park and took the little round white pills he carried with him. I talked to him about my miserable life and he told me about how bad his was. A *folie a deux.*

After a few weeks of this I wrote him a note in class: "Why don't we commit suicide together?"

He wrote back: "I'm not interested in dying."

The next day he stopped talking to me or even looking at me. It never occurred to me to ask why; my life was already surreal and this was just one more, strange incident. I missed his little white pills as much as I missed him. I had no idea how to go about finding another source.

After breaking the engagement and failing to find a suicide partner, I spent a frenzied summer working full time in the library of the *Sun-Times* newspaper, going to concerts and plays, and generally staying in motion until I was exhausted every day. At the end of the summer, I collapsed and slept for two entire days.

I wrote to my aunt and uncle in California: [I] *keep me so busy that I haven't got too much time to think. This is a very desired condition…because thinking sometimes produces some very unwanted results. So, as you can see, I'm doing myself a favor on all counts.*

In an effort to get away from Chicago and all of the problems I seemed to have there, I applied to universities all over the country. It was June 1962 and already too late for most of them. When the University of Wisconsin in Madison accepted my late application, my mother convinced me that 150 miles would be far enough. I only had enough money saved up for one year, but I couldn't think beyond that. I would deal with that issue when the time came. Luckily, my parents pitched in for food and housing.

LOS ANGELES

Before I moved to Wisconsin at the end of the summer, my sister Judi and I went to Los Angeles to visit my aunt and uncle and cousins. It was our first time away on a trip without our family and our first time on an airplane. The flight out was on an old-style propeller plane. There was rough weather all the way across the country. Those were the days of up-chuck bags, and the stewardesses were busy collecting them and providing new ones for the whole trip. I hadn't thrown up since I was twelve, and I was one of the few who didn't.

Our cousins, Gary and Joel, were about the same ages as my sister and I. We went all over the place in the two weeks Judi and I were there: tourist places, like The Huntington Estate and Gardens; down to the ocean; and into the streets of Old Los Angeles. With our cousins, we took long bike rides and walks and talked endlessly.

Gary and Joel fixed us up with a couple of their friends, Richard for me and Steve for Judi. We spent time just hanging out with them, mostly at Richard's house. Brilliant and wild, he said he had missed an entire year of school because of mononucleosis, but kept up with his classes anyway.

Richard taught us dirty drinking songs when he joined us on walks. He led all of us into antics like calling people from pay phones and swearing at them. I'd never done anything so obviously obnoxious and possibly illegal. I was appalled and at the same time excited by how bad we were. Had drugs been as available then as they are now we would have been stoned the entire time. None of us drank—we were obnoxious all on our own.

Sometimes Richard and I stayed behind at his house while the others went on. I let him touch me in places and in ways I'd heard about but never tried. I let myself feel what he was doing. I was surprised and a little alarmed by the sensations I felt. My sister was more experienced than I. She told me about getting aroused, which was news to me. Richard didn't seem to want to go all the way. As intrigued as I was by all of the interesting things he was doing, I didn't think about what might have happened if he had been more aggressive. Later I learned he was gay.

I came back late for dinner one evening, my clothes all crushed, worried a little about the response I might get, and amazed at what I had just been doing. Richard and I had been taking full advantage of the fact that his parents were never home.

"Oh, there you are," my aunt Deb said. She was apparently more annoyed by my being late than anything else.

No one else commented on either my appearance or late arrival, so I sat down at the round dinner table with the rest of the family. The subject of the conversation quickly moved elsewhere. Their lack of response was fascinating.

In fact, a lot about their household was fascinating. There were arguments: loud, intense, short, and infrequent. They blew up like summer squalls and were over just as quickly, barely dampening the soil before moving on, or so it seemed to me.

In my household, fights seemed much more dangerous. The arguments I got into with my parents often left me confused and humiliated. As I matured, I realized that my father had a talent for changing the subject and speaking as if he were saying something important, when he was really not saying anything at all. My mother supported him no matter how incomprehensible he was. The idea that a family could have simple, comprehensible arguments that were merely loud, but not dangerous, was incredible to me.

Near the end of our two weeks in Los Angeles, the entire family embarked on a day trip to San Diego, quite a distance from their home. By the time we were headed back, it was dark and everyone was tired. Judi and my cousins fell asleep in the back seat. I sat in the front with my aunt and uncle.

We had a long, easy conversation all the way home. This wasn't a time for great confidences. Rather, they seemed genuinely interested in me and what I was doing and where I thought I might be going. They listened and asked questions that didn't seem to have a correct answer that I had to figure out. The conversation was simple just as the family fights seemed to be simple. They were people who seemed to love me just as I was, without needing me to be anything or say anything to take care of them. It was a blessed time, riding in the dark, our faces slightly illuminated by the lights on the dashboard. More than forty years later, my aunt Deb still brings it up, a fond remembrance of a time that touched her as well as me.

After we got home I wrote to my aunt and uncle:
Tell me something: is it possible to feel homesick for a place and people you hardly know at all?
I feel…great confusion as to why it doesn't feel good to be home again.
A few days later, I wrote to them again:

I've been ridiculously depressed since Sunday, but I attribute that to my complete dissatisfaction and displeasure with being in Chicago. This existed before California and is greatly heightened since returning. It is the oddest feeling in the world to be completely surrounded by things and people you grew up with and live with and yet to feel a complete stranger to them all.

On the one hand they [my family] *encourages my break from the house as something desirable and good. And, on the other hand, they smother me with so much affection that by Tuesday* [when I was scheduled to leave for the University of Wisconsin] *I shall undoubtedly feel like an ace number one cad slinking away into the night.*

Please don't look at this as a problem to be solved, but merely an added thought to our previous discussion. Undoubtedly the situation has been magnified and maybe even misinterpreted beyond its rightful proportions.

I wrote letters to my aunt and uncle and cousins and my strange new boyfriend, Richard—a torrent of letters, breathless with hyperbole—because I was desperate to hang onto the new awareness I'd experienced in California.

UNIVERSITY OF WISCONSIN

In the fall of 1962, I moved to Madison and started school. It was the first time I was living on my own, and it was a great relief to be away from my family. I had never been away from my family any longer than spending a night at my grandmother Libby's apartment on Rockwell Street or the recent trip to Los Angeles. I didn't know anyone in Madison or very much about the University. The mixed feelings, ranging from excitement to fear, threatened to be more than I could manage, and the turmoil let loose by breaking my engagement had been only partly contained by a summer full of distractions.

I went to Wisconsin hoping that a totally new environment would magically settle my turmoil. The girls' boarding house where I lived was on Lake Street near State Street. That placed me as close as one could live to the libraries and the Student Union, with its multitude of activities. In addition to taking a full load of classes, I found a job in the library and did as much else as I could, flirting with frenzy again.

About six weeks later, John Kennedy and Nikita Khrushchev got into a potentially deadly game of chicken over the installation of nuclear missiles aimed at the United States from Cuba. I remember walking through the halls of the Wisconsin Student Union during the height of the crisis. Young men and women filled the space talking in low, panicky voices, terrorized. I wasn't terrified at all. Rather, I felt a strange sense of calm. The nuclear war that had hung over my entire childhood was finally going to happen, and soon I would be dead. Finally I would have relief.

The world crisis settled down before October was over, but I didn't. With a sense of desperation I went to the student health center and was directed to do group therapy with Dr. Gammel, a psychiatric resident. The group met once a week in the University of Wisconsin medical center, about a mile from where I lived. We were eight or ten undergraduates, talking mostly about relationships, whether we ever stole something, how we were doing at school. I spoke up occasionally.

There was something comforting about having a place to go to talk about how I felt about things, even though I didn't say much about what was really troubling me.

Dr. Gammel also put me on medication. I didn't care what it was for, and didn't notice that it made any difference.

One very cold night, near Christmas, I gave Susan, the closest friend I had in Madison, a small box with my most precious belongings.

"Hold onto this for me," I said, "I'm going out and don't know when I will be back."

Susan looked at the box and then at me. She seemed surprised and a little worried, but she didn't say anything. I was distraught when I left the house, somehow expecting to just evaporate into the air, or perhaps just disintegrate. I wasn't thinking about suicide exactly. I wasn't thinking at all. I was just certain that I would not return or even live out the night, although how I would disappear was entirely unclear. I was a little crazy. I wandered far from campus and got lost. The Wisconsin state capitol building has a tall dome and is brightly lit every night. One side of it faces the university and was less than a mile from where I lived. At some point, I saw it and found my way back, defeated.

I told this story to Dr. Gammel and he started seeing me individually, as well as with the group I had entered in the fall. We met in a small, plain room. He chain smoked on his side of the standard-issue wooden desk and looked interested. I was uncomfortable with his attention and was anxious and hesitant.

I remember almost nothing that he and I talked about, except that I continued to try to present my family as basically loving and normal. Once, he said something to me that was closer to the truth. I struggled not to cry, but when I got back to my room I broke into unaccustomed sobbing, thinking over and over: *My parents don't love me; my parent's don't love me.*

Just before Christmas break, I told him that I didn't want to go home. He suggested I spend a few days in the hospital during the break. There was something so reassuring about the offer, knowing that someone took my distress seriously and didn't try to talk me out of it, that I felt better and went home for a few days instead, staying away from my family most of the time.

Throughout the school year, a few friends and I tried out all of the churches we could get to on foot. I went with a detached curiosity. The Unitarian church in Madison that had been designed by Frank Lloyd Wright was the most interesting architecturally, but the service was too much like the Reform Jewish service I left behind. The Lutherans were too negative to be taken seriously. I liked the mysterious nature and sense of ritual of the Catholic Mass. It was still in Latin in those days, so I had no idea what was going on. I never considered looking up any of the area synagogues. The Jewish student center, Hillel, was only a few blocks from where I lived, but I never went in.

I might have pursued Buddhism, had it been as popular then as it is now; but in the winter of 1962–1963 in the upper Midwest, Buddhist studies were part of graduate programs far removed from my undergraduate life. There were no such things as public meditation groups or seminars.

I lived in a small boarding house with a large kitchen in the basement, which the students shared. The house-mother lived in an apartment on the first floor with her husband, a graduate student, and young son, George. I shared a two-room suite on the other side of the first floor with three other girls.

Of the two-dozen girls who lived there, six of us were very nonobservant Jews. At Passover time in early spring, we got permission to have some wine and made a *Seder*, the ritual meal in which the Passover story is retold. The six of us searched our memories for what was needed and how the service went. We had none of the *haggadot*, the Passover prayer books that are the essential script to the service. It never occurred to any of us to ask for help. Yet, we held an earnest Passover service, the most meaningful Jewish anything that I'd ever experienced.

Just when I thought I had divorced myself from Judaism, it was apparent that I'd been circling around looking for another way in.

MEETING RUSSELL

When I came home from Madison for the Thanksgiving break, my friends Bonnie and Ed fixed me up with Ed's older brother, Russell. Bonnie had lived across Bernard Street since she was twelve. We were almost always in the same classes through high school. She was dating Ed, another classmate, who I knew since early elementary school. There was another connection between Russell and me—our mothers had been in the grade school PTA at the same time years before.

At five foot six inches, Russell was the tallest member of his family and a couple of inches taller than I. He had light reddish hair, which was thick and wavy like his mother, Mollie. While he was (and remains) short and slender, he was broad shouldered with a quiet strength about him. The four of us went out on a double date that has left no traces of memory, except for what followed.

I didn't think much about Russell in the weeks after I returned to campus, absorbed as I was with my emotional unraveling to the point where I was invited for a hospital stay over Christmas break. When I ended up going home instead, I was surprised and pleased to hear that Russell had called wanting to know when I was available. I was only home for a long weekend, but we went out several times. Russell appeared to like me, and I found him approachable, gentle, and thoughtful. He was a doctoral student in physics at the University of Chicago. I thought that physicists were the ultimate in rational human beings. I imagined such rational beings to be far above the emotional turmoil I was in most of the time. I was impressed.

On our second date, Russell and I went to a nightclub. Russell was so easy to talk to, soft spoken with a calming voice. He's since told me that I was easy to talk to as well. I was in a very strange mood. What I noticed was that my mood didn't seem to disturb him. Much later, he told me that he thought of me as a delicate butterfly. He asked me out again before I went back to Wisconsin.

I was fragile as well as delicate and in need of a safe, stable place to alight. Our unspoken pact, almost from the beginning, was that Russell would take care of me. Years later, one sign that I was really starting to change was when his solicitousness felt overdone and unwanted.

After I went back to school, we started writing to each other almost every day. These were easy letters, similar in a way to my conversations with my aunt Deb and uncle Abe. Russell seemed to like me and didn't want too much from me. I went home about once a month, and he came up to Madison once a month. He was very comfortable to be around.

We made out often and once spent the night together, a tricky business that involved sneaking out of my dorm after hours and getting back in without being caught. We didn't make love. We moved very slowly, and after awhile I began to enjoy being sensual and even sexual with him in a way I never did with Stanley.

By the end of the school year in June 1963, I was much happier. Dr. Gammel had taken me seriously and hadn't tried to talk me out of my distress, as my parents would have done. Having minimal contact with my parents was probably a factor as well. I thought I was done with therapy. I had made few friends with anyone in Madison, and most of them were not returning the next year. The few men I dated at the university never connected with me as strongly as Russell did. I had never had enough money to afford more than one year away from home anyway, so the decision to move back to Chicago was an easy one. I reapplied to Roosevelt University and was quickly accepted.

At Dr. Gammel's suggestion, after moving back to Chicago, I told my parents that I wanted to move out and live on my own. As I recall, they didn't say anything, which I took to mean that they didn't object. I was absurdly naïve about what was involved in supporting myself: I was still a university student and had no source of income large enough to pay rent, and I really knew nothing about cooking or maintaining a household. However, my parents continued to say nothing as I went about finding roommates and looking at apartments in the neighborhood.

The day I told them I actually meant to move, they both exploded at me. My mother was worried about what people would think about me and, ultimately about her, if her unmarried daughter was living away from home. According to her, doing so would ruin both of our reputations. I don't remember exactly what my father said, except no daughter of his was going to live on her own.

Once again it seemed they had led me to believe something was all right and then changed the rules at the last minute. This time I yelled back and, very uncharacteristically used the word "damn." My father got furious and shifted the subject to the language I had used.

Changing directions midstream was a favorite tactic of his to throw me off. At twenty, I was old enough to know what he was doing, but I wasn't strong enough to withstand his assault. I crumbled and capitulated. I felt crazed trying to squelch all my rage. I pushed the crazy feeling, the rage, and all the rest I didn't know what to do with, into an already full cache of energy and anxiety. I knew how to give my parents the performance they wanted. I didn't say anything important or meaningful to my father again until after my mother's death, twenty-seven years later.

I didn't move out.

THE L-SHAPED ROOM

In mid-November, after I returned from Wisconsin, Russell and I went to see *The L-Shaped Room*, a film about an unwed mother. The Brahms *First Piano Concerto* played throughout in the background. Afterwards, we sat on the landing outside my door on Bernard Street, talking and necking as we often did. Russell said, in his usual noncommittal way, "I was thinking how it would be nice to come home to you every day."

I looked at him.

"I think so, too," I replied, trying to keep my response low key to match his. Inside, I was alive with excitement.

When I went into the house, I told my parents that I thought Russell had proposed. I was certainly excited as if he had. On the other hand, despite the look on his face and the happy tone in his voice, I called him the next morning just to be sure.

I was delighted to be able to get married even before I graduated college. It was a clear sign that I had done enough things right so that I would not have to remain single. I didn't know if I loved Russell. He was safe and I trusted him, which seemed far more important. I easily imagined living with him.

The following Friday, John F. Kennedy was shot in Dallas. I stood in the library at Roosevelt University, incredulous and stunned as people talked about the news. Russell was at the Medici restaurant in Hyde Park having lunch with a friend and unreachable immediately. Everything in the country ground to a halt for days as everyone found a television to watch the aftermath of the catastrophe play out. Russell and I debated whether to spread our happy news in the middle of such national trauma. We only waited a little while, and then we got back to making announcements and plans.

We decided to get married the following June, when I was twenty-one. My mother asked me what I had in mind for the wedding. When I said I was thinking of a large wedding, she went to work and had a grand time with the planning. I was consulted very little, which was just fine with me because I was still in school and busy enough.

Happily and safely engaged, when I turned twenty-one I decided that it was time to actually have sex. Even though I was a little more experienced than when I dated Stanley and more willing to be touched and to touch, I wasn't really any more interested in sex than I'd ever been. I did know, however, that it seemed that most women my age had made love already. Russell wasn't likely to break the engagement if I was no longer a virgin, as my mother and grandmother had warned.

Russell and I planned the event carefully. I went to a pharmacy on Michigan Avenue near the *Sun-Times* building and bought a contraceptive. Russell came equipped, also. I easily lied to my parents about where I was going that night, saying we were going to someplace in the northern suburbs when in fact we intended to go south to Russell's Hyde Park apartment. I lived a lie in my household all of the time, so telling such a blatant lie wasn't much different. Russell made sure his roommates were gone for the evening. It was more of an adventure than a night of passion, an accomplishment I was very pleased about at the end of the evening.

We married on the summer solstice of 1964, a hot steamy day. I dressed in the rabbi's study, which was the only air-conditioned room in Temple Beth Israel. Someone told me I would be too excited to notice the heat. I was excited, and in fact, I did notice the rivulets of sweat dripping under my voluminous dress with the sheer Filipino-styled sleeves. My bridesmaids had their moment of rebellion when they unanimously rejected my wish that they dress in garden-party styled dresses and insisted on a cocktail dress that they could wear again. At least they capitulated on bright yellow, which I refused to negotiate.

I was enormously pleased to be getting married to Russell. He, on the other hand, looked very serious as he walked down the aisle of my temple, just ahead of his mother and father. My mother's brother and sister and their entire families had come in from out of town. My grandmother Libby's many sisters and her brother came with their adult children. Libby was at that moment in the hospital following a heart attack. My father's family was well represented, as well as Russell's—both of our sides had invited a good complement of friends. Russell was the first in his family to marry, and I was the first on my mother's side.

When the ceremony was over, we moved on to a banquet hall on the far west side of Chicago for a formal dinner with dancing and festivities. It was a fine celebration. Afterwards, we stopped by Edgewater Hospital to see my grandmother, Libby, and then on to the airport to fly in two stages to Quebec for our honeymoon. We got on the plane very happy to be married and very happy to be alone and away from the commotion of the wedding.

Russell was still a graduate student, but he had put some money away to make a real vacation of our honeymoon. We decided on Quebec for a variety of reasons, not the least of which was that it was the closest thing to going to Europe without having to leave North America, because the local people spoke French. For the first part of the honeymoon, we settled into a place in a house with rooms to let in the older part of the city. The concierge recognized us as newlyweds right away, and she teased us kindly about our new status.

I had just finished a year of college French, and Russell, who was more linguistically talented than I, was armed with the Berlitz phrase book. We had read *Winnie the Pooh* to each other as part of our courtship. For the honeymoon, we read a French edition of *Le Petit Prince* by Antoine de Saint Exupéry. Between the two of us we did very well, enjoying how we managed to fit in and not look like tourists.

We spent about five days going up and down the Gaspe Peninsula along the St. Lawrence Seaway. The farther we traveled away from Quebec City, the less people were willing or able to speak English when our elementary French proved inadequate. The Quebec separatist movement was heating up in those days. There were several small bombings in the province while we were there—nothing close to us, with only minor damage done—but it was enough to make us glad that we could blend in most of the time.

Russell and I returned from our Canadian honeymoon to housesit for his doctoral advisor in Hyde Park. The big, turn-of-the century, clapboard house had three floors, many bedrooms, and a huge gourmet kitchen, which was mostly bewildering to a novice cook such as myself. But I had a palpable sense of freedom, knowing I didn't have to live on Bernard Street any more, and my freedom far outweighed any qualms about how I was going to make supper or be a wife.

Two weeks after we got back, on a hot July night, we went for a walk in the evening. That was an ordinary, unremarkable thing to do in the Albany Park neighborhood we had grown up in, but this was Hyde Park, an integrated, liberal neighborhood surrounded on three sides by the south-side ghetto. We approached a small group of teenage boys who turned on us as we passed. Russell and I started to run, but the sandals I was wearing, while hippie-chic, would not stay on without effort. I had to stop or trip and fall. It was an opportunistic robbery for the robbers. They took money from Russell's wallet and his watch. They missed my small diamond engagement ring.

We got home and locked the doors. I wasn't sure what else to do. I didn't even think of calling the police at first. Russell did but thought it would be futile, so we just went to bed. The next morning we finally placed the ultimately useless call, as we hadn't gotten much of a look at the boys in the dark. I was more numb and depressed than usual for days afterwards.

A few weeks later, I took a walk in the middle of an afternoon to visit Cindy, a friend and classmate from Wisconsin who transferred back to Roosevelt when I did. As I came up to the walkway of her apartment building, a large man, perhaps in his thirties, came barging out of the front door, paused momentarily as he saw me, and ran off. I froze. He had just burgled one of the apartments. That time, when I was sure he was gone and wasn't going to attack me, I went to Cindy's apartment and immediately called the police.

My new life seemed to be getting off to a dangerous start. I didn't know what to do with the fear these two events produced except to push it away and pretend that it didn't matter. The discrepancy between my inner and outer life grew.

When Russell's advisor and his family came home in the fall, we moved into married-student housing across the street from the Fermi Institute where Russell spent most of his time. There we finally settled into ordinary married-student life in a four-room apartment furnished with used furniture, except for our bed. This included an original Duncan Phyfe dining room set I didn't begin to appreciate until we sold it years later for $100 to a woman who could hardly contain her excitement about her find. The university was in an urban renewal phase, clearing entire blocks to make space for new construction. Our multiunit building was the only one left standing on our block, which created a strange sense of isolation in the middle of the city.

Our apartment had a number of serious locks on both the front and back doors, and the window on the back door was boarded up. I felt a little safer than I had in the big house we had tended over the summer, with its multiple possibilities for invasion. For the first six months after we married, we settled into an agreeable routine. Some of the sense of futility and helplessness from the summer robberies subsided.

SONIA

In January 1965 I graduated from Roosevelt University. Russell and I took a brief vacation to Starved Rock State Park, about two hours west of Chicago. It was a place we liked, and we could go there by train, an important consideration because in those student days we didn't have a car.

We arrived the day after a big snowstorm—a day that was bitterly cold, clear, and dazzling in the high pressure that often follows a midwestern winter storm. It was the middle of the week, and there were only six or eight guests in the entire lodge including us. There must have been one enormous furnace for our entire floor or our entire section. It was on and there was no way to modulate the temperature. Our room was extremely hot, so much so that when we first opened the windows, the hot air poured out, rather than the subzero air coming in. We left the shower going for long periods, trying to get some moisture in the room. We took off our clothes. Despite contraception, our daughter was conceived.

As befit an English major, I applied for editorial assistant jobs at several publishing companies. My interviews were the week after we came back from Starved Rock. As part of the first interview I was asked to take a lengthy mental health test, which asked about and assessed my mental status in very intrusive ways that would be illegal in most circumstances today. I felt worse and worse as the long afternoon wore on. About a week later, I learned that I didn't get the job. Somehow I wasn't surprised, but I mustered the courage to call and ask why not, as I had done very well in school. The person I spoke to hedged and said the company didn't think I would fit in very well.

I knew the person was being evasive and polite. I imagined he was thinking I was too crazy or weird to work there. I could have been angry and humiliated. What I recall is that I assumed I was, in fact, too crazy and weird, and wondered how I would find any job where I would fit in.

The second interview was with a trade journal called *Rock Mining and Processing*. This time there were no questionnaires or tests, only an interview by the senior editor. He mostly wanted to know if we were planning on moving or having a baby—in short, was I going to stick around. I said I didn't think we would be moving for at least several years or starting a family any time soon, unaware that I was already pregnant.

I started work on the trade journal shortly after that. I also started to get nauseated in the mornings and ravenous at meal times. Then I missed my period. The only other time I missed a period was around the time Dr. Gammel invited me to stay in the hospital for Christmas. I hadn't been sexually active then, and knew I wasn't pregnant, but in February 1965, I knew I could be.

I went to see Dr. Lash because he was the only gynecologist I knew. After the examination and confirmation, he instructed me to come back in a month. That wasn't my intention. I remembered very well how cold and judgmental he had seemed when I first met him seven years earlier. I meant only to verify that I was pregnant and then find someone else. However, I was very unassertive, especially with authoritative people, and I was accustomed to being compliant without making a fuss, so I made the next appointment.

I was the first of my generation of friends and family to get pregnant. Both of our families were excited and happy. This baby would be the start of a new generation on both sides of our family.

I liked the idea of being pregnant but was unprepared for the hormonal upheaval. I was more depressed than usual more of the time, and I had less to distract me. Although it was now more of an effort to keep my unhappiness to myself, it never occurred to me to talk to anyone about how I felt. I was too worried that anyone I confided in would try to convince me that there was no reason to be unhappy.

I remember sitting with Russell's parents and grandmother at their house watching the televised return of Vladimir Horowitz to the concert stage in May 1965. It was an exciting event, as Horowitz hadn't played in public in over twelve years. My mother-in-law, Mollie, had been a student in a master class with him years before, and she listened with great interest.

Horowitz stumbled in the first bars of his first piece, a Bach toccata. I don't know if it was that moment of public embarrassment or something else, but I slid into despair. I left the living room and went to the far other side of the house to the tiny room off the kitchen that had been Russell's room. I lay out on his bed wishing someone would intuit how miserable I was and come to rescue me. The bungalow wasn't a big house. I heard the concert, which was perfect after that first moment. I heard the cheers of the ecstatic audience. I knew why no one was coming, but that didn't stop me from feeling sorry for myself.

As the fetus grew it often pressed on my bladder. Once it kicked near my bladder and I wet myself as I was walking through my apartment. I didn't miss the opportunity to scold myself, something about not acting my age.

Real grown-ups didn't have accidents. The second time was in bed while we were spending the weekend with my in-laws. That time I was extremely embarrassed. I managed to get up and get the sheets washed before most of the family awoke, but I was sure they knew. I didn't know my mother-in-law well enough then to talk to her. I got more depressed.

I was unassertive about many things, but not all. I was intent on having natural childbirth. Dr. Lash was entirely unenthusiastic. I asked him for exercises to do so I could prepare. He said to just walk every day. I asked him all kinds of questions about what was going on in my body. He had the same answer for all of them: you're pregnant.

When the time came, I arrived at Michael Reese Hospital in the small hours of the morning. Once in the labor room I heard someone say that Dr. Lash was lecturing that morning and wasn't in the hospital yet. One of the nurses told me not to push, obviously trying to slow the process until he arrived. They also told me not to scream because I would hurt my throat. The nurses couldn't give me anything for the pain without a doctor's orders, and he wasn't available.

Despite the admonitions from the nurses about sore throats, I somehow decided that I had permission, so I did scream, again and again, full out, with abandon. I screamed not so much from the discomfort of having a baby; I screamed because I knew this was one place where no one would tell me I didn't have anything to scream about. I didn't mind the sore throat that followed.

I could feel my child in the birth canal when Dr. Lash hurried in, telling the nurse to put me out. I knew the birth was only minutes away. I shouted, "No!" and prevailed. Sonia was born a few minutes later.

In those days new mothers stayed in the hospital five days. I had arranged for "rooming in," which put me in one part of a suite of two patient rooms with a small nursery in between that held four newborns. That meant I was with my daughter much more than women whose babies were housed in the main nursery. The nurse brought her to me and taught us both how to manage nursing. She showed me how to bathe and dress this little person.

I was keenly aware that, while I was happy to have had an unremarkable pregnancy and to have delivered a healthy baby, I knew nothing about caring for a child and nothing about this child in particular. Postpartum depression hit hard in the middle of my hospital stay. Despite feeling very overwhelmed and hopeless, I somehow remembered that this was normal and would probably pass, and it did.

I insisted on nursing, even though I didn't know anyone else who was nursing. I figured that women had been nursing for thousands of years, so I would, too. My pediatrician was unhappy, because if I nursed he couldn't be in charge of what was in the formula. This was nonnegotiable, and I nursed Sonia for eight months, until she decided she had enough.

After my daughter was born, I struggled in ways that I imagine must have been similar to my mother's struggles with me. Like her and her mother before her, I read books on how to be a good parent. I read Dr. Spock's book on childcare and was comforted by his advice that young mothers had to take care of themselves as well as their children. I read Bruno Bettelheim's book, *Love is Not Enough*, and worried about destroying my infant's psyche. These books were perhaps more sophisticated than those my mother had read, but I didn't find what I was looking for either.

I had no idea how to manage my baby's uncontrollability and raw emotions and the uncontrollability of my own emotions. I remember thinking she was like a storm over which I had no control whatsoever. I thought more about suicide, but the thought of my helpless child stopped me.

RUSSELL'S FATHER DIES

On a cold, damp February day, when Sonia wasn't yet four months old, I got a call from Mollie. She told me that Russell's father, John, had died of a massive heart attack. I called Russell to come home, and we packed up to spend the week with his family on the north side. It was the sort of damp winter day when it never seems possible to wear enough clothes to be warm. As we turned onto Lawrence Avenue to head west from the Outer Drive, we got a flat tire. Fixing it was cumbersome—Russell in sweaters and overcoat struggling with the tire, while I held onto our infant. Standing in the cold added to the melancholy of the moment.

Observant Jews mark a death with a quick funeral and sitting shiva, seven days of intense mourning during which people come to comfort the mourners. The house was full of people, most of whom I didn't know or knew very little, including Russell's family.

I hardly knew my father-in-law. He had suffered a serious stroke six years prior, which left him impaired enough that he had to stop working as a physical education teacher and soccer coach. I knew him as a disabled man with slurred speech in a household dominated by two powerful women, his wife and his mother-in-law. I was shy, and he had difficulty talking. I don't recall ever having a conversation with him.

John had been a very popular teacher and coach. Many people came to pay their respects, and there was a deep sense of loss in the household. When the house quieted down for the night, I wished it had been my father who died. There was great disparity between how much John was loved and how much I hated my father. My guilt was overwhelming.

PREGNANT WITH JONATHAN

I was already pregnant again when Russell received his doctorate in March 1967, in an elaborate, colorful ceremony in Rockefeller Chapel. As depressed as I'd been before, I was far worse during the second pregnancy. I was ashamed, too. I'd had a year of therapy in Wisconsin, even twice a week, and had felt better afterwards, so what was I complaining about now? I never complained out loud, but I berated myself, instead, for being so unhappy. I slept at every opportunity.

Since Russell was no longer a student, we didn't qualify for subsidized housing, so we moved into a small high-rise building about a mile away, on the corner of Fifty-Fourth Street and Harper. There we had a two-bedroom apartment on the twelfth floor with bars on the kitchen window, which opened onto a fire escape. The living room had windows that looked out over the entire west side of the city and north to downtown. Inside, the space was cramped and uncomfortable. I was reluctant to call this place home and didn't hang any pictures on the walls for months.

Jonathan was born in November 1967. This time I had a new gynecologist, Dr. Platt, who was far easier for me to get along with. Russell's brother Ed and his wife, Bonnie, now lived a few miles south of us, while Ed was in graduate school at the University of Chicago. Assuming that this birth was going to be similar to Sonia's, when it was time to go to the hospital, we took our time delivering Sonia to Bonnie and Ed's apartment, which was in the opposite direction of the hospital. However, things moved fast, and by the time I got into the delivery room, Dr. Platt instructed me to push. He angled a big mirror so I could watch the proceedings, but I was too busy. With two or three shoves, Jonathan arrived. Russell and I were very happy to have a son after a daughter.

We decided to have him circumcised in the hospital rather than having a *brit*, the Jewish ritual circumcision performed eight days after the boy's birth. I knew nothing about this kind of ritual, and Russell knew very little more, so we didn't think it was important. His mother and grandmother may have been upset but never commented about our choice.

Sonia was barely over two when I brought Jonathan home. She was intrigued and often tried to copy my behavior with her dolls. In anticipation of her growing jealous of her little brother, I doted on her. In particular, nursing time for him was story time for her.

In the spring of 1968, Martin Luther King was assassinated. We had followed his career with great interest and sympathy. Many Jews joined him in voter registration drives and antisegregation marches. We were horrified by the murder. We were also horrified as we watched the great clouds of smoke and the flashing lights of fires as the west-side ghetto neighborhoods burned in the riots that followed the assassination. Our living-room windows gave us an unobstructed view, which was particularly vivid at night. Despite its liberal, inclusive intentions, the Hyde Park area was tense, surrounded by the angry ghetto areas to the north and south and west. Someone was murdered down the block. Whether this murder was related to the general unrest was never clear.

In June, a few months after King's assassination, Robert F. Kennedy was murdered. The violence in the country and in the neighborhood was stunning and frightening. I wanted to do something, but the feeling, while urgent, was vague. What could I do that would matter?

In the midst of the national pandemonium, I ran into my friend Cindy's husband Sigurd, who was out riding his bike. Sigurd was deeply committed to social justice projects, often biking from his Hyde Park apartment to tutor children in the ghetto south of Hyde Park, as he was that day. He was the one person I thought might answer my questions so I called to him to stop for a moment.

"I'm sure I'm not the only person who feels completely helpless and surprised by the chaos that erupted in the west-side riots," I said. "It seems important that we do something to help, although I am not at all sure what. What can or should I do?"

"Help yourself first," he said, without further explanation, and then excused himself.

It seemed a very odd thing to say. I always thought that attending to myself was only proof of what a self-centered, selfish person I was.

I should only be helping others. What kind of help do I need? I pondered. *How would helping myself possibly help anyone else?*

I was embarrassed to ask Sigurd to explain what he meant, so I remained perplexed about what to do in the moment and did nothing except take care of my babies and husband.

MOVING TO NAPERVILLE

Russell's first job was as a particle physicist at Argonne National Laboratory in west suburban Lemont. Living in a troubled neighborhood in a tiny apartment was confining and frightening. Argonne was a long commute from Hyde Park, so we decided to move.

One Sunday in June, after the 1968 riots subsided, we drove out to the near western suburbs, not far from Argonne, to look at apartments. Every one listed in the newspaper that day had already been taken, so we looked farther west. We finally took an apartment in Naperville, a village we had only heard of for the first time six months previously, when we were invited to a Christmas party there. On that occasion the Chicago area was wrapped in a thick blanket of fog, with minimal visibility. We had to drive slowly and took a very long time reaching our destination. In June, I was still unclear about where Naperville actually was.

The apartment was pleasant and adequate enough, with a laundry in the basement. It was only two and a half miles from the East-West Tollway, which we took into the city, and less than a half mile to the commuter train. It was important to me that we could get into the city easily, even without a car. That helped with the sense of being cut off from familiar city life and friends.

In those days there was only one stoplight in the center of the village and only one on the way to Argonne, so Russell's drive was much easier and faster than the Hyde Park commute.

We now lived about thirty miles due west of where we had been in Hyde Park, but it felt like a world away. Russell and I had both grown up in Albany Park, which was Jewish and middle class and boring. "Downtown" had no other meaning for us than Chicago's downtown. Russell had lived in Hyde Park during the ten years it took to get through all of his schooling, and I'd been there since we married. I loved being in the world-class intellectual atmosphere of the University of Chicago neighborhood, but we could never afford the money for a baby sitter and tickets to the many cultural events happening only blocks away. I fancied myself a liberal intellectual, as were all of the people I knew. Hyde Park was full of folks like us. Aside from what we read in the newspaper, we knew very little about what was happening in the rest of the Chicago metropolitan area.

Naperville, in the late 1960s and 1970s, was an almost entirely Euro-American, conservative Christian community. Long hair was anathema; drugs, a scandal. I heard that we were the twelfth Jewish family to move into Naperville, but it was a while before I met even one other Jew. Possibly worse than that, my cousin Marilyn, ever the liberal social activist, warned us that there were precious few Democrats in all of Du Page County, where Naperville occupied the southwest corner.

As I feared, our Chicago friends found the distance daunting. There are still jokes that Naperville is somewhere near the Iowa border (which is actually about 150 miles further west). We were far from our friends and even farther from our families.

At first it seemed to be impossible to meet other people. Most of our neighbors were Naperville natives, who were not at all interested in newcomers. Some resented any outsider's intrusion in their village life. Almost every weekend we trekked into the city, especially to the north side to visit our families, and the city people sometimes came west. I pushed one-year-old Jonathan in his stroller with his three-year-old sister holding onto the side, all over the neighborhood looking for signs of other families with small children. I was twenty-six and very lonely in a community that was not only new to me but also completely different from anything I'd experienced before. Sometimes I rang the doorbell of a house with toys left out in the yard. More often than not, no one answered. On the few occasions when the mother of the house answered and I told her we were looking for playmates, she let me know she wasn't really interested.

I met Edna, the wife of Russell's car pool partner, and she introduced me to the American Association of University Women (AAUW). I thought this would be a place to find like-minded women because all of the women had to have college degrees in order to join. However, most of the AAUW women were much older than we and were more interested in having tea and gossiping than tackling the topics that were the heart of the AAUW agenda. It was a lonely time.

I didn't really get acquainted with other people until Sonia started nursery school when she was almost four. There were only two preschools in Naperville at the time, a church-sponsored school and the Hobson Cooperative Nursery School. The choice was obvious. Because Hobson was a cooperative, all of the mothers were expected to help out at the school once a month. That meant we all needed babysitters for our other children, so a group of us started a cooperative babysitting club. After awhile, it became clear to me that the cooperative nature of the school was as important for the parents as for the children. Finally, this was a place where I started to make friends.

In the fall of 1968 I went back to Roosevelt University to begin work on a masters degree in urban affairs, inspired by *The Death and Life of Great American Cities* by Jane Jacobs. I figured I would take one class a semester while the children were very young and teach at a community college when I finished. I was never an "earth mother": I didn't care much for cooking, didn't know how to sew (an accomplishment since I am a descendent of several generations of tailors, including my mother), and was a somewhat indifferent housekeeper. In honest moments, I knew I didn't like being with young children all day long. There wasn't any intellectual challenge to being with them. They were a constant reminder of how inadequate I thought I was as a mother, because I didn't like all the things that I thought good mothers were supposed to like. I worried about how much damage I might be doing with my inadequacies.

I loved being back in school. Studying, writing papers, participating in class—those were the things I knew how to do well. School kept me busy and distracted. Most of my classes were in the evening, because almost all of the students worked during the day. This was also a good arrangement for babysitting, because I could count on Russell to take over when I had to drive downtown.

Although the distraction of school was satisfying, I was still depressed most of the time and continued to think about suicide almost daily. Whatever I did to care for my family never matched my ideas of perfection, and anything less was awful. There was no middle ground in my thinking and no hope of ever being good enough. I berated myself endlessly about not liking so many aspects of being a mother and housewife, sure signs that there was something basically wrong with me.

The roads were relatively clear when I returned home at night after class as soon as I got out of the city and onto the East-West Tollway heading west. Even then, suicide was always on my mind, never far from awareness, like a persistent drip from a corroded pipe. In the quiet of the drive home I would often hear the drip.

There was a place just beyond where the highway became elevated as it crossed Route 53, at the southern border of the Morton Arboretum, before it made a slight curve to the south and then headed west again as it went up what passes for a hill around here. Often I would imagine not making the curve and careening off the highway. The impulse wasn't very strong, but I almost always thought about it at that spot.

Years later, I realized that I thought about suicide the way an alcoholic always has a drink on her mind, or a person with an eating disorder always thinks about food. For me it was easier to think about how to die than about why I might be so interested in dying.

EXPERIMENTAL DRUGS

I imagined myself as a hippie sympathizer, but the truth was that Russell had his profession and a job and we were married with two babies. We were both first children and much too responsible and too encumbered to actually be hippies. Instead, we skirted the edges. Before we moved to Naperville, one of Russell's friends had given us some marijuana to try. I liked the idea that it was frowned upon, especially by my parents, and I liked the heightened sensations I experienced, which were so unlike the numbed-out state I was usually in. However, almost every time we smoked marijuana, I got paranoid to some degree or another and imagined that everyone around me thought I was a disgusting, crazy person. That, I did not like.

In the summer of 1969, we went to Vancouver, British Columbia, to visit Fred, Russell's youngest brother, who had gone there to avoid the draft. Fred was a real hippie in my eyes, expanding his mind with almost any substance he came across. He was far less interested in pleasing people than Russell or I were, and he was not at all afraid of flaunting rules when it suited him. He went into exile to be true to his principles.

He offered to have someone watch the children if we wanted to try some really good LSD. Of course we did. We tripped out at Lynn Canyon, in a provincial park near Vancouver. It was a clear, cool day in the beautiful park forest. I noticed a fallen log that was slowly being chewed up by carpenter ants. As the LSD began to take effect, I became fascinated with the soft, slight mounds of sawdust the ants left behind, and the interesting play of light and dark as the sunlight sprinkled through the leaves of the surrounding trees. The experience wasn't as much hallucinatory as intense. I'd read about LSD, and I figured this was a mild, good trip.

I was unprepared, however, for how difficult it was to come out of it. The first effects of the drug wore off after eight or ten hours, but the sense of being slightly drugged persisted for almost three months. It added a strange overlay in my mind to the depression that was already there, deepening it into despair. Because it was so unchangeable and persistent, it felt even worse than the ordinary depression I lived with. I became more paranoid, much like when I was high on marijuana.

When we came home to Naperville, I lost interest in most of what I had been doing. I thought about quitting graduate school. I had changed my focus from urban affairs to public administration, which prolonged my program. That summer the subject didn't interest me much anymore. When I told Russell what I was thinking, he strongly encouraged me to finish. He said I would never get any credit in the work world for the courses I took, only from the degree I earned. A degree would be like a union card. I kept going, and eventually the effects of the LSD wore off.

JEREMY

We decided to adopt our third child for all kinds of reasons, only some of which were well thought out or even conscious. Partly, it was a response to the Zero Population Growth movement of the time. For many months, *The Chicago Daily News* ran an article every week about children available for adoption who were not newborns or who had some kind of difficulty. Russell and I both came from families in which three children were the norm, so our little family felt incomplete with only two, but I didn't think I could survive the emotional upheaval of another pregnancy. Despite my concerns about being an adequate mother, taking in a child who was already here seemed like the right thing to do.

When Russell and I decided to adopt, we already knew that we would only be considered for a hard-to-place child because we could still make babies on our own. In our first adoption interview the social worker described a child who might be available to us: an otherwise healthy, Caucasian baby boy who was considered hard to place because he wasn't a newborn. He had been held back because there was some concern about potential problems due to his birth mother's drug use when she was pregnant. After a few months, it became clear that the problems the doctors were looking for had not manifested, but by then he was too "old" for a quick adoption.

I was excited by what the social worker told us because his birth parents, who were students at an Illinois university, seemed enough like us—studious and musical—for the child to possibly be a very good fit with our family. In an auspicious coincidence, his foster family had named him Jeremy, the boy's name we had picked out during my first pregnancy.

Four months later, the social worker told us that we had been approved, and by the way, did we remember Jeremy? He was eight months old by then and even harder to place, so he was still available. We immediately said we wanted him.

Jeremy was living as the baby in a foster family with four children, two of whom were adopted. His foster family had cared for him like one of their own. The first time we met him, in May 1970, Jeremy came for a short visit with his four-year-old foster brother, who was being shown where Jeremy was going to live after he left "home." The next week, when the social worker brought Jeremy by himself to stay, she also brought a baby album filled with baby pictures and photographs of special days in his foster family's life, such as Jeremy all dressed up and sitting next to a big Easter lily plant. He invariably looked happy. In November, we went to court, and he became officially ours.

I was very happy to add to our family in such a painless way. Our entire extended family welcomed our new baby as if he were homemade. Sonia wasn't so sure. At four and a half she was old enough to understand that her new brother came from someplace else and had arrived much bigger than the babies in her friends' homes. Once, when Jeremy was annoying me, she asked if we couldn't just send him back. I assured her that no one ever got sent back for any reason.

To the great relief of our landlords, whose apartment was beneath ours, and who did not rejoice in our enlarged family, we decided to buy a house. We found one a few blocks away that we could afford with a loan from Russell's mother. We moved a few months after Jeremy became ours for good.

EUROPE

In the summer of 1972, Russell was asked to visit the four high-energy particle accelerators in Europe to observe how they operated and to see how what he learned might apply at Argonne. All of his expenses would be covered, and if I paid my own way, I was welcome to go along. Neither of us had ever been to Europe, although it was on the agenda for some day when the children were old enough and we had enough money and all the other considerations that put things off into the indefinite future. This was an excellent opportunity, and we decided I would go along.

Arranging the trip was no simple matter, but in time we figured it out. My mother-in-law, Mollie, with whom I was getting more comfortable all the time, was a schoolteacher who had the summer off. She took the children some of the time. My parents took them on weekends, when they were not working. My sister was married with an infant by then, but she pitched in where she could.

We traveled with another couple, who were very late getting to the airport for the long check in. By the time we were at the counter almost all of the seats were taken and we were asked if we would mind sitting in first class. We tried hard not to look too excited as we giggled our way into the 747, the classiest airplane of the day. There we were presented with bowls full of caviar and hot towels to wipe our hands. There was an upstairs lounge where the first-class passengers could sit around little tables and sip wine. There was freshly squeezed orange juice with breakfast. We had quite a grand time crossing the Atlantic.

I was very nervous about being so far from home and so far from my children. But I also had no idea if or when I would ever be able to come again. I wanted to see and do everything.

Our first stop was Oxford, England, where Russell and his colleague were going to visit the Harwell Laboratory. A driver from Harwell met us at Heathrow airport and drove us to our hotel. In the days that followed, while the men were at meetings, the other woman and I wandered all over.

Over the weekend, we all took the train into London and walked everywhere, seeing as much as we could.

One day, the four of us were invited to tea at the home of a colleague who had lived in the United States for a while but had returned to England and now lived in a small village outside of Oxford. Tea was a feast of tasty light sandwiches, sweets, nuts, and of course, tea. After we had all eaten, our hosts invited us to walk around the village. It wasn't long after we set out that I realized that what I had poured in was ready to pour out.

I had rules back then—rules about not interrupting someone else's agenda and rules about not appearing to need anything lest I be humiliated. Everyone at the tea except Russell was a new acquaintance, and I was uneasy among strangers in a new place. I was particularly anxious about what they might say or think of me if I interrupted the walk to go back to the house.

I kept my mouth shut and grew increasingly uncomfortable. By the time we reached the house and relief, I was desperate. I was also caught in a battle between the need to speak up and my dread of doing so. The more urgent my need to speak up, the higher my anxiety rose, until it blossomed into a full-blown panic attack. From then on whenever I felt trapped, especially in the presence of anyone who I thought might be put out by my attending to myself instead of them, panic almost overwhelmed me. I was very skilled at pretending all was well, and kept this new flaw in my personality from Russell.

After Oxford, the four of us went on to the CERN Laboratory, outside of Geneva, Switzerland, where we parted company with the other couple. Russell and I enjoyed a few days of sightseeing. There were some days when I was on my own. On one of those solo days, I was walking down the sidewalk toward my hotel, when two men approached from the other direction. As they passed, the closest one reached out and grabbed my breast, squeezed it, and walked on. I stopped, startled, and turned around, but they kept on walking as if nothing had happened. I grew intensely depressed, went to my room, and slept until Russell came back. I had no idea why I was so depressed.

From Geneva, we went to Paris for a few days, where Russell visited the SACLAY Laboratory, and then to Hamburg where he went to the DESY Laboratory. The hotel in Paris was delightful in an old-fashioned way, but the toilet was down the hall. That really wasn't a problem, but I was learning to fret any time I thought there might be a delay getting there in time.

I found the Louvre intimidating because I never could figure out just where I was with respect to the restrooms. The Mona Lisa was surprisingly small, well protected, and surrounded by a small crowd of people who were probably tourists like us. Even with Russell with me I felt lost and trapped. I was too frantic to be disappointed about how little we could see.

What impressed me about the ancient headless statue of Winged Victory was that it was on a landing of a stairwell, which meant it wasn't within the warren of galleries that seemed to comprise each floor. I felt less trapped in the stairwell, where I could see how to get out.

In Hamburg, I was surprised that my first impression of German people coming and going reminded me of Naperville, a town with a great deal of German ancestry in its original inhabitants. There was something about their posture, their gait, and their gestures that was hard to define but strangely familiar. Hamburg was more intimidating than home. It was difficult not to imagine anti-Semitism in every corner. I found an English language bookstore and bought a novel by Henry Miller, and I spent most of my alone time reading or sleeping.

I was never sorry that I went to Europe, but I was sorry that I was anxious and depressed so much of the time. I slept away many afternoons, unable to manage the challenge of my new panic and being so far from what was familiar. Thousands of miles away from my children, I missed them terribly.

By the time we got home, I was anxious any time I left my house. I could have become more and more housebound, as many people with anxiety problems do. But it was more important to look "normal" to others around me than to avoid the discomfort that going out caused.

As much as I tried to keep my distress to myself, sometimes I had to tell Russell that I needed to find a washroom. He didn't seem bothered, perhaps because he didn't know how upset I was by the time I said something, but I thought that panic was a serious character flaw and a clear sign that I was crazy. I was too embarrassed to think much about whether it could be treated or fixed or lessened. I had no idea how to make it stop.

PLAN COMMISSION

In early 1972, one of my Hobson Nursery School friends and I chaired the AAUW Urban Affairs committee. After one of our meetings, a Naperville city councilwoman asked if either of us would be willing to serve on the Naperville Plan Commission. My friend wasn't interested, but I was, especially with my academic interest in city affairs. I asked the councilwoman what the time commitment would be since I was still in school working on my master's degree in urban affairs, active at the nursery school, and raising three small children. She said the commission met only twice a month in public session, with occasional additional meetings. I agreed to the appointment.

Naperville was already growing rapidly from the small farm town it had been before World War II into one of the five largest cities in Illinois that it is today. The City Council approved the Plan Commission recommendations about 95 percent of the time, which added a level of importance to what we were doing. Unlike what I'd been told, we met about twice a week almost every week. I was probably the youngest member of the commission and often took the position of gadfly, looking out for the interests of young families.

I had been on the Commission only a few months before our trip to Europe. After we returned, my anxiety jacked up every time I went to a meeting, as I worried about being trapped up front, about being embarrassed when I excused myself to go to the washroom, about someone surmising that there was something wrong with me that I couldn't sit still through a several-hour meeting like the other adults in the room.

However, I liked the fact that we were making a real contribution. Judaism teaches the importance of social action. What better place to be active than on an important public commission?

THE JEWISH COMMUNITY

The first Jewish family we met in Naperville was the Prasteins from our nursery school. They, too, had started out in Hyde Park before moving to Naperville with their five children several years before we did. For a long time, they were the only Jews we knew in town. When Sonia was five or six, she thought the only Jewish people in the world besides the Prasteins were her relatives.

In the spring 1972, I received an unusual invitation. A small group of Jewish women decided to invite any other Jewish women they could find in our area to come to an afternoon tea party at the home of Naomi Rubin. The Rubin family had been in Naperville since the early twentieth century.

When I arrived at Naomi's home on Columbia Street, I was startled to find about thirty women sitting in her spacious living room. We all looked around at each other, amazed at how many we were and from how many nearby towns. We all knew that there were other Jews around, but no one had known how many there were. That afternoon there was talk of starting a community.

In the fall, a group of us gathered in the basement of one of the families to celebrate the High Holidays. We were all young with babies and toddlers who needed tending from time to time. Just as with the Passover *Seder* in Madison that I had participated in, this was very much a do-it-yourself service. We had no rabbi, no Torah (the scroll of the first five books of the Hebrew Bible), no sermons. Our counterculture prayer book was a compilation of traditional prayers and readings interspersed with quotations from contemporary poets, the lyrics of "Where Have all the Flowers Gone" by Pete Seeger, and something from John Lennon of the Beatles. Services consisted of taking turns reading portions out of the prayer book with interruptions for diaper changes and snacks for the children. It belonged to us, and it was precious.

The next year, we did the same thing. This time, Yom Kippur services were interrupted by turning on the television set to see what was happening in Israel, as her Arab neighbors chose the holiest day on the Jewish calendar to attack.

As with the impromptu Passover service at my dorm in Madison, these holiday services touched me in a way no formal service had ever done. Both services were partly of my own creation and made rich with my own intentions and longing. Something was going on in this small crowd of young families, and once I had a taste, I wanted more.

Although Sonia and Jonathan had been going to a Sunday school in another Jewish community ten miles away, by the spring of 1974 we had formed our own very small Naperville Sunday school. We took turns having the classes in our homes, two weeks in one place and then two weeks in the next. The youngest children met in the kitchen, where they could do messier crafts. First grade was in the dining room, second grade in the family room, and so on. Our first paid staff person was someone to coordinate the volunteer teachers. We quickly outgrew this arrangement and began holding our classes in the City Hall building in downtown Naperville, where the Plan Commission met. There, we had paid teachers who were all shipped in from the Jewish communities on the north side of Chicago, along with a few volunteers.

This emerging Jewish community was very different from the organized and established one I had grown up in. In our Naperville community, if we wanted a worship service, we had to do it ourselves. Some people, like Russell, were very well educated, while most, like myself, were poorly educated or more secular than religious.

I wanted to be one of the service leaders so I could experiment with how to create the spiritual atmosphere I hungered for. However, I started from a base of very little useful knowledge. When it was our turn to lead, Russell did all of the Hebrew readings, and I did the English. I couldn't read the Hebrew alphabet, but I could chant along with many of the prayers because I had learned the words and melodies when I sang in the Temple Beth Israel choirs. Now, I learned as I went along.

All of us who cared about making this Jewish venture work needed to stretch ourselves. The effort enlivened some embers of longing for a place in the Jewish world that had never completely gone out.

THE FIRST TEN YEARS OF MARRIAGE

During all of this time, I kept our parents informed about what I was doing. My mother-in-law, Mollie, was interested in my many activities. Although she was working full time as a special education teacher, she always found ways to learn and study, and she supported my own studies. While Russell's family wasn't Orthodox, they were far more observant and intentional about their Jewish practice than mine had ever been. Mollie gladly entered into serious conversations about Judaism, God, and religion, without belittling my ignorance or my questions. She listened to my ideas, asked questions, and offered suggestions when asked for them. I came to value her wisdom and cherish having her in my life. Sometimes I joked with Russell that if he ever left me I was going to keep his mother.

I don't remember my mother or father having much to say about my school or the various community projects I was involved in, except this: about once every three or four years my mother told me she thought I was a poor wife and mother and that I was not taking good enough care of my husband and children because I was so busy outside our home. As I recall those pronouncements about my inadequacies, I realize was a variant of the "self-centered" speech she had delivered years before in her bedroom. As an adult, I was just as devastated as I had been when I was fifteen. When I asked Russell if he thought I wasn't taking care of him enough, he invariably assured me that he was content and satisfied with me as his wife. I was never quite sure whether or not to believe him because his response was so different from my mother's.

Looking back now, I can say that in the first ten years of my marriage I struggled to demonstrate that I was the perfect wife, the perfect mother, the perfect human being. I didn't understand then that perfection is an idol that demands greater and greater sacrifices until the supplicant is consumed.

As I tried harder to do what was basically impossible, I never told Russell about what was going on with me. I would not risk the possibility that he might belittle my distress or humiliate me for being less than happy, although he was (and is) the least likely person to do so. He often helped where he could, taking on babysitting and household chores without complaint. I almost never asked for help. He noticed that and offered when it seemed necessary. Even then, it was difficult to back away from the belief that I had to do everything myself in order to be acceptable. My mother had taught me all too well that a good wife lives to keep her family happy, which meant, among other things, never bothering her husband with her own wants and needs and feelings. I put up a good enough front that even Russell never realized how unhappy I was.

I failed to be perfect, of course, which only fueled my misguided attempts to try harder. Failure increased my desperation and despair, which was increasingly difficult to live with, especially trying to maintain a happy face. By keeping busy or unconscious (or both) I could sometimes avoid noticing the agony I was in.

Mounting rage and old, mysterious terrors threatened to escape whenever I slowed down; they fueled my increasing frenzy. I couldn't imagine where such strong, terrible feelings might be coming from or what they were about, and I knew they were out of proportion to anything going on in the moment. I just wanted them to stop.

As a mother of young children, I sometimes broke into ferocious rages when I couldn't hold back any longer. I managed to not hit any of them, but I sometimes had to leave the room in order to stop myself.

Once, when Jonathan was about eighteen months old, he teased and played and squirmed while I was trying to change his diaper. I don't know why I was so fragile that day, but my tolerance was near zero. I walked out of his room, leaving him bare bottomed for the moment, thinking that I understood completely how a parent could beat a child. I terrified myself with my murderous intent.

I was safe from these dangerous feelings only if I was moving fast enough or too exhausted to care. In effect, this strategy led to my abandoning my children to my schedule and my naps, and my husband to my meetings and classes, which were the hallmarks for my mother of what a bad wife and mother I was.

Between graduate school, nursery school, the Plan Commission, and our new Jewish community, my schedule was quite insane. In the fall of 1973, my last semester of graduate school, I took three classes instead of only one and studied for my comprehensive exams. I was exhausted most of the time. I consistently underestimated the amount of time and energy raising three young children took.

When my children all finally entered grade school and I finished my degree, I thought that the frenzy of my life would finally settle down. It did not. I didn't know how to slow down or stop. I also didn't know how to say no to any request for my time.

One summer day after I graduated, I sat with Edna, my first Naperville friend, on the stoop outside of her house. I said I needed some time off, maybe a week. No, I corrected myself, maybe a month. I read an article about workaholics and had decided I was one. Shortly after that, feeling more and more like I was losing control, I decided to try therapy again.

COLLAPSE

It was a mild day at the beginning of October 1974, a few months after talking to my friend Edna about needing time off and almost ten months after I finished my master's degree, when I drove east to Clarendon Hills to see Phyllis, my new therapist, for the first time. I got dressed up in a dark skirt and a pretty white blouse with long, puffy sleeves, as if I were going to a job interview and appearances mattered. I was so anxious before, during and after the session that I could barely pay attention to my driving. After that I took the Burlington commuter train to my sessions.

From the beginning, I was more comfortable with Phyllis than I'd been with anyone else. She suggested that I keep a journal. Rather than an instruction or a piece of advice, I took her comment as permission to write about myself. I had rarely written anything about myself since I married, over ten years earlier. If she had suggested it, then it wouldn't be merely self-indulgent to do so. I started to write regularly.

The fourth time I saw her, my efforts to put up a good front began to unravel. She mentioned how scattered I seemed, and I felt caught. Waiting for my train afterwards, I fantasized about being under the train rather than on it. This time my fantasy had some energy behind it. I was startled and scared. Later I wrote:

It is taking a long time to settle down. Death has rarely been so close. I am hysterical. I am numb. I want to go home and be unconscious. I think of pills. Most of them are used up. No matter. The promise [to not kill myself] *is made, if unstated. I want to fight. I feel very weak. Maybe a death is necessary to make way for a rebirth. I am dissolving. I am nameless. The stomach tightens and reminds me that the body remains.*

Splits of panic. All it would take is to doubt an ability to keep a promise. I am sitting still. I am flailing about, screaming for help. Where is reality? In the words? Behind them? In the ones you hear but are not spoken? Death would be so easy; so easy to give up an identity made of words I do not understand.

The children were all in school when I got home from seeing Phyllis. I was upset and dizzy and breathless and thought I was dying. I called Edna.

"Why not call Phyllis?" she asked.

I would never have thought of that myself, devoted as I was to not bothering anyone. But, then, I couldn't think of anything else to do. I called. Phyllis could hear my panicky breathing—fast and shallow—as I gulped in air and barely exhaled.

She said, "Slow your breath. You are hyperventilating."

I did and calmed down but only for a moment. Strange, unfamiliar, and unpredictable things were happening to my body and mind. I had heard a song by Leonard Cohen who wrote, "Your life is a leaf that the seasons tear off and condemn." I thought the lyrics described me perfectly. All my efforts to control myself were failing.

I did not settle down. My anxiety made my body feel like I was plugged into an electric socket. I was frightened by the intensity of my feelings and my failure to stop them. I didn't know what to do with myself.

The next day I wrote, trying to both express myself and keep my feelings as far away as possible:

The winds of death drift over me as gently as the early morning sun. A sheet pulled up against their chill becomes a shroud. Among the winds and whispers my children speak. Today my children will protect me. Their raucous shouts, their fights, their noise. I will hang on to their commotion. I feel weak and unsteady, awakened by that constant breeze and blown about already. I forgot my reasons and my choices and must remember and recite them. There is no wind I did not choose to make; there is no decision I must take.

A few days later, I could barely get out of bed. It was a school day, and Russell took care of getting the children to school and then stayed home from work. We went to the Morton Arboretum nearby and lay out on the grass in the warm October sun. I could have stayed there forever.

The next day wasn't any better. I saw Phyllis again. She insisted on a no-suicide contract: I would not take my life by accident or on purpose, no matter what, for at least several days. Later I wrote:

Our contract rattles around in my head like an impatient percussion section. I can't stop thinking about it, paying attention to it. It is a responsibility trip, a promise of things to do as well as not to do. Accident implies neglect. Preservation of the body requires action, fundamental, life sustaining. It is powerful, that contract. I still don't want to see it written. It is noisy enough without being visible, too.

My mother called, and I spoke to her briefly.

"How are you," she asked, by way of opening a conversation.

"I'm fine," I replied, but didn't say much else. I'm sure I sounded tense. I wrote: *I almost hung up on my mother. I can practically taste the discomfort I am causing her. I am bitter to us both.*

She sent a bouquet of flowers. There was a smiley face on the card, which read, "Always look to the bright side."

I wrote: *They would kill me again! They will never know or understand what an awful gift they sent.* "Don't be what you are, be something else, anything else but what you are."

Today, I can say that I wanted to bludgeon her to death with smiley faces. Then, I didn't know how angry I was. Instead, I tried to kill myself in the unobtrusive manner I had perfected all of my life, by rendering myself unconscious.

Sleeping was good enough. I could put myself out in a minute. I called Judy, a nearby Hobson Nursery School friend, and said enough that she invited me to her house. Judy offered me her bed, where I slept until school was over, safe from flowers and cheery missives from my mother. The next day, Phyllis suggested that if I couldn't be safe enough at home, perhaps I should be in the hospital.

My mother-in-law, Mollie, who I thought was very perceptive about people, once said she thought of me as the Rock of Gibraltar. I had fooled her, too. My foundation was all sand and rotted timber.

Russell and I together saw Phyllis two days later. We talked about my going into the hospital, what it would entail, the logistics, and especially whether it was necessary. We all concluded that it was a good idea, and I checked into Riveredge Hospital the next morning.

When I went into the hospital, I was horrified by the idea that anyone would know just how defective I was. That was the main secret I knew I was keeping, and it was leaking out all over the place.

"How I could feel so depressed," I had asked my Hobson friend, Judy, "when everything was so good in my life? I had a husband who said he loved me and who was kind, a house, three kids, and a cat. What else could I want?"

"Do you know that people love you," she asked.

I said, "No."

The only explanation I had for my mental state was some profound flaw about which nothing could be done.

I wrote this about my parents and me while I was in the hospital:

My parents say, "If we hurt you, you deserved it."

My parents say, "You hurt us, you must stop and protect us— we did not deserve it."

They say, "If you do not protect us; we, who are weak, will fall apart and the blame will be yours."

They say, "You are not good. You are not good because you hurt us."

They say, "We cannot love you if you cannot be good enough."

I say, "I am unconvinced that I am good enough to be loved. I've run out of things to do to prove my worth."

And yet, even in the midst of unraveling, there was something else. A few days before I went into the hospital I wrote:

Perhaps I have a guardian. Mine works as an advance agent setting things up to happen at the right time. The one absolute constant in my life has been that things always happen at the right time. My guardian does not require my acquiescence or recognition to work.

I thought that going into the hospital was ultimate proof that I'd completely failed at the only thing that mattered: being able to keep myself together and take care of everyone else. At moments I was so distraught that I would force my mind to go blank—I was unwilling to even think the words that described my failure.

I felt an unprecedented collection of sensations, some too unfamiliar to identify. I didn't have the vocabulary to describe the sea of shame I was drowning in. I felt like I was scrambling to keep my footing on slippery slime and grabbing for handholds that disintegrated as I touched them. I was thoroughly confused and desperate.

And, as I went into the hospital, there was an odd kind of hopefulness as well. It was a kind of surrender when the struggle had overwhelmed me. I wrote:

Thought-less
Care-less
Emotion-less. Not cold. Not empty.
Quiet as the fall furrowed fields.
My worrisome harvest is in.
Now it is time to be still,
To prepare for winter's waiting,
Storing up the sun and wisps of wind,
Gathering the hidden energy of dry
Stalks and the year's first flurries.

HOSPITAL

My sense of failure notwithstanding, I was also glad to be in the hospital where the doors were locked. I had no interest in being anywhere else, so I didn't feel trapped. At my request, my parents did not have permission to visit. The locks kept them out. The locks also kept out all of my ordinary activity. They said "no" to everything except the hospital agenda. I didn't worry about my children or my husband or anyone else. Russell told me about the child-care arrangements and they seemed good enough. I felt very chaotic and cut off from the people in my life and helpless to the point of indifference. I didn't, I couldn't, worry about anyone else. I barely had the energy to be in therapy all day long.

Another thing I liked about the hospital was that everyone there was some kind of crazy, if not exactly psychotic—you had to be in order to get in. It was a great relief not to have to hold myself together or try to impress anyone with my sanity. I was fascinated with the variety of reasons people were there. There was comfort in their company. There was comfort in knowing I didn't have to be responsible for anyone else. There was comfort in knowing that I didn't have to be responsible for staying away from sharp objects and bottles of pills and trains. Members of the hospital staff checked on me every fifteen minutes. If I was being watched so carefully, I could relax my vigilance a little.

I was glad to be in the hospital, but it wasn't a place to rest; rather, it was a place to work. I saw either Phyllis, or Ray, my psychiatrist, or his associate, Peg, five days a week. I was in all kinds of group therapy: I learned to make clay pots in art therapy. I went home on the weekends, but I chose to stay in the hospital for Thanksgiving so I could avoid my parents.

Phyllis was interested in my dreams. I told her one dream in which I wanted to cross a busy street to get to a bakery, which had wonderful pastries in the window. The street was very icy and full of cars. It didn't seem possible to cross without slipping and getting hit.

We talked about how I couldn't imagine safely getting what I wanted. We also talked about my own slipperiness and my feeling that I was as out of control as the cars seemed to be.

In another dream, I went home to a very large, empty clapboard house set on a hill, reached by several flights of crumbling stairs. The house was desolate, broken and empty—a place where no one had lived for a long time. The image of the house was clearly how I thought of myself: almost too large, empty, desolate, and broken.

For many years after, I had recurrent dreams of food and houses. I could gauge my emotional and mental progress by the availability of the food or the state of repair of the houses.

Shortly before I went home I wrote:

I imagine a net, each strand strong and flexible in delicate readiness, its lines graceful and harmonic.

It is a net to catch, but never hold captive; a net that I may weave and shape.

Perhaps it has always been here.

Now it sparkles and shines as I stand in the center in wonder.

As each strand flows to me, I reach out and take hold and feel that it is real and warm and full of life.

The strength and love of the sender of each strand are full of the energy of the sun, the care of a gentle rain, the richness of deep, black earth.

For a moment, at least, I remembered that my story was part of a much, much larger story, a story of life and wonder, a story touched with divine serenity. For a moment, I forgot my mistaken beliefs about the reality of my shame and my failures.

After thirty-two days, rather suddenly, I found the hospital schedule boring and said so. The next day I went home. I'd been there for thirty-three days, just a bit over the month I had told Edna I needed the summer before.

HOME AGAIN

When I got out of the hospital, it was suddenly easy to say no and to resign from everything. For the next year and a half, my only activity outside of my household was therapy: group once a week with Russell, led by Ray, and private sessions with Phyllis. I don't recall what my goals were, if I'd even really thought about them. Feeling better seemed like a good idea, but it was several years before I could begin to imagine what feeling better might be like.

One of the first things that changed with my hospitalization was my relationship with Russell. In the first ten years of our marriage, I had worked hard to be the kind of wife my mother taught me to be: undemanding, affectionate, endlessly taking care of my family and asking nothing for myself, and so on. During my therapy in the hospital I began to realize that in adhering to her model of a wife I was not in fact paying much attention to what Russell actually wanted or thought. I also realized that sometimes I was angry with him, but didn't know how to say so. I was enormously dependent on him, and terrified that he would leave if he knew how I felt. The more aware I became of what was wrong between us the less tolerant I became of our situation.

When I first came home I didn't want him physically near me. I thought, *if Russell wanted a divorce, this is the perfect excuse*. He was not happy with my insistence that he not touch me, but said often that he had married me for life, and was not going to leave. *Words are just words*, I thought. Russell stayed, did what he could, went to group therapy with me, and eventually I softened.

A few weeks after I came home from the hospital, my family celebrated my father's parents' anniversary. They were married on Christmas Eve 1908, because Jewish workers could get Christmas Day off. There had been regular Christmas Day anniversary parties long before I was born. In 1974, the guests were my grandmother (my grandfather having died in 1969), my aunt and uncle and their children and grandchildren, and my parents and their children and grandchildren.

For as far back as I could remember I had never missed this party. I was still very shaky and in the earliest stages of recovering from whatever had precipitated my collapse. It mattered to me very much that I go, even though everyone presumably knew that I was crazy enough to have just gotten out of a mental hospital.

The party always was a very predictable event. The rituals changed from time to time over the years but not very much. In those days, we gathered at the Como Inn just north and west of Chicago's downtown in one of their party rooms that could accommodate our small crowd. Dinner was always the same menu from year to year: an antipasto, minestrone soup, main dishes of Italian sausage, chicken and beef, and a pasta side dish with marinara sauce; dessert was spumoni ice cream with cookies and fruit. After dinner, we exchanged Hanukah gifts, whether or not Hanukah coincided with Christmas, then gathered our belongings and went home. Conversation revolved around the growing family and very little else.

Going to the party in 1974 was my display of how I really wasn't crazy, of how I wasn't going to disrupt the montage of one big happy family. I didn't expect anyone to comment on where I'd been or why, and nobody did. Each of us in that party room was one part of the design. The appearance of harmony and happiness was the most important thing, and we all played our part.

Below the level of thought, or off to a side where I only occasionally noticed, there were other goals beyond not disturbing the family fantasy. One of the biggest was to keep my panic hidden and continue to give the impression that I was normal. As much as possible, I didn't want anyone to know how depressed or anxious I was.

For all of the no-suicide contracts I made, some short and some longer, I never really wanted to give up suicide as an option; I just didn't want to feel suicidal all the time. Thinking about suicide and how I might do it was an escape hatch, a distraction, a comfort, and an excitement.

BEING SLIPPERY

I think I was like many people who go into therapy, wanting to feel better, but not wanting to touch what really bothered me. I had some secrets that I kept well out of sight of everyone, including myself.

I was aware that I wanted to follow where my therapists were leading, because that was a way to demonstrate that I was cooperative and helpful. I was usually unaware of how much I wanted to stay completely in control of what happened.

There were also moments of insight. Nine months after I got out of the hospital, I wrote about an interaction with Ray:

I won't let you push me.

I will let you push me.

If you push, I can get stuck because you are pushing. Then I can blame you for pushing and for my being stuck. If I let you push me, if I encourage you to push me, then I can disown responsibility for where I land— my place will become your fault, not mine.

I am impressed with how I do not let me know what I know, how I could be in such a shit spot and be so unaware, how I could hear myself say inside that I wanted Ray to take responsibility for me and still not hear what I was saying.

It is complicated. Ray does push, and I do ask him to, and he will do what I ask [in this respect]*, and I will not let him.*

I wrote that. I knew how manipulative I was, at least when I wrote it. I forgot and had to relearn it dozens of times, many dozens of times. Ray called it "bear trapping" when I presented myself as eager and cooperative and then blanked out or got numb or stonewalled in some other way. Over the years, Ray wasn't the only one to get angry with me for my slipperiness, while I usually remained miserably (and at some level, deliberately) unconscious of what I was doing.

It's not that no one told me. I didn't listen. I wanted to be found—I kept coming back. I never wanted to be found. I trusted Ray some, and Phyllis a great deal, but at a deep, unconscious level I didn't trust either of them to know the parts of me that I hid from myself. I didn't trust me to know my deepest secrets either. I took a very long time before I let someone find me. I took a very long time to stop hiding.

I wasn't just being obnoxious, although there probably was some of that. One time, I told Phyllis about how important it was to be good.

She said, "Behind every good girl is a brat."

Not me, I thought. But, it was me.

Phyllis and Ray both practiced Gestalt Therapy, which they had learned from its founder, Fritz Perls. This psychotherapy method uses structured experiences to heighten awareness. It is particularly effective and powerful in bypassing the client's intellect to get to the emotions. Smart, verbal people like me could talk around all kinds of things indefinitely. Gestalt techniques are primarily experiential. Experience is much harder to talk away.

We did a lot of what is called "empty chair work," which basically involved having a conversation between various parts of myself. A classic in Gestalt circles was the conversation (which was sometimes a fight or a debate or a silent standoff) between the Top Dog and Underdog parts of self. The theory was that the client could learn about herself by listening to what she was saying as she played the alternate parts, back and forth.

I had a bunch of parts. The idea of talking to them, and them talking back, wasn't foreign to me, although I didn't usually talk out loud to myself as I did in therapy sessions. It was easy to slip in and out of those parts, which left me thinking that I was doing something right. On the other hand, I was intent (consciously, some of the time) on appearing forthright and keeping my most vulnerable parts of myself well out of sight. The work did not go smoothly, and progress was very slow.

SHOSTAKOVICH

Ray led workshops and marathons for all of his groups. These were intensive fifteen and thirty hour weekend therapy sessions, modeled somewhat on the encounter groups of that era. He often put on recordings of music for people after they had done especially meaningful work.

Once, at such a time, he played the second movement of the Shostakovich *Second Piano Concerto* for me. It was a section of heartbreaking beauty that broke open my heart. Exhausted by the late hour and the effort to contain myself, I lay down on the floor. I knew the piece but had never *really* heard the piece. Somehow the piano's simple melody caught my mood precisely. I struggled so hard with the urge to both open up and stay closed. Not only did Shostakovich write a melody entirely devoid of struggle, but Ray knew that this music was perfect for the moment and for me. It was wonderful that Ray knew me so well. Listening to the music was a time of surrender.

The concerto still takes me back to the sense of surrender every time I listen to it.

MEDITATION: A BEGINNING

Not long after I left the hospital, someone told me about learning to meditate from Swami Rama, a yogi master who was the guru of the Himalayan Institute, about an hour away from home. I had been curious about meditation for many years, but this was the first class I'd heard about. I signed up immediately. The beginners' lessons were about learning diaphragmatic breathing, systematic tension release, and learning to smooth the breath so that there were no pauses, jerks, or sounds being made. Swami Rama recommended practicing twice a day for twenty minutes each time.

About six months later, I made an appointment with Swami Rama to receive a mantra, a Sanskrit word that would be the focus of my meditation. After a long ride and a long wait, I was shown into his room, where he made a sweeping movement with his arm and hand indicating that he wanted me to sit on the floor. He asked me a few questions and said something about needing to learn to stop hurting myself. Then he told me that my mantra would be *Shama*, pronounced with one syllable on the inhalation and the other on the exhalation. He wrote out the meaning of the word on a small scrap of paper, which I still have: peace, prosperity, perfection, health, happiness, light, love, and two more words I no longer can make out. He told me to say the mantra and focus on my heart center, about midway down the breastbone, and then said something about how closed my heart was. I was impressed with what he discovered about me after so short a conversation. Then the interview was over.

I liked the two-syllable word, *Shama*. I particularly liked how close it was to *Sh'ma*, the Hebrew word for listen, pronounced almost as one syllable. For me this was a Sanskrit link to my Judaism.

When I tried to do the meditation as I was taught, my perfectionism made each session more frustrating than relaxing. I thought there was something the matter with me if I couldn't do what sounded so simple, and once again I didn't ask for help. I didn't know then that my difficulties with the practice were common, perhaps universal among beginners. I quit with a sense of failure.

A NEW NAME

One weekend in mid-April, about five months after leaving the hospital, I participated in a movement workshop with a choreographer from San Francisco, whose name I have long forgotten. He began by asking what name we wanted to be called by for the weekend.

What an odd sort of request, I thought, but without further consideration, I said my Hebrew name, Yonah, which means, "dove."

I had already been playing around with referring to myself as Yonah in my journals. I liked the sound of it. I liked the hint of mystical mystery in using a Hebrew name. I was called Yonah all weekend.

By the time I returned home, something had shifted in me. It was as if my skin had painlessly expanded, as if I literally grew in the night. If a name is a kind of garment, I had acquired a new wardrobe. The new name seemed more mine than Toby.

On Monday morning, Phyllis and I spent the whole session talking about what changing my name might mean to me. During my group therapy session with Russell on Tuesday night, I brought the matter up again. As an exercise in awareness Ray asked me to introduce myself to each member of the group with my new name. As I introduced myself to each person in turn I could feel an almost physical shift until, by the end of the exercise, the shift was complete and permanent.

Coming home after group Russell said that "Toby" had never seemed to fit me, that he liked "Yonah" much better. I told my children the next morning. To them this was just another piece of information, new to the day. I went to the bank and changed my signature card and mailed out applications for a new Social Security card and driver's license. By the end of the day the change was public and legal, because first name changes didn't require any legal action.

When I told my parents, they sounded mystified but they didn't ask why. All the other people I told about the change told me how much they liked "Yonah." I liked that people liked my name, and most even found it beautiful. When meeting new people before the name change, a common response was some degree of incredulity and puzzlement about how a female had ended up with a name like Toby. (My birth name, Toby, was actually a common girl's name in the Jewish community, coming from the Yiddish word, "*toybe*," which means "dove," which is why Yonah is naturally my Hebrew name.) From then on none of my family or friends ever mistakenly used my old name, nor did I.

I vaguely realized at the time that changing my name, especially in such a natural, easy way, meant I was changing. Toby seemed limited and limiting in some way that Yonah didn't. This first emergence of a new sense of self was also accompanied by the first hints of self-compassion, which had been missing almost entirely beforehand.

That was the first result of the movement weekend.

A MOVEMENT MEDITATION

The choreographer who led the workshop in which I tried out my new name had described to us how he set up certain creative movement exercises for his troupe. He watched what the dancers did and then used their movements to create his performance pieces. While he had no intention to produce anything performable at the workshop, he went through the same process with us as he did with his dancers. He would give us an idea, such as the evolution of humankind, and instruct us to find a way in unstructured movement to suggest what the idea meant to us. Then, he would quietly watch for an hour and a half or two while we moved. There were breaks and an opportunity to talk about what had happened. Most people stayed silent. There were also breaks for meals and when we went home for the night. We danced Friday evening, all day on Saturday, and into Sunday afternoon.

    I loved the silence. I loved the sense of being able to move myself, without having to take the other dancers or the choreographer into account, beyond not bumping into them. I loved that there was no technique that I could do well or poorly. I loved dancing without structure— without a right way and a wrong way to do it. I loved the possibilities of expressing myself through movement, which had almost never happened when I had studied ballet. I loved that no one expressed any interest in what I was doing. I loved the brilliance of my senses when we left on Sunday. Years later, I realized that the entire weekend had been one long meditation with pauses.

    I wanted to know more about how to do this activity, which didn't seem to have a name beyond dancing. A few months later, I heard about dance/movement therapy from someone, and figured that was what we had been doing at the workshop. Movement can be a much more direct route to emotions and expression than talk therapy, because it bypasses language and the intellect entirely. Intuitively I knew this well, and was so guarded against my own feelings that I never just danced by myself. Today I suspect that my interest in learning to lead dance/movement therapy was inspired at least in part by a desire to be in control of the proceedings.

By the time I tracked down a place to study this kind of dancing, the year-long program had already begun, and I was shut out. I was disappointed but resigned to waiting. In the meantime, I was hired by the City of Naperville to work part-time on the capital improvements budget, which became my first job after getting my masters degree in public administration. Working for the city turned out to be far less interesting than I had imagined when I was a student.

The next year, barely two years since my collapse, I enrolled in a certificate program to become a dance/movement therapist. The entire program was taught at Riveredge Hospital, where I'd been a patient, in conjunction with Northeastern Illinois University. To be back in the hospital as a student was odd. I vividly remembered being a patient and how I felt then. As a student, I prided myself in the fact that I was learning to be a therapist and was no longer a patient. But I was barely beginning to recover. The experiential sections of almost every dance therapy class aggravated the old issues of wanting to look competent and all put together despite my inner pandemonium.

The academic part of the program, which was a basic introduction to counseling theory, was interesting and easy enough. The exercises we did in the dance therapy class were similar to the ones from the workshop but much shorter. In class, our emphasis was on learning to be deliberate in what we chose to do with our clients and how to be mindful of the likely effects of our choices. During the experiential section of each class, it was often difficult to keep myself in the student's persona and not that of a client—I had to remind myself that this wasn't a therapy group but a class.

But I was good at being a student and did well. At the end of the twelve-month course, in the summer of 1977, I quit my city job and went directly from my internship into employment as a dance/movement therapist at a day-hospital, where chronic psychiatric patients came in for therapy during the day but went home at night. That was a challenge and a triumph.

Almost immediately, I started training with the Gestalt Institute in Chicago to increase my therapeutic skills. Phyllis was on the faculty. I was excited to be learning how to lead the kinds of things she had done with me, and the theory behind the method. We students did a lot of practicing with each other.

The basic idea behind Gestalt Therapy is that awareness can yield insight, which then can produce psychological growth. The technique is all about increasing self-awareness. I got myself into the same kind of trouble as I had during dance therapy training—I was being very affected personally by the exercises we were doing. As always, I kept my distress to myself, not even bringing it up in my own therapy sessions.

Sometimes I slipped beyond my attempts to look good and was more honestly expressive. Years later, a classmate from those times said that the intensity of my responses scared the rest of the class. I hadn't noticed the class reaction in my struggle to believe that I was only having a "deep" experience.

Sitting in the counselor's chair didn't come easily to me, but I was diligent in the training. I read all of the books on Gestalt Therapy I could find. Becoming skilled in what I was doing helped me maintain an illusion that I was really all right. In the second year, I did an internship with the Institute, had lots of supervision, and tried to put everything I learned into practice with my dance-therapy groups.

Although spiritual matters were outside the realm of orthodox Gestalt Therapy, several of the faculty members and one of the students were very interested in the spiritual ramifications of focusing on awareness. From them, I learned about guided meditations and Spirit Guides.

To invoke a Spirit Guide, the meditation leader first used peaceful imagery to help the class get into a meditative state. Then, imagery was used to bring us up to a high place, like a mountain-top (signifying our Higher Self that is connected to Divine wisdom), or down into a deep place, like the bottom of a cave or pool (signifying the place where our deepest wisdom resides). We were instructed to ask for our Guides to appear and wait for them to come forth. Once our Guides appeared, the leader of the meditation asked open-ended, evocative questions about the state of our lives and the direction we were going or thought we wanted to be going. We were then to listen or see or intuit the answers our Guides could provide. Often, we were instructed to ask our Guides our own specific questions about our lives, then to wait for the answers.

If the Guide failed to appear, perhaps we were not ready. If an answer was not forthcoming, perhaps we had asked the wrong question. Everything about the techniques of using Spirit Guides was presented in a completely nonjudgmental, self-compassionate way.

The Guides were understood to be parts of ourselves that had access to our deepest inner wisdom. They were very useful in contemplating what we were doing or what we wanted to do with our lives. In time, I named my most important Guide Shama, the same word that Swami Rama had used for my mantra. Shama was androgynous, round, and sort of soft in appearance. S/he was also miraculously compassionate and, as I learned later, demanding.

MY FATHER'S HEART ATTACKS

In 1977, my father had two heart attacks, four months apart. In those days, a heart attack survivor stayed in the hospital for many days. After the first heart attack, he was hospitalized at Edgewater Hospital on Chicago's north side, which was the same hospital where I was born.

While he was there, I attended a Gestalt Therapy seminar about exploring Jewish identity. Apropos of something, I announced in a matter-of-fact voice that one of my uncles had molested me when I was sixteen. I mentioned that I'd never forgotten the incident. People's eyes widened, their expressions freshened, as they suddenly grew alert.

"But it was nothing, really," I continued. "It doesn't bother me at all."

Later, in response to my saying something about my father's heart attack, the facilitator suggested I do a classic Gestalt style, empty-chair conversation with my father. During the conversation, I would play the roles of both him and myself.

After a moment, I replied, "This is silly. My father is just down the street. I'll go and talk to him directly."

So I did. He was in a small room in intensive care. In my memory, the walls were entirely covered in stainless steel. The serious, shiny equipment, the tiny sink near his bed, the lack of anything remotely soft or comforting marked this a room set apart. My father was lying down, neatly covered and tucked in a way that I think only nurses can do. He looked more drawn and scared than I'd ever seen him. I was tight all over with the effort to not know or show any of the multitude of feelings that must have been there, barely contained. Above all, I was scared—perhaps he would die. He was only fifty-nine years old. I don't remember what we talked about; more importantly, I told myself I was there lending whatever support I could. I, of course, needed nothing for myself. It was a brief visit.

My mother was there, too. After we left my father, we went across the street to a small restaurant. Over coffee, she started to talk about her relationship with my father. She said that she was aware that she had given up a lot in her life to keep my father happy. She said she thought her effort had been well worth it.

I remember thinking that her efforts had also come at a cost to her children. I did not share my thoughts with her.

My father's second heart attack occurred four months later while he was going about his business as a hardware salesman some place on the far south side. He ended up at Little Company of Mary Hospital on Ninety-Fifth Street. This attack frightened him more because he thought he had been making a good recovery from the first episode.

When I called him, he told me his doctor had talked to him about reducing stress. I knew several relaxation exercises, and he accepted my offer to come and teach him one.

Except for the Hyde Park neighborhood, the south side of the Chicago metropolitan area has never been very familiar to me. The nighttime ride on Interstate 294 to Ninety-Fifth Street and then the miles driving east to the hospital seemed very long. I was worried and no more prepared for him to die than I'd been after the first episode.

After visiting a few minutes we started the exercise.

"Close your eyes," I instructed. "Be aware of the top of your head. Let the muscles of your scalp relax. Be aware of your forehead. Let the muscles of your forehead relax."

In time I came to the lower part of his body, and he made a sexual innuendo. Startled and flustered, I didn't continue.

This was a genuine opportunity for me to actually help you, I thought angrily, *and all you can think of are crude jokes.*

I left resolving to never help him again with anything.

As I write this, I realize that this little story is more complex than I thought thirty years ago. My father knew how to bully, how to demand, how to charm and play when he was feeling good, but I think he knew almost nothing about intimacy, at least not with me. Perhaps the intimacy of my offering, in a moment when he was scared and vulnerable, was too much for him, and he pushed me away in the one way he knew best.

He died sixteen years later of respiratory failure at a time when I was too scared and vulnerable myself to let him anywhere near me. Our paths were orthogonal, starting at a singular point and taking off in directions that would never really meet again. We missed each other entirely.

YOUNG MAN INTERRUPTED

In the late 1970s, when I was a student at the Gestalt Institute of Chicago, my class was held in an old building on Wabash along the El tracks just south of Adams. We met once a week for thirty weeks during the academic year, plus four weekends. On one of the weekends, I went downstairs to the Mexican fast-food place next door to pick up some lunch. As I returned to the tiny lobby of my building, a young man followed me, with a swagger in his step and a "gotcha" grin on his face. He looked behind himself for a second, as if to see if anyone was following us, and then he entered the lobby right behind me. Suddenly, the door next to the elevator opened, and a guard, whom I hadn't noticed before, stepped out and asked the young man where he was going. The swagger disappeared, and he ran out of the building.

Only then did it occur to me that I had been vaguely aware that the man was following me out of the restaurant; I knew that he was following me into the lobby; and I knew from the way he moved and the look on his face, that he had no business in the building. I'd been in a trance almost from the moment I saw him. Only being startled by the guard broke it.

On the way up in the elevator, I wondered briefly why I, who wasn't naïve about staying safe in the city, had done nothing to protect myself. I thought about that question from time to time, but I could never stay focused with my curiosity long enough to find an answer. I worried that I would be an easy target in a dangerous situation, unable to protect myself, so I took to trying to be even more careful about not getting into potentially dangerous situations in the first place.

In February 1978, my Bernard Street uncle died suddenly from a heart attack in the night. We all gathered in my aunt's apartment for an abbreviated shiva, or mourning period. The layout of the apartments on Spaulding, where my parents, aunt and uncle and grandmother had moved in the early 1970s, allowed for the flow of people from the front to the back either through the dining room or through the main bedroom, which shared a wall with the dining room, and had doors on both ends.

One afternoon during shiva, my sister and I were alone for a few moments in my aunt's bedroom.

I think Judi spoke first.

"He molested me," she said, "when I was so sick with mononucleosis. He would bring me lunch on the days when mom was at work. Once I was awake enough to notice what he was doing."

I was surprised, and told her about my own experience with him when I was sixteen, the same one I mentioned at the Gestalt Jewish Identity workshop before going to see my father in the hospital.

I told her that when it happened I'd gone downstairs to his apartment looking for one of my cousins. She wasn't there. No one was there but my uncle. I sat down on their couch to wait for her. He sat down next to me on my right, smelling of beer and sitting too close. He put his right leg over both of mine and started to turn his body towards mine. I pushed his leg away, got up and walked away.

Judi was just as surprised to hear my story, as I was to hear hers. We both had a sense of relief that telling a secret can bring. Then, someone walked into the room, and we seamlessly changed the subject. Neither of us spoke about this moment again for almost twenty years.

My uncle's behavior with me was certainly inappropriate but not horrendous. The memory remained very vivid, however. When my daughter Sonia was big enough to go up and down the stairs on Bernard Street by herself, I told Russell about that incident. I told him Sonia was never to be allowed to be alone with my uncle. Russell listened with full attention and didn't question my story or my concern. At that time, I didn't remember anything else troubling about my uncle, but what I did recall scared me into warning Russell.

DANCING WITH FRANCES

Gina, a dance therapist friend, told me about Frances Allis, a dance teacher who had a studio downtown. I recognized her name from the directory of the Fine Arts building, when I studied with Miss McRae. Gina said she had learned more about dance therapy from Frances than any other teacher, even though Frances only taught modern dance and some ballet. Classes with Frances were held on the same days that I needed to be downtown for the Gestalt Therapy classes, so I enrolled.

Frances' current studio was in a small, old, mostly empty building, fronting on the El tracks along Jackson, across the alley from Goldblatt's department store. We were frequently admonished to make sure the elevator was empty before going up to avoid getting caught with a vagrant or worse. The studio had the requisite unvarnished wooden floor, barres and mirrors, two small dressing rooms, and dirty windows that looked out onto the wall of the building next door. The studio also had a pianist, who composed new music to go with the new choreography Frances created for each class, and an elderly artist who used our classes for figure drawing practice. This worn-out old room vibrated from the creativity within it.

Frances sat through every class, disabled by two arthritic hips, calling out her instructions and corrections. She taught us that every movement, from the set-piece of our warm-up to the most inventive piece of choreography, was an expression of some kind of motivation, not just a response to an instruction.

"Why are you moving your arm?" she asked. "Where does the movement of your foot begin? What is the motivation for moving at all?"

I had danced over a period of about twenty-eight years, including the previous five years with someone in Naperville, although there were many fallow years in the middle. Even though I was a trained dance/movement therapist by then, Frances was my first dance teacher who connected the idea of formal, artistic dance with inner intention. She cared deeply about the form of the dance, the technique, the precision, just as Miss McRae had. But she also cared about the feeling of it. I had never connected inner feeling with outer structured movement before.

This was a revelation. At least since high school, I had cultivated living as much in my head and as little in my body as I could manage. My experience with the San Francescan choreographer was fascinating but unique—I never tried self-motivated movement by myself. In my dance-therapy studies I kept myself as removed from the experiential parts of the class as I could, more frightened than curious about what I might do and experience. As obvious as it seems now, I never considered the possibility that dance could be an artistic expression of feeling. My own dancing flourished.

PALO ALTO, CALIFORNIA

In 1979, Russell accepted a two-year assignment to help move a mammoth super-conducting magnet from Argonne to the Stanford Linear Accelerator Center at Stanford University in Palo Alto, California, and to help install it there as part of a particle-physics experiment using the colliding-beam facility. I thought this would be a great adventure. I had always wanted to move somewhere far away from home, and northern California always seemed to be the best place to go.

I finished my therapy with Phyllis and the second year of training at the Gestalt Institute, the children finished school, and we found renters for our house. We gave away a lot of stuff, left a few pieces of furniture, stored some things in my mother-in-law's basement, arranged for someone to take care of the cat until Russell came back a month later and brought him back to California by plane, oversaw the movers, packed up two cars (one with a top carrier), and set out for a two-week trip to California right after the Fourth of July.

We figured that with camping and Russell's travel stipend, we could manage the trip with very little additional expense. I drove the year-old Chevrolet Impala, and Russell took the 1972 blue Dodge Dart with the top carrier attached. We spent our last night in the Midwest at my mother-in-law's house in Chicago, dropping off more things for storage there. The Dart lost a hubcap within an hour of leaving Chicago, a harbinger of minor, but important crises that accompanied us all the way: we stopped for small repairs in Rapid City, South Dakota, and a radiator replacement in Boulder, Colorado.

I was never a big fan of camping, and doing so after driving all day was exhausting. It didn't help that with goods packed in two cars and a top carrier, I often couldn't remember where anything was. The biggest advantage to camping was that all five of us could get some distance between us for a little while. With my penchant for hyperbole I imagined we were like the pioneers in the great wagon trains of the nineteenth century, leaving home forever, enduring unanticipated hardships, and facing an uncertain future. Of course, our trip wasn't at all as arduous as those taken one hundred years before. What was true was that I was nervous, facing unanticipated challenges and an unpredictable future.

The summer of 1979 was a time of gasoline shortages and high prices, so there were relatively few people on the road. Keeping up with Russell was very easy. Because he had had so much trouble with his car, I drove behind him for the whole trip. The children made big posters to put up in the windows to signal times to stop for a break, a huge coffee cup signaling the need for caffeine, an open hand for a general need to stop (such as exchanging children if the two riding together were starting to quarrel), and a walkie-talkie to signal when we needed to turn on the real ones to talk without stopping.

If we grew too tired of camping and wanted to stay in a motel, we had no trouble the entire trip just showing up and finding a room until we reached the town of Lake Tahoe in California on a Saturday night. We intended to stay in a motel that last night on the road. The traffic at five o'clock on that Saturday night in Lake Tahoe was like five o'clock rush hour around Chicago on any workday—impatient drivers and bumper-to-bumper traffic. It took a very long time to cover very short distances. Every hotel or motel we encountered was full. We were all hungry and tired but decided to keep driving west until we found a motel, which we did four hours later on the outskirts of Sacramento. We arrived at the adjoining restaurant just before they closed at nine o'clock, happy to finally get out of the car and eat a meal.

I was startled and dismayed the next morning to see the brown landscape. I probably knew that summer was a dry season in California, but I was expecting green anyway. To a Midwesterner, everything looked dead. Palo Alto was close enough that we only had to endure the dreary landscape for another half day.

We reached Palo Alto and moved into a motel for a week while we waited for the moving van. Then we moved into a rented house on Loma Verde, a few doors off of Middlefield, a shopping street somewhat similar to Lawrence Avenue in the neighborhood I grew up in. The house was partly furnished. It was also dirty, with dust balls in every corner and dried spaghetti and pasta sauce on the dishes from the previous tenant's last meal. By then, I was more than dismayed, wondering if this whole venture was a mistake.

In the summer of 1979, the neighborhood was all small ranch houses that were probably built in the 1950s. The houses may have been modest, but a number of them had three or four cars parked in the driveway: Mercedes Benzes, Porsches, BMWs, and the occasional Bentley or Lamborghini. Our driveway held our 1972 Dodge Dart and the 1978 Chevy Impala. Surveying the automotive landscape one day, Jonathan, our emerging adolescent, wondered out loud if we were on welfare. This prompted one of the rare occasions when Russell totally lost his temper.

Our new house was considerably smaller than our house in Naperville, having neither a basement nor an attic. The boys' room was manageable with bunk beds, and Sonia's room was just tiny. The house wasn't elevated off of street level, as many are in the Midwest where basements are more common. When we finally collapsed into bed on the first night (in our own bed which I was very glad we thought to take), we heard voices from people walking by on the sidewalk, not far from our bedroom window. The curtains were closed, but I still felt very vulnerable and exposed. In my more paranoid moments I imagined a man sneaking through the window and raping me. I didn't know if I was safe. But everyone else seemed more happily excited than scared, so I put my own feelings aside.

In the early days of our stay in Palo Alto, my enthusiasm for this great adventure disappeared like the illusory summer greenery in the unwavering summer light of day outside of Sacramento. The first week we were in our new house we didn't have a phone. There was a public phone in front of a liquor store across Middlefield, so I went there to make calls. Russell had his work. The children had school. I knew no one. Besides getting the house in order, I had nothing to do.

I called my mother and told her about my loneliness. She chided me for feeling bad. I was sorry I called and didn't talk to her again about how I felt.

After about three weeks, with some trepidation, I decided to try volunteering until I could figure out how to find work as a dance therapist. I took a deep breath as I picked up the phone to call the temple we had already joined and announced that I was available. I don't remember what tasks I was asked to do but it was a place to start.

Not long afterward, someone suggested I look into a job as a part-time singles-group coordinator with the Jewish Community Center. Several months into it, after arranging a weekend event at a retreat center, I was told that about twenty hours of unavoidable extra work I did would not be compensated but should be considered a contribution. No one had said anything about donating my services. I got angry at being taken advantage of, and I quit after only five months. I surprised myself with what felt like a very bold move. I was pleased with this evidence of my recovery.

In the middle of the first year we were in Palo Alto, I joined Hadassah, an international Jewish women's group that raises funds for several major hospitals in Israel. I had never been involved in a women's service organization before. My mother-in-law and her mother had both been active in Hadassah from the time each was a young woman. I had come to admire Mollie's intelligence and insightfulness. If she thought so highly of this group, I thought I would try it too.

The women I met through Hadassah were also bright, creative women. After a while, it seemed to me that many of them poured all of their considerable intelligence and talents into the organization for lack of other places to put them. This was still a time when most women older than I didn't work outside of their homes, particularly if their husbands earned enough money so additional income wasn't a necessity. Some of them were hostile to people like me who didn't invest Hadassah with as much importance as they did.

Too quickly, I was asked to join the Hadassah board as vice president of education. The responsibility of this position was to produce ten monthly educational meetings for the membership. Being very new to the area, I didn't have the contacts to do this by myself. The president assured me that I would get all the help I needed, so with great reservation I allowed my arm to be twisted and said yes.

I knew I was in trouble at the June board installation. There was a beautiful luncheon, set outside on one woman's patio, as can only be done in a predictably sunny and dry climate. The moderator introduced me as someone with a long-standing commitment to Hadassah and its goals—I who had only joined for the first time a few months before.

Who are they talking about? I wondered. *What I have gotten myself into?* I was very uneasy by the time I left.

Over the summer, I received no help at all. One woman told me that her immense apartment, which I'd seen, couldn't possibly be big enough to hold a meeting that might only attract a few dozen people. Other people had all kinds of reasons why they couldn't do what I asked of them.

The first of the High Holidays, Rosh Hashanah, always begins at sundown on a day in September. Although it had never been our family's practice, many people have a major family dinner before the first services. The morning of the first evening of Rosh Hashanah, I called another member of the board, frantic about my lack of progress. The board member was very angry that I interrupted her dinner preparations and scolded me for not having done the job I agreed to do. Between Rosh Hashanah and the end of the High Holidays ten days later, I went to the president and resigned.

Before this episode, I rarely let myself know I was angry if someone took advantage of me. I had never stood up for myself like this. At least I knew enough not to be shamed for being set up to do an impossible task. But, when I recall how anxious I was about the Rosh Hashanah incident, how I avoided even going to Hadassah meetings or events, how my stomach tightened painfully when I did go, I think it would be more accurate to say I was enraged. After all the therapy I'd already done, I was still very afraid of my anger. I may have taken better care of myself than I had in the past, by getting out of a difficult situation, but I was very unsettled by how easy it was to get painfully anxious.

After a year of looking around, I finally found a paid dance-therapy position with the local community college, mostly working in senior facilities and nursing homes. I liked what I did but grew to realize that I wanted the greater responsibilities of actually being a psychotherapist, rather than just adjunct staff.

DANCING WITH NURIT AND EHUD

There were several very good dance studios within a few miles of our home. Sonia studied at one and I at another. At the Zohar studio I studied modern dance with Nurit, who had danced with Martha Graham; jazz with Nurit's husband, Ehud, who had been a professional volleyball player before becoming a dancer; and ballet with a young woman, whose name I have long forgotten, who had been a member of the Sadler Wells Ballet Company in London.

Once again, I was dancing many hours a week, but this time with adults and without McRae's harshness. Nurit's passion was choreography, which she pursued and taught without Frances's attention to motivation. Every few months, she produced a concert in which all of her advanced students were invited to participate. No union, no pay, no hats and gloves coming and going, just opportunity after opportunity to perform in public, which I did several times. When I could keep McRae's scolding voice out of my head, I had a fine time.

Nurit was intense but gentle as she made corrections or suggestions for doing something better. Sometimes when she touched my leg or my arm, an incredible longing filled me, almost to the point of tears. At the time I was stunned by the intensity of my longing; but as with other mysterious feelings and sensations, I couldn't stay focused on thinking about it. Today, I realize I wanted more of her gentle, nonjudgmental touch, more of her kindness.

Ehud, on the other hand, was a flirt who loved the sexiness of jazz. I took jazz because that is what advanced students at Zohar did, not because I liked it. Frequently in his class I held back from doing a movement fully because the sexiness of it was too apparent and unnerving, another intense feeling I couldn't explain or manage.

Jonathan, our older son and middle child, entered adolescence fighting, mostly with me. Somehow he figured out how to do a good approximation of my father's crazy-making talk, seeming to say something intelligible, but not actually saying anything. Sometimes he shifted the subject as my father had done the day I swore at him. There were times Jonathan was actually speaking nonsense syllables but quietly enough that I could barely make out whether he was saying real words or not.

After a while, my anxiety rose and my stomach tightened every day when he was due to come home from school. Feeling out of control and crazy around my son, it was difficult to keep a steady hand. I'm sure I was furious with him. Russell only knew what was public about our clashes.

One day, I decided that I would have to move out because I couldn't stand being around Jonathan.

Then I thought: *Maybe he should move.*

That wasn't a better solution, but I briefly felt better knowing that I didn't always have to be the one who accommodated to everyone else. When he came home from school that day, I did something unprecedented: I told him what I'd been thinking and how his chatter sometimes sounded too much like my father—how that made me feel intolerably upset, and he had to stop. He knew exactly what I was talking about and complied, needing to be reminded only once after that. I was relieved that he stopped and even more relieved that Jonathan knew what I was talking about and didn't try to deny it or suggest I was crazy to think what I thought or feel what I felt.

At the same time as my confrontation with Jonathan, Zohar was putting on a two-performance, end-of-season dance concert. I danced in several pieces. In the dressing room as we got ready for the first performance, one of the women talked about her career with one of the New York modern-dance companies. Somehow her story represented everything about dance that I'd lost, particularly the uninhibited joy of moving, and the pleasure of performance. I was very upset.

I'm sure grief was part of it. But there was also terror and rage. The dancer in me had already grieved my losses many times. I knew nothing then about my rage at feeling like I had been forced out of dancing and forced out of much of the pleasure of dancing by a teacher who took out her bitterness on her students. What I did know was that my rage felt as dangerous as a nuclear warhead that only needed the flip of a switch to detonate. My rage terrified me. I didn't know what to do with the great upwelling of feelings that night except what I usually did with strong feelings: I became deeply depressed and so numbed out that it was an effort to move at all.

The night after the first performance I dreamt that I walked into a room to find Jonathan hanging from a noose made from a belt. In the dream, I was hysterical, screaming and crying, but no one paid any attention. This may have had something to do with Jonathan (who had threatened suicide from time to time). More to the point, I knew from my Gestalt training that each element of a dream represented a part of myself. After so much therapy, I was still killing myself—screaming and crying out but in a way that no one could notice.

The next day, I brought the dream to the dance therapist teacher I was studying with, and who was also my personal therapist. As we worked on it, the dream seemed to be a recapitulation of the prior six or seven years of work. When we finished, I was much calmer and settled.

Now the depression is finally done, I thought, certain that I was right.

For that evening's performance I danced with an open heart.

JEWISH LIFE

By the time we left for California, our little Naperville Jewish community had grown to the point of incorporating. We were still doing a lot on our own. We hired teachers for the children and a rabbi for the High Holidays and once a month for Sabbath services. Our learning and praying was fervent with intention. All of our energies went towards creating an institution that would serve a group which encompassed almost the full spectrum of Jewish observance except, perhaps, the most orthodox. Organized adult education was either nonexistent or haphazard.

One of the best parts of our time on the West Coast was our involvement with a very large, wealthy Reform congregation, which was completely established and organized, and big enough to provide the richness of possibilities that our Naperville Jewish Community Organization simply couldn't. A group of us formed a *havurah*, a small group of people who gathered regularly to study together. We called ourselves the *Chai* Society, a play on "High Society," and the fact that eighteen was the number on the door of the classroom we met in. (In Hebrew each letter has a numerical equivalent. The two letters of the word *chai*, equal eighteen when added together, and *chai* means life.)

One couple had lived in Israel for seven years before deciding to return to the United States. Another couple had recently arrived from Russia. A Stanford professor and a psychologist made up another couple. Other people came and went.

Many of the participants were much more knowledgeable about Judaism than I, and our conversations were exciting. The adult-education program at the synagogue also offered classes that had been unavailable in our home community. Adding this to what I had learned from Mollie and Russell, I thought more about the likelihood that the Jewish experience I grew up with was only a small sampling of what was possible.

BACK TO NAPERVILLE

We went to Palo Alto in 1979 with the intention of checking out the possibility of resettling there permanently. The area around San Francisco had always seemed the most attractive place in the country to live. Once there, we discovered that much of what seemed so attractive from a distance was far less so up close. Public schools were not as good as in Naperville because so many people sent their children to private schools. Competition for jobs in mental health was so intense that a doctorate was considered an entry-level degree. The roads were crowded, and housing was exorbitant.

As Russell watched colleagues hoping to stay in California try to get jobs, we realized that we couldn't afford to stay in or near Palo Alto without both of us working full time. It had been very difficult for me to find even a part-time job. After almost two years, it was still difficult to find friends. Most people I met were very busy with jobs and school and going away for the weekend and the myriad things there are to do in an interesting location with mild weather. I never spotted the apparently rare laid-back Californian in all the time we lived there.

In the process of trying to decide whether to stay or go home, Russell decided that physics had lost its flavor and fun. Projects, such as the one he was involved with at Stanford, involved more and more people doing smaller and smaller parts of the work. Funding, which had always been at the pleasure of Congress, became less and less certain in the late 1970s and early 1980s.

Many of Russell's colleagues who decided to return to Illinois looked for and found jobs at Bell Labs, three miles from our Naperville house. Russell did too, taking a job as a telecommunications software engineer. A sour joke by the end of 1981 was that the entire high-energy physics department from Argonne National Laboratory was now working for Ma Bell, at better salaries and much saner working conditions.

We returned to our Naperville house twenty-two months after leaving it. I decided that rather than going back to finish the third year of the program at the Gestalt Institute, I would work on a doctorate in counseling. One of my classmates at the Institute, Betty Bosdell, was a professor in a counseling program at Northern Illinois University. I liked the flexible nature of the Northern program. Also, I had been learning from her informally almost from the time I met her, and I wanted more of what she had to teach.

Betty asked me why I wanted to earn a doctorate rather than a less demanding master's degree in counseling. A doctoral program involved a great deal of class work and the daunting challenges of comprehensive examinations and a dissertation. I told her that I wanted to teach at the university level some day and also do clinical work. In those days, a doctorate was a requirement for university positions. In order to be credible to referral sources for a psychotherapy practice, I needed some more impressive credentials than two years of dance therapy training (the second year done in California) and two years of Gestalt Therapy training. A professional license wasn't required in Illinois then.

There were several things I didn't mention to her. For one thing, I associated my master's degree with having a nervous breakdown, and I somehow thought working on another would lead to the same conclusion. Logically this may not have made sense, but the feeling of aversion was very strong.

More importantly, I wanted the status of a doctoral degree. In the service of protecting my mental health, I decided to give myself permission to quit the program any time it felt overwhelming. Since I couldn't create the kind of intimate friendships I wanted, I thought I could settle for possibly being admired for my accomplishments. And I thought that having a doctorate would give me an upper hand in any attempt by my father to tell me I didn't know what I was talking about. I applied to the Northern Illinois University doctoral program in the spring and was accepted.

We returned to Naperville in June 1981, this time shipping all of our camping gear in the moving van. What remained of the summer after we returned was spent stripping wood, painting, buying new carpeting and furniture, and generally having a good time trying to see what we could get done by the start of school. Russell eagerly took on learning all the new things he needed to know to do his new job. He always loved the challenge of mastering something difficult. Our two boys were at transition points in school: Jeremy starting middle school and Jonathan beginning high school. They moved into their new schools easily. Sonia, however, was unhappy and angry at having her well-established Palo Alto social and dance life interrupted, and she remained so until she left for college a few years later.

In many ways this was a good time for our family, and in some ways it wasn't. I loved the intellectual stretch of my classes at NIU, which I began just before Labor Day. I also loved the long, relatively empty ride to school on the East-West Tollway west almost forty miles to De Kalb, where NIU is located. Like many who have grown up in urban Illinois, I always thought that the central flatlands of the state, with their unending corn and soybean fields, were beyond boring. After the commotion of California, however, these same flat fields, with their gentle swells and occasional small stands of trees, seemed solid and soothing.

In the fall of 1981, there was very little traffic beyond the western edge of Aurora, about twelve miles west of home, even during the day. I came to enjoy watching the subtleties of the seasons: the patterns of snow and black earth and straw in the winter; the misty lace of new leaves in miniature forests at the edge of unplanted fields in the spring; the progress of the corn during the summer.

When I came home alone at night, for over twenty-five miles the land was dark except for the lights from farmhouses. During the hour or so the trip took, many times there was no one to talk to and nothing to do except lightly pay attention to the road. There was usually nothing to look forward to when I got home except a brief visit with Russell and going to bed. I discovered that the flatlands were not boring, but quiet. On the many trips to De Kalb and back, I learned to love the quiet.

Two of my classmates, Nili and Catha, were women from my area, so we formed a car pool for classes we took together. The long rides to and from our university and our generally chatty natures were the incubators for the deepest friendships I'd ever known.

I felt emotionally healthier than ever much of the time. Some of that better feeling, I'm sure, had to do with being in the familiar circumstances of school. Betty drew students to her who liked her rigor and the fact that she taught classes that explored spirituality and psychotherapy, such as Psychosynthesis and Transpersonal Psychology, that were unavailable almost anywhere else, certainly not anywhere in the Midwest. A group of us took all of the same classes from her, creating a friendship among us that persists to this day. The doctoral counseling program at NIU at that time was exciting, even intoxicating.

Each semester I took classes with Betty, starting with a theories class at the beginning of the program. In it we studied theories of mental disorder and change, theories that underlay all of the psychotherapeutic techniques we brought into our consulting rooms to treat our clients. The week we studied Adlerian psychology Betty told us that Adler found great meaning in a person's earliest memories.

I thought about the horses and the shallow river, my earliest memory. It was an image that came up from time to time. I had always regarded it as a curiosity notable only for its vividness, an antique from a mostly forgotten era. I never assigned any meaning to it and couldn't do so after Betty's class.

I also mentioned it to Nili, who had trained as an Adlerian. She wasn't able to find the meaning in the image either.

I rarely thought about suicide. After being in the hospital, one of the ways I thought I would know that I was making significant progress was when I stopped thinking about suicide every single day. By the time I left Phyllis, before our California odyssey, I thought I'd put suicide away for good. Putting it away, as it eventually turned out, wasn't the same as giving it up.

To myself, I pronounced the era of being depressed over.

Then again, we were moving into a high-intensity period with our adolescents. Our children are close enough in age that there were three years when simultaneously we had three teenagers.

Jonathan, our older son, got involved in band and sports. The track team he was on bored him after a while, and he stopped. He was an excellent clarinetist, but music wasn't the route to friends for him as it had been for me.

He was sneaky, in the way of second children, but not quite sneaky enough to avoid all detection. Once, when Sonia was away at college, Russell and I decided to try going away for about twenty-four hours, leaving the boys to stay with the families of friends. Jonathan and his friend arranged a big party at our house, which ended, including the cleanup, in time to get back to the friend's house by curfew.

When we walked into the house the next day, it was very clear that a party had taken place. There was a big pitcher of beer in the refrigerator and soda cans behind the couch. The linens on one of the beds had been changed with mismatched sheets – not something I would have done. A cushion from one of the living room chairs was missing and never turned up, nor did an explanation. It was clear that they had tried to straighten things up but they left so many telltale clues that Russell and I ended up laughing. When I spoke to the friend's mother, she told me she could tell that the boys had been up to something almost as soon as they walked in the door. It only took a few questions from her to learn the whole story.

When Jonathan was a senior, some of his friends wrote in his yearbook about that party, and another one he threw, being the highlight of their high school years.

Jeremy watched his big brother and tried some of the things he saw, including an unauthorized gathering at our house, which resulted in the police being called. After hearing about Jonathan and his friends driving over a nearby bump in the road fast enough to leave the ground, Jeremy tried the same stunt on a rainy night and totaled the car he wasn't old enough to drive. The unbelted boy and girl sitting in the back seat escaped with minor cuts and bruises. Miraculously, the parents did not sue us. None of his acting out involved more than misdemeanors, but sometimes it seemed that he was getting caught every week doing something he patently should not have.

Or was it that between the two boys someone was getting caught almost every week? There were calls to pick up a drunken son, a small marijuana horticulture exhibit I found in our attic, and a trip to the emergency room when one of the boys drank too much (which we only heard about later). Despite too many encounters with the police, only one resulted in a night in jail on charges that were later dropped. It was still too much.

Nili assured me that this was only a rough phase and not a blueprint for the rest of their lives. I often despaired of them reaching adulthood, much less maturing. My guilt over not being able to prevent the trouble they were getting into spilled easily into shame.

My daughter was another story, adamantly not acting out, as her brothers were. She longed to be with the popular kids but refused to go to parties where there was drinking. She wanted to begin dating, as so many of her girlfriends were doing, but was shy to the point of appearing indifferent when around a boy she found attractive. She dated very little and fretted about her lack of social life.

I was reminded frequently of a story about my mother's mother who was thirteen when she set out alone to come to the United States. As she boarded the train to leave her hometown in the Ukraine, my great-grandmother told her to be afraid of men. Not to be cautious and careful, but to be afraid. That was the whole story. Much later I learned that she took her mother's admonition so seriously that when a suitor casually touched her shoulder, she fainted. The man who eventually married her, saw the touch and the faint, and took care not to touch her at all until after the wedding.

I don't remember either her or my mother telling me to be afraid of men, although I heard the "getting-on-the-train" story from time to time. But I knew, with the exception of Russell, that I was at least standoffish around men and sometimes afraid of big men. As I listened to some of my friends talk about men approaching them at parties or other places, I realized that I presented myself in a way that never invited sexual advances. When Sonia talked about her own experiences, especially as she described her own aversion to seeming interested, I could only wonder how that message to be afraid of men had silently traveled down into a fifth generation, perturbing all of us.

It was difficult trying to guide my daughter into understanding her developing sexuality. It wasn't a subject that was easy for me, either. In my therapy with Phyllis, I never talked about sex. She brought up the subject from time to time. I always said my sex life was just fine and refused to pursue the matter. I couldn't teach what I so little understood.

SHAME-BASED FAMILY

When I discovered both of my sons were drinking, as were all of their friends, I joined Al-Anon. As I studied with Betty, I became more and more interested in spirituality, so I liked the idea that Al-Anon was a spiritual program. Much of what it taught dovetailed nicely with what I was learning elsewhere. I liked the connection of a Higher Power to the process of healing, and I liked that it seemed to support many of the things I learned in therapy.

Al-Anon is for people who are absorbed in someone else's drinking or drugging and who are trying to control the drinker's out-of-control behavior in a manner not unlike the alcoholic trying to control her drinking. Attempting to control the uncontrollable and then trying harder to maintain control when one inevitably fails can make people miserable and even crazy.

What I learned right away was that I was trying too hard to be in charge of my children's lives; in fact, I was trying to be in charge of everybody's lives, so I could ensure that they would all be happy. When the boys did things I didn't approve of, like getting drunk, I'm sure I felt more shame and guilt about their behavior than they did. I wondered about that, realizing quickly that I had been trying to make everyone happy for as long as I could remember, long before my sons' drinking.

I heard about shame-based families, an idea that was popular in the early and mid-1980s in the counseling community, the model for which was the alcoholic family. In this model someone is doing something like drinking to the point of creating problems. This creates shame in the doer and in the rest of the family, as they all try strategies to stop what is beyond their ability to stop. That failure, in and of itself, adds to the sense of shame. In time, the entire family's focus can be reduced more and more to dealing with their shame.

As I talked with colleagues and read a few books and articles about shame-based families, it certainly seemed that the family I grew up in fit the descriptions, although no one in my parents' generation was actually addicted to anything as far as I knew.

After years of therapy, I knew that my depression and anxiety had been responses at least in part to how I'd been raised. The same was true for my brother, who started getting in trouble at school in the first grade, and who also was eventually treated for depression.

In a classic shame-based family, everyone is trying to be in charge of what is basically uncontrollable. But what was the root of the shame in my family? Yes, we were dysfunctional, and if one believed the press that the word dysfunctional was getting in those days, so was everyone else. Even if every family was dysfunctional almost by definition, most people didn't need to be hospitalized or think about suicide as much as I did—so what was my problem? All I knew for sure was that all the therapy hadn't made a dent in my belief that I had to be in charge of everyone's happiness and that my constant, inevitable failure in this regard kept depression and the thought of suicide constantly fueled.

The more I learned about shame, the stronger my sense of being in denial grew. But, about what? Isn't denial at its best and most creative when the person in denial truly has no conscious idea what is being denied?

During this time of thinking about shame and denial, I had a dream where I was driving around in a car, running people down, shooting at everyone in sight, and nearly causing accidents as I drove past a train.

What, I wondered in my journal, *is with all of the violence and terrorizing everyone?* An inner voice responded, *shoot me. I'd rather die anyway.*

This time I stayed focused enough to wonder further about that voice. I wrote: *Sometimes I wonder if you are protecting me from some awful early memory. No! Don't! What? Or am I just getting caught up in my own imagination? Is there any difference between memory and imagination?*

A few months later, after a conversation with my sister, Judi, in which I talked more about sex than was usual for me, I wrote:

I talked to Judi about sex and touching, etc. Got very upset. It is a young-place upset. After meditating yesterday I approached Shama [the Spirit Guide I discovered while at the Gestalt Institute] *to ask about what was going on. S/he said, "not yet." I had trouble staying with it, and finally gave up.*

I then gave myself a fine little pep talk:

If the time is not yet, perhaps I am getting ready. I am solidly on the side of sanity. No need to push or hurry, at least on this issue. If there are terrors in the past, they are in the past.

And after that I wrote:

I think I do not know what I know. I forget what I know.

Today, I know what was hidden and "forgotten." I know what I was denying, all in the service of protecting my mother and of ensuring that my problems didn't upset her. I was sure that my story would kill her.

Unconsciously and carefully, I waited until she was dead before I uncovered my secrets.

SPIRITUALITY

When I was working on my doctorate, I became more interested in spirituality. In my first class with Betty, which was an overview of counseling theories, she taught that psychological growth laid the foundation for spiritual growth. Spiritual development then proceeded until it ran into psychological issues that had to be resolved in order to move to the next step. These two kinds of growth stair-stepped with each other throughout a person's life.

Later, Betty taught Psychosynthesis, a Freudian based counseling theory that includes spiritual growth as well as psychological repair. Psychosynthesis also proposes a model of inner parts and a step-by-step process leading to integration and wholeness. Those of us who took her Psychosynthesis classes were invited to join Betty once a month to study and practice techniques with each other. Nili, Catha, and I, and some of the others in our classes, took her up on the offer.

At the monthly meetings Betty taught us Voice Dialogue, another technique, devised by Hal and Sidra Stone, for exploring parts of the personality. All of these techniques were very compatible with Gestalt Therapy. Although I wasn't in therapy at this time, classes and Betty's group kept my own inner work moving.

Betty also introduced her monthly group members to Carolyn Conger, a spiritual teacher and doctoral student in psychology at the time, from Santa Monica, California. Carolyn led weekend retreats around Chicago and in Indiana in January. She loved to dip into real winters, and still does. In time, she became one of my most important teachers.

Carolyn is a heavy woman, a little taller than my moderate height. When the group was working she sat quietly attentive, fully present and never fidgety the way I was. She was grounded and centered, giving herself over to whatever she was doing, whether it was teaching, telling stories, or laughing.

One thing that I was aware of from the very first retreat in January 1983 was that Carolyn framed her comments and instructions in a manner that made it very clear that she had no investment in what I or anyone else did with what she said. It was equally fine if we went along with her exercises, or not. Often, before a guided meditation she told us not to concern ourselves with listening.

"You will hear what you need to hear," she said calmly. "Even if you fall asleep, you will get what you need or are ready for, whether you are aware of it or not."

The fact that she could be interested in us, in me, without wanting anything from us was wonderful. My therapists, Phyllis and Ray, also were careful not to appear to want anything from me, but Carolyn's attitude seemed even deeper and more genuine than theirs.

After a few retreats, I could feel myself begin to relax as we drove up to the retreat site at the George Williams College campus on Lake Geneva in Wisconsin. The critical part of me went off duty for the weekend.

I learned more about meditation from Carolyn. In addition to guided and silent meditations, we did long freeform chants and eventually, after a number of years, long freeform movement sessions, with even less structure than I experienced with the San Francisco choreographer.

I also learned more about Spirit Guides and techniques for accessing higher wisdom after having first encountered these ideas in my work with faculty at the Gestalt Institute and then with Betty. Carolyn sometimes used loud, evocative music, and sometimes carefully crafted guided meditations to induct us into altered states of consciousness from which our inner wisdom was more accessible. She was also fond of using Tarot cards to spur our imaginations. All of her teaching ultimately was about learning to access and to trust our higher wisdom.

Carolyn's retreats were experiences of joy and peacefulness that remained a model of what might be possible throughout the year.

EXAMS

My first comprehensive examination, about two years after I began my doctoral program, was on the clinical aspects of counseling. It was a long day of nonstop writing, but I was very confident that I knew what I was doing and passed easily.

The second exam, about four or five months later, consisted of a small number of questions from a booklet we had been given when we entered the program. All of the students knew from the first day the exact questions we might be asked on this exam. These questions covered all of the nonclinical material, particularly research design and statistics, educational psychology (this being a degree from the School of Education), and American educational theory, all material I knew less about and was less interested in.

I studied with classmates. I carried flash cards around with me. I wrote outlines. I read. Preparing was intense.

It was also the nature of these exams that if failed, in whole or in part, the student could retake either the whole or the part only once more. If the student failed a second time, the program ended. I definitely had a sense that my entire career was on the line the morning I walked in and took my place, not too close to anyone else, examined the page where the specific questions were spelled out, and began to write.

In the afternoon, we were given three hours to design and describe a counseling research project, covering the theoretical question to be addressed, what factors had to be taken into account, and what kind of statistical analysis would be used at the end. I finished the assignment in about two hours, and then I began to consider what I wrote. The more I thought (and wrote down what I was thinking) the more my design fell apart. It appeared to be flawed in every particular. I described every one. When I finished, I was crushed. I considered throwing the entire thing in the trash. Contrary to the rules, I got up and walked out of the room and down the hall. I don't know where I was going or what I expected to happen. I reached the end of the hall and came back and sat down, feeling completely defeated. Finally, I turned in the paper and left.

During the hour drive back home I sank into a deep sense of failure and depression. Any hope that I might have passed was destroyed. I forgot entirely that if I did poorly on any sections of the exam I could take them again.

Part of the ritual of doctoral comprehensive exams was that the results were disseminated simultaneously by mail to everyone who took the tests. Faculty members were not permitted to tell a student in advance whether she had passed or not. It didn't seem to matter because I was so sure I failed.

During the several weeks that the exams were being graded, I visited with Betty one afternoon. I told her I was sure I had failed and why. Being careful not to actually say that I passed, she told me that I wrote the best exam of all of the students who took it with me. At some level, I understood that I had passed, but the news came too late. I was too depressed to be cheered at all. When the confirming letter arrived, it had no impact either. I had managed somehow to blacken my world enough to prohibit almost any light from penetrating.

I stayed deeply depressed for over a year afterwards, and struggled to keep working on my dissertation, a theoretical paper on the relationship of Dance/Movement Therapy and Reichian Bioenergetics. Fortunately, it was a library research paper, not an experimental project. At least I really enjoyed the process of reading and writing.

The more I explored my idea that these two kinds of body psychotherapy had a common core, the more I came to conclude that my original hypothesis was wrong. This time the result was interesting rather than distressing because I didn't feel like my career was on the line, but I remained very depressed.

In January 1985, I was again at Carolyn Conger's annual retreat. I no longer recall anything we did during that retreat, but by the end the depression was totally lifted. To this day I have no explanation for the complete change. Perhaps I was buoyed by the sense of safety and the possibilities for peace and joy that seemed to typify my experiences with Carolyn. Perhaps my capacity for optimism returned after a weekend of being with people who went out of their way not to be critical or judgmental. By Sunday night, I was charged and ready to make the sprint to the finish line.

On Monday morning, I called my dissertation chairman and asked when my project had to be finished in order to graduate at the end of spring semester. When he told me, I decided to try to meet the deadline. I told my family to more or less forget about me doing much around the house for the next couple of months. I think they caught onto my excitement because everyone pitched in to help without complaint.

I was on a high for about eight weeks, writing, making copies for my committee, getting their feedback, writing some more, again and again, some days barely stopping long enough to eat or use the washroom. I loved the energy. I loved the high. I could see how people became work or excitement addicted. I made every deadline, the last one only by calling the office I had to go to and telling them I would be two or three minutes late.

I graduated in May 1985, anxious and without the tranquilizers I used to get through my master's degree ceremony, but glad to be done. My parents were in Europe, Sonia had yet to come home from college, and my boys were not interested in attending the ceremony. Only Russell came to my graduation. I was disappointed in my family's response but not enough to spoil the day. I spent the next few months calming down.

It was time to get my career launched. For the first few months after I finished my degree, I floated around in a great cocoon of confidence that I actually knew something and had the paper to prove it. However, although I had started my therapy practice two years before, in the first four months after graduation I didn't get one referral. I thought this was a bad cosmic joke, or, perhaps, an antidote to hubris.

In the fall, I took a three-day workshop on alcoholism and drug addiction at Parkside Lutheran Hospital in Park Ridge. I was appalled that I knew so little about so important a factor in people's mental health. I also noticed, again, the similarities between families distorted by addictions and my own.

At the end of the workshop, the presenter announced that Parkside was looking for someone to colead an adolescent addiction prevention program. I said I was interested, and within a short time I was hired and immersed in the world of addictions.

The program I ran with a coworker was an early intervention for high school students found with drugs or alcohol at school or school events. We did assessments of the students and their families and taught mandatory classes to both groups on addictions and the effect addiction has on families. Full participation in the program was the only way to avoid a two-week suspension from school.

I learned the material quickly. I think I have performance genes, so I wasn't daunted by the idea of presenting classes to groups of people, most of whom didn't want to be there.

What was unsettling was my own perfectionism. I worked two evenings a week. As I recall, almost every time I drove home I examined every minute detail of what I did that night and found fault with most of it. My self-criticism and perfectionism were absurd. My coworker and I worked closely together. She was also my immediate supervisor. She rarely commented on my self-perceived imperfections.

I was slipping back into the same state of overworking with outrageous expectations that I had been in before the hospitalization. I was very unhappy that in the twelve or thirteen years since that episode, despite all of the learning and changes that I'd made, so much hadn't changed at all.

YOU MUST KILL PRIDE

One quiet autumn afternoon, I decided to try accessing Shama, my Spirit Guide, to ask about how to deal with my chronic distress. I got into a slight meditative state, as I had been taught, and then imagined going up to the mountaintop where I usually visualized meeting Shama. I imagined my Guide as a chubby, middle-aged androgynous character, dressed in a shapeless robe. Most often s/he didn't say much but held and comforted me.

This time when I "went up" Shama was sitting off to the side, and another character was there. It was Death, himself, in black robe and hood with a scythe—the full standard image. I was very surprised and scared.

"Am I going to die soon?" I asked.

"In time, but not now," came the response. "You must kill pride."

There were a few more questions and answers, mostly on the order of assurances that I wasn't about to die immediately. And then the incident was over.

What was that supposed to mean, to kill pride? Did that mean not to take any pleasure in my accomplishments, which were about the only things I did take pleasure in? That didn't make sense. Was I to cultivate shame for myself and what I did? I thought I had too much shame, not too little. I thought about pride a lot.

True to form, I read everything I could find about pride and shame, which at the time wasn't much. After a while, I realized that pride was just the grandiose flip side of shame, and what I needed was to undo both and develop humility. Both pride and shame, in my definitions, presumed that I was held to a different standard than anyone else on the planet. It seemed like a great discovery, although I wasn't sure what humility was. Humiliation was my area of expertise. I had no idea how to go about what Death had commanded, but the insistence of the Death figure remained very vivid.

As I contemplated Death's message, I realized that one of the factors in killing pride was developing self-compassion, and recognizing that it wasn't the same thing as self-absorption or selfishness. Self-compassion was a trait that I repeatedly found and lost in my thicket of shame. Each time I reclaimed it I immediately noticed how connected self-compassion was to loving others as well.

In the period after the hospitalization, about ten years before Death appeared, the beginning of self-compassion was the first indication I had that I was beginning to recover.

At that time I had written:

It is only by loving myself that I can hope to love another. When I am filled with self-contempt my "loving" is but a longing to fill my empty space and ease my pain. When I hate myself, my emptiness is infinite— there is no amount anyone can give to make me whole again. But when I love me, my empty place is just the right size to hold the gifts of the world. When I love me, I know what to take from my fullness and send back out to someone else in return.

Shame and pride hobble the heart, closing it to love. Even small amounts of humility were like a balm, soothing my heart enough so it naturally began to stretch and open.

JUDAISM AND MEDITATION

Experiences such as I had with Carolyn left me wanting more. They also left me wanting more from my own Jewish tradition. I didn't know anyone Jewish who knew anything about the mystical side of Judaism; no one who was as curious as I was. No one I knew had ever heard of Jewish meditation. Throughout my life, I had always known and talked to many Catholics. I admired what I heard about Catholic interest in mystery and mysticism. I thought that a tradition as old as the one I lived in must certainly have included the spiritual, mystical side of life, or it would never have survived so many millennia.

I remember the day in 1985 this thought came to me. I was walking north on Wabash Avenue, under the El tracks in Chicago's downtown, headed for Kroch's and Brentano's Bookstore, then the largest bookstore in the city. The store had a large basement section and two upper levels. The section on religion was on the top floor, which is where I was headed that day. The first thing I saw when I ascended the stairway enough was a display rack of books facing the stairs. In the middle of the rack was Aryeh Kaplan's new book, *Jewish Meditation*.

Kaplan's book was the answer to my question. Yes, there was a long, significant mystical side of Judaism. This book was one of the very first to contain translations of some of the mystical texts into English. Kaplan begins the book by saying that he had decided these old texts needed to be available in English to make them accessible to a wider audience because so many of the students and teachers of Jewish mysticism had died in the Holocaust.

I read the book quickly but didn't absorb much. Kaplan assumed that his readers had a deeper knowledge of Jewish learning than I did. Jewish mystical writing was often deliberately intended to add to the mystery of God, not explain it. I didn't know how to read it or what to do with what I read.

These difficulties didn't matter. What mattered was that I finally had an answer to my question of whether there could be a spiritual home for me in Judaism. I was satisfied for the moment that the answer was yes.

MY MOTHER AND MOTHER-IN-LAW

On a Wednesday in June 1986, my mother called to tell me that she had been diagnosed with inflammatory carcinoma. She had had some terrible pains from her back and down into her leg, so I thought the cancer had something to do with her legs. However this was a breast cancer. Her pain was related to arthritis. She told me that her kind of cancer is typified by many tiny tumors, so pinpointed treatments, such as surgery and radiation, weren't appropriate. What none of us knew then was that the prognosis for inflammatory carcinoma was usually death in about six months.

The day after my mother's cancer call, my mother-in-law and I set off for a place outside of Philadelphia for a long weekend shabbaton, a kind of retreat that included prayer services for Sabbath and time for study-workshops. Neither of us had ever done anything quite like this, but she was the right person for me to be with on this spiritual adventure.

Our airplane arrived at Philadelphia about the same time as a massive storm system that kept us airborne an additional hour. During a lull, we landed and then made our way to get our rental car and headed off just before the downpour began again, right in the middle of the evening rush hour.

In the confusion of unfamiliar roads, rain, and heavy traffic, I took a wrong turn onto an enormous loop that added another hour to our trip. I was very upset about being lost, being late, and the fact that my mother was possibly dying; however I managed to keep myself under control long enough to drive safely and get where we were going. Mollie understood how upset I was, and she was careful to simply support me so I could focus on finding the retreat site. Was it genes or training that passed those same calm, nonjudgmental qualities to her son?

By the next day, I settled down enough to take in what we were doing, although I was still reeling from my mother's news. Again, Mollie was calm and comforting, interested and concerned. Most important of all, she didn't need me to take care of her.

Even before we returned, I was aware of how happy I was that I could share this experience with her and how I couldn't imagine spending so much time in close proximity with my own mother. I felt pulled to my mother by her illness and guilty for sharing precious time with Mollie and loving my time with her.

DEEPENING

1987

The second weekend in January 1987, I set off for Carolyn Conger's annual retreat with great excitement and anticipation. This was an opportunity to see many of my friends from my doctoral program. The George Williams College Wisconsin campus site was always beautiful in the winter. Most of all, the exercises Carolyn had us do were powerful tools for inner healing and growth: meditations to evocative music, dream interpretations, and work with Tarot cards. In previous years, I had come away from each retreat in a wonderfully peaceful state of mind, which I hoped to repeat again.

After one early exercise I wrote:

What is waiting to be healed? Hanging on to those old ways and beliefs, the old craziness and fears that keep my life dark.

What is waiting to be empowered? My awareness of the Light.

At the '87 retreat I met Pat, a tall, thin man who identified himself as a Tibetan Buddhist from St. Louis. He was my partner in an exercise in which we attempted to intuit truths about each other.

"There is so much more," he told me. "There is so much MORE!"

I knew with unusual certainty that he was absolutely right. But what was the more and where was it? And, most of all, how could I find it?

Carolyn liked to use Tarot cards as tools for accessing our deeper selves. Tarot decks contain twenty-one cards with pictures of various archetypical characters, such as the Fool or the Priestess or the Hermit, and archetypical concepts, such as the Wheel of Life or the Sun. When laid out in order, the twenty-one can be read as the hero's journey from innocence to spiritual enlightenment. The rest of the deck is arranged in suits with various evocative pictures on them. In the 1980s and 1990s, Carolyn almost always used just the first twenty-one cards to stir our imaginations, to set our intent for the weekend or to provide guidance for particular tasks.

We were to work with the cards as if they were dream images. Carolyn always suggested that we not look into their traditional meanings until we had finished with our own, idiosyncratic interpretations. We never explicitly used them for divination, although sometimes they did seem prophetic.

On this occasion, Carolyn asked us to randomly pick a card from a picture-side down deck to represent what we needed for healing. I chose the Death card. I couldn't say why, but it seemed very right. Something in me needed to die in order for me to come to life. The card I chose to represent the energy that was coming into my life was the Tower. It is an image of two people falling out of a castle tower that is being hit by lightning. That seemed right, too. The picture is an ominous portrait of pandemonium, destruction, and impending death. I was strangely excited and eager rather than scared.

Yet, I held little hope that I could ever have "more." I wrote simply and without hyperbole or metaphor for a change:

I am guilty for being who I am.
I am wounded. I have lost the means to stand on my own.
I am afraid to try again.
God, I said, where are you when I call and do not know what to do?

I was trying very hard to be the one who was finally finished with therapy and ready to focus entirely on developing my spirituality, but I wasn't succeeding very well. Despite having heard about the idea that the seeker must wander in the desert a good long time, letting experience kill off the vestiges of slavery (emotional and spiritual as well as physical in the Biblical telling of this tale), I really didn't understand what any of that meant. All I knew for sure was that all of the inner work and study hadn't made much difference at the deepest levels of what I believed about myself.

In the months that followed my encounter with the Tibetan Buddhist from St. Louis, the excitement of the moment wore off. In the course of the rest of the year, my life seemed to get more chaotic. The "more" that the Buddhist spoke of remained a complete mystery to me.

In late winter, I quit my job with Parkside after the working conditions deteriorated and I was promised a substantial raise that was actually only fifty cents an hour. My private practice was still very small.

I decided that I needed to find a spiritual teacher who I could see more often than at a once-a-year retreat. Many traditions, including mine, admonish that when the student is ready the teacher will appear. I was anxious and impatient and didn't want to wait.

I greatly admired Rabbi Victor Amster, the Orthodox rabbi who acted as the principal of our congregation's religious school, even though I wasn't interested in becoming more Orthodox. I made an appointment to talk to him about his becoming my spiritual teacher. Just as I began to tell him what I wanted, he got a phone call informing him that his father had suddenly become ill and was rushed to the hospital. Of course that was the end of the meeting. He ran out saying he would call me later. I waited for days and then weeks, but he didn't call back. I could have called him, but somehow I understood that this wasn't the time.

In June, my family and I took a trip to Israel because Russell's youngest brother, Fred, and his family were in Haifa for a sabbatical year. He was a teacher in a northern Canadian school district that allowed its teachers to put aside a percentage of their salary to save up for a year off. Some of the time we stayed at Fred's apartment and some of the time both families traveled around the country together. I was uneasy about going, afraid that I would be overwhelmed by the challenges of being in a country so different from home. On the other hand, perhaps being in the land of the Jewish Bible, the land of my people, would be a source of inspiration as such trips had been for many people before me.

It was indeed strange to be in a place where I knew almost nothing about the language, except how to recite the liturgy. Even my children, who were unenthusiastic Hebrew students at best, could make out letters and words better than I could.

By 1987, when we were there, the European influence of the creators of Israeli independence had been modified by the geographic fact of being in a tiny corner of the Middle East. The variety of people from all over the world, the smells of cities in the desert in summer, the abundance of produce and other goods in the souks, the great open air markets, and even the fact that most of the people I saw were Jewish—all of these sensations were unfamiliar and overwhelming. I tried very hard to be enthusiastic about this trip, which is so important for many Jews. All these sensations plus being in a place where I didn't know my way around only escalated my anxiety. My nervousness quickly produced an inner worry: Why couldn't I enjoy what we were doing as much as I imagined everyone else was.

I lasted three days. On that third day, our first in Jerusalem, we explored the shadowy corners of the old, walled city. We stood at the great Wall of Solomon's Temple, sweating in the desert sunshine. My worry about where the washrooms might be was mixed with awe at being in such a fateful place. After a snack stop at a falafel stand, I became the only one of the two families who got food poisoning. The English-speaking doctor who came to our hotel in Jerusalem said that in Israel my malady was called "Mohammed's revenge."

The next three or four days, we traveled to Ein Gedde for the famous mud baths and then to Massadah, where everyone else climbed to the top to see where an entire community martyred themselves when under siege two-thousand years before. I spent those days sleeping in different hotels, sipping tea, avoiding the mineral water that the doctor said would only make matters worse, eating white toast, and going to the toilet while the rest of the family were sightseeing. I wasn't feeling well, but my anxiety dropped as the challenges of traveling diminished.

Just as the diarrhea was beginning to ease, something else made me even sicker, this time with a fever. It was Friday afternoon, when the entire country gets ready to observe the full rest of Sabbath. By then, we were back in the Klem apartment in Haifa, and everyone was hustling to prepare Sabbath dinner. I slept and went to the toilet.

My family was due to leave on Sunday for a few days in France. Sonia was going to show us around Dijon, where she had spent a semester a few years earlier. By the beginning of Sabbath at sundown, it seemed a poor idea for me to travel around so much, just to be sick in another hotel. However, all Israeli businesses close for Sabbath, so there was no time for rearranging travel plans.

In the midst of a feverish fog, it occurred to me that our travel agent in Illinois was still in the middle of Friday afternoon. We reached her, and within ten minutes she had arranged for Jeremy and me to come home from France, while Russell, Jonathan, and Sonia continued on to Dijon. Jeremy had been the least interested in going on this trip, and he was easily the most eager to get home to "real" food, like hamburgers and French fries. We also reached my parents who agreed to meet us at the airport.

My mother brought a pot of chicken soup, not knowing if I wanted to go home or go back to their place. I gladly let my parents take Jeremy and me to their apartment for a day until I felt well enough to go home. I was clearly sick, and my mother had no need for me to take care of her, so it was a comfortable arrangement for both of us.

The next week, I started teaching a graduate class on group counseling at Northern Illinois University. I was still so weak from my illness that Catha, who had business on campus, drove me the first few times. The class and I got off to a poor start, one week late because my trip had already been planned when I agreed to teach it. It took me several weeks to get my energy up to a level where I could be as sharp and attentive as I needed to be. It took the class several weeks to realize that I meant what I said about the work I expected them to do. Many were school counselors who were taking a summer graduate course to add to their resumes and thereby add to their paychecks. Several were indignant about having to actually study or produce anything.

At the end of the term, one of my students, who had a vision problem, made a complete botch of the main project of the class, and she then complained about discrimination when I didn't give her an A. Despite the fact that she never once approached me for assistance, my department did not support me. Perhaps my department chairperson thought she would sue.

When all of the negotiations were done, the student got her A. I finished the course exhausted and very disappointed.

That year I was also the chairperson of Religious Affairs at our synagogue (now named Congregation Beth Shalom) and in charge of much of the logistical planning for the High Holiday services right after Labor Day. Just as the decision was being made about my student's grade, weeks after the class actually ended, the person I was counting on to arrange babysitting services for the holidays became unavailable. Now it became my responsibility to find sitters that had been promised for congregants with very young children. Everyone I called to take this on was a model of assertiveness: every one said no. I went through my entire list of possibilities and couldn't find anyone else to do this piece of grunt work. With only a few days left I scrambled and found some sitters. I was too frazzled and exhausted to fully notice how angry I was.

In addition, my mother wasn't doing well with her cancer.

And there was ordinary life: getting Jonathan and Sonia back to college, seeing clients, and trying to be an attentive wife. I was getting close to burnout, as I'd been thirteen years earlier when I ended up in the hospital.

The pandemonium of the image of the Tower was manifesting itself in every aspect of life.

Russell was the one steady part of my life. He was and is a quiet man, supportive of everything I was doing as long as my activities didn't intrude on his work obligations. In turn I was very careful to always check with him to be sure that I was not disturbing him.

Carolyn Conger's announcement of the coming January's retreat came in the summer. Just the idea that the retreat was coming in five months was reassuring, a lifeline of sorts. At least there was a time coming up where I might get replenished. A few months later, she notified us that she wasn't coming after all. I tried to convince myself that I was only disappointed as opposed to being distraught at having this lifeline cut.

I had a dream at about the same time that Carolyn cancelled the retreat: I was in a decrepit old school. The few students were listless, and the building was falling apart and crumbling. I went away to a large house. Someone was giving a lecture, but it was irrelevant and I didn't stay. I was told I must go east for what I need. I didn't know which way was east. I was told it was opposite of the way from which I'd come.

I wrote:

From this I learn it is time to move on, not to go back. The old lessons have fallen apart. What I need to learn is further on.

JAMES

My mind was still in this unsettled state when a colleague invited me to join her for a weekend therapy marathon in November—thirty hours of therapeutic work between Friday night and Sunday evening, with Ray and his associate, James. I knew that unfinished psychological work could interfere with spiritual work, and that my spiritual life was what I was most interested in and most distracted from. I knew how anxious I felt almost all the time, and how easy it was to be washed with shame and depression.

Perhaps, I thought, *I needed to do just a little more therapy, to clean up a few minor spots.*

I knew the two therapists running the workshop. Ray had been my psychiatrist thirteen years earlier. Fifteen and thirty-hour marathons were part of every group I did with him, so I was familiar with the format and its intensity. I first met James in 1975, when he had just finished his masters degree in social work and joined Ray's psychiatric practice.

The first time I worked with James he led a small group of people in a guided imagery exercise in which we imagined ourselves rising above our bodies and observing our own deaths. I went into a very deep trance state, from which he did not have the skill to help me get completely out. For several days I drifted in and out of a very spacey altered state of consciousness. I was frightened by this strange experience that I couldn't seem to stop. Ray wasn't available, so I made an appointment with one of his more experienced associates, who didn't seem to know what to do either.

Finally, I called Phyllis, who understood exactly what had happened.

"Oh, you just got into a trance," she explained. "It will stop on its own."

I must have relaxed, and a moment later it was over, but I took a very dim view of James's ability after that.

About six months later, James and I both participated in a counselor training class that Ray led. Then, in 1977, James and I were students at the Gestalt Institute of Chicago together, until I left two years later. Five years later, during my doctoral training he was one of my internship supervisors.

He was obviously much more skilled by then, but I still didn't think much of him. I think I was a therapy snob, considering Ray and Phyllis as masters and James as just not measuring up.

I had not had any contact with James for another five years until the marathon in 1987. I heard, in the meantime, that he had been studying Reichian Bioenergetics. I'd written my dissertation on a comparison of Dance/Movement Therapy and Reichian Bioenergetics, so I was very curious about what James had learned. I was also ready to be quite critical. After all, I had immersed myself in Bioenergetic theory, if not practice, and had some opinions on the matter.

Before the marathon I had another dream: I went looking for my car where I thought I parked it. I couldn't find it anywhere and decided I would have to walk home. From this I realized that whatever came next was going to go slowly and take a long time.

The marathon involved some movement and other kinds of body-work, as well as some kinds of awareness and expressive exercises I was familiar with from other workshops I had attended. In addition, all of the participants did individual work with Ray and James as well. Much more intense feeling came up than I expected, which was startling and unsettling, as if this was all somehow too much, too fast.

After one of the times I worked individually with James, with a strange sense of knowing I said to him, "I scared you once, but you don't seem frightened of me now."

"That's true," he said, and added, "I've changed a lot." That seemed to be crucially important.

By the end of the weekend, my anxiety level shot up as if it were on top of a massive geyser that would not quit. Unlike other times in my life when I felt anxious, now I was literally trembling much of the time. There was no bringing it down. I needed help.

As a practicing therapist myself, it wasn't easy to figure out who I might see for my own psychotherapy—many of the clinicians whose work I admired were friends of mine. I still wasn't sure about James, but the fact that he wasn't afraid of me was crucial. He was also not a friend. With those thoughts in mind, I started to see James regularly, and in short order was going to him twice a week. It never seemed to be enough for me to really calm down.

In time, it occurred to me that James was the teacher I was ready for. Spiritual growth wasn't on his agenda, but his offering of psychotherapy and his confidence that he could now manage anything I presented to him were just what I needed.

FIRST MEMORIES

A few weeks after the marathon, when I'd just begun to work individually with James, Russell and I made love. In the course of things he put his hand on my belly. In an instant I was deeply depressed. I pushed the feeling away, and we continued. That night I dreamt of being paralyzed with fear as a man, black in silhouette, came at me with a full erection. I wrote:

I am angry, confused. I want to push the image away. I want to keep it. It is so strong. I think it is important. I want to know about it. I think, you fool, what did you wake up for? It would have been better to stay with the dream and see what happens. I think, you always make much about nothing. In fact this whole therapy is a lot of fuss about nothing. Nothing ever did or ever will happen. You're wasting time and money entertaining J with your hysterics.

Underneath the fright is rage; underneath the rage is terror. They always said I made it up. I probably did. No one did anything, they said. Someone did something. I thought, J will find out that it is all made up and send me away, a fool for trying to create such drama.

My Critical self said, you are self indulgent, you think too much about yourself. Don't waste so much time on you, making up stories. Unbelievable stories.

The scolding was no different from what I had written thirty years earlier. But then, I continued:

Hands all over; I remember hands all over. I feel helpless in this memory. They are so big. Everyone says I must let him touch me and hold me and hug me and kiss me. Hands all over.

Is it sexual? I don't know. Stimulated. Excited. Anxious. Scared. I can't get them off of me.

Despite all the previous therapy, these kinds of things had never come up before. I was embarrassed by my story. I wrote:

Even when I tell my husband bits and pieces I half expect him to discount it. I am ashamed that I have this story that wants to be told; a story I fear someone will find foolish, will not believe, will say I made up and then walk away and not hear it.

Another day I wrote:

I get confused by others telling me what is true. I feel hopeless that I will be believed.

Actually, Russell listened attentively and never questioned my version of events.

There was more. I had a strange sensation of being wild with excitement, over-stimulated (but was it sexual stimulation?) and having to be still. That was all. What happened and when, remained a mystery.

I went to an art exhibit and saw what I took to be a picture of a whore, although it was only a naked woman, sitting on a chair with her legs spread slightly apart, like a person who is very relaxed. I was washed with shame, as if it were me, as if I sat like that and was seen and condemned. I had no recollection of ever doing such a thing.

I connected some of these images with my uncle from Bernard Street. I clearly recalled him doing something that felt sexual and creepy to me once when I was sixteen. On that occasion, I pushed him away and left. That was all. My sister had remembered him molesting her once, too.

I wanted to tell my mother and father what was coming up in my memory for me. I wanted to tell them there was a reason I'd been so depressed. I wanted them to hear me, to believe me, to care about my story, and not just their fantasy version of my story.

My sister, my brother, Russell, and I went to see them. My mother sensed immediately that this wasn't a simple social call. My father was so oblivious of the tension in the room that my mother had to call him to attention. I told them about what I remembered and the new feelings and images that were coming up.

My uncle had died ten years earlier. My father was momentarily aghast, and quickly tried to move the conversation elsewhere. My mother was very serious as she listened. She related an incident from when she was very little: a male cousin had chased her into the bathroom and only stopped when she crawled behind the toilet. Somehow she was certain he had meant to molest her. As soon as she told this story, she retracted it as nothing important.

"It was just as well your revelation wasn't made much earlier," my mother said, "because it might have torn your aunt's and uncle's marriage apart and alienated the two families."

Perhaps it was just as well! Indeed! This way only I was going nuts with my secret. What about the damage to me! I thought, outraged. I spoke it to Russell and to James. I didn't dare to say it to my parents.

Soon afterwards, James invited me to do a sexual history: had I ever done this, had I ever done that? I answered no to almost everything. The clinician in me could see that there was too much missing.

"Do you think there's more?" I asked James.

"Yes," he said, without elaborating.

Later during that session, when my voice dropped to a whisper, he asked me to make a sound. I wondered what was behind my quiet voice. I thought I could hear the sound James was asking for. It was a scream from the earth, a scream from my feet. But my throat tightened, and I was silent. Where was my voice? Why could it get no further than in my imagination?

Later I wrote:

The answers to these questions are like ghosts, who do no less damage just because no one knows their names. They do more, just because no one knows their names. They come at night to haunt me, and because I don't see them I think I'm crazy, and because my parents don't see them either they say to me, "maybe you are crazy to feel haunted when of course there are no ghosts." If there are no ghosts, then why so many ghost trails?

WORKING WITH JAMES

My work with James was intense and exhausting every time I saw him. Dreams and images and frequent contact with Shama and other Inner Guides provided resources I hadn't known how to use the first time I was in therapy. My growing reliance on these Spirit Guides provided a means of hope and understanding that helped me fight off the despair that regularly threatened to overwhelm me.

The metaphors I was so fond of spoke truthfully at times when I was stubborn or went through contortions of equivocation to hide the truth. For the first time the language in my journals was more direct. I may have been literally silent, but my voice was becoming clear.

One afternoon, a few months after I started working with James, I left my session distraught. It was February and very cold. Even so, I didn't start the car when I got in. Instead, I sat for a few minutes thinking that I would just go home, put the car into the garage, hook up a hose to the exhaust pipe and kill myself. Then I fell sound asleep for about ten minutes. As I awoke, I thought about my plan again.

I can't stand this, I thought.

Later, at home, I wrote:

Did I look for them? Did they just come? The Healer and Shama. They bathed me in love and warmth and healing. I thought, "Maybe I do need to go back into the hospital."

James said, "How you've been hurt, you've been hurt so bad."

Anything to stop the pain. The Healer and Shama came through stronger. I talked to them.

I said, "I can't stand this."

They said, "Yes, you can. Yes, you can. We will help you stand it. The pain will not kill you."

"At worst," I said, "I only see blankness, and feel desperate for it to go away. Will I know what is behind the blankness?"

"If you need to know, you'll know," they answer. "You can tolerate this."

They're right, of course. It is not that I want to die, only that I think I cannot stand the pain. They know. They know I want life, fully. Later they promised me joy. I want that. I want life with joy.

Their certainty, their uncontaminated assurance, without anger or criticism, is comforting.

Shama told me to go home and make a list of people I could call for help when I felt suicidal. S/he said, "Call them all up and ask if you can ask them for this kind of help."

I was startled and miserable. I went home, made a list of friends I thought might say yes, and made the phone calls.

I CAN'T ASK FOR HELP

But there was another problem. A short time after the incident in the parking lot, I had another dream: I went onto a platform to wait for a train. I looked down and saw a slush-covered road, not tracks. I was rather high up. I watched a car and a small truck coming around a corner toward the station. The car rounded the corner too quickly and sank into the slush as if into quicksand. I was horrified and ran back into the station to try to call for help. There were many people and desks in the first office I came to. The people were friendly enough, but no one seemed to understand my urgency. Someone finally showed me the phones, but the equipment was incapable of handling a 911 call. In another office I finally found a phone from which I could dial 911. The person who answered was very, very slow. I was vaguely aware that whoever was in the car was long gone. Even if help came immediately, it would be too late.

Later, I thought about the dream and decided that the drowned driver was my mother and that there wasn't a thing I could do to save her or find help for her.

With a sense of complete failure, I thought, *"I'm too late for all of them."*

That was true. However, the dream was about me more than it was about my mother. The train I hoped to get on was never coming to the platform where I was waiting. I was drowning quickly. The only ways I knew to call for help were totally inadequate, mostly because I kept my distress to myself. Friends said they would help, but would I actually ever call them and ask for it? (This is why counselors, like physicians, do not try to heal themselves.)

I didn't trust James to ask him for help either. I only went to see him because I was desperate and had no better ideas about what to do. I wrote:

I try him out, and he is equal to the task. He does not flinch. He does not make me stop because he cannot stand up to me. He is not afraid of me.

It mattered enormously that he wasn't afraid of me, that the intensity of my feelings and the terrible implications of my memories were not too much for him to handle, although why remained a mystery.

And yet, even at this beginning, which was proceeding faster and harder than anything I anticipated, I also dreamt that I found a hidden locked compartment. It had been lost for many years, but someone nearby had the key. The key was never lost. Inside the compartment was the title to my house. It really was my house. Whatever it looked like, whatever its shape or condition, it was mine and no one else's. I was cleaning my house of old stuff. I was glad there wasn't more than there was and that the task wasn't impossible.

I knew this was a dream of acceptance and optimism. Today, looking back, I can see the self-compassion and hopefulness, too.

A MAJOR PRODUCTION

I struggled in those early months. What I thought was going to be a minor tune-up was turning into a major production, for reasons I could not figure out. I had all kinds of ambitions in those days: a book and articles I was going to write and teaching to do. However, my own therapy and the small counseling practice I had and what little housework I did left no energy for anything else.

Professionally, I was coming into my own, with frequent meetings with a clinical consultant to keep my own material from intruding on my professional sessions. Somehow I got to be quite skilled at leaving my own distress outside of my office door. Some weeks it seemed that all of my clients and I were working on some variation of the same themes: shame, one week; anger another; difficulties with parents; and so on. Frequently, what I learned with James got passed along to my clients as fast as I learned it.

It is a truism in the counseling world that the therapist can only lead the client as far as the therapist has gone. Without having to be deliberate about it, the deeper I went with James the deeper I was able to lead my own clients.

I kept thinking something was terribly wrong. After all, I had already done years of therapy and thought I'd made significant progress. Almost from the start, the current work was deeper and more difficult than anything that had preceded it. What was I to do about all of my professional ambitions? Stopping therapy wasn't an option. I just about lived from session to session.

Only a month after James and I started to work together, I wrote:

I have been opened and left raw and vulnerable. I asked for it. I knew and didn't know it would be so difficult and painful. There is no hope for this pain, I fear. That is the fear, indeed. There is no hope for it; that it is a forever festering sore. From time to time the bandages must be removed, the scabs and pus cleared away, broken again to let fresh healing blood flow forth, only to be rewrapped and set to fester again. What will have to be amputated? Or, will I die of gangrene?

Shama is silent. S/he has nothing to offer but his or her presence, unfailing and constant.

I couldn't imagine canceling a session for any reason at all. I imagined that if I stopped, the pain would be so overwhelming that I would die within the week. I would not and could not let James help me very much. But just by seeing him, seeing that he didn't tire of me time after time, I slowly came to rely on his hope for me. I wrote:

I imagined myself as a flock of forest creatures who creep or slink forward to taste, to sniff, to poke. Who is he anyway? Will he hurt, too? I tried him out; I tested him. Will he stay, I wondered? Will he allow me to stay? I know so much more than I can say right now. Does he think I'm lying? I am not. I have secrets, but I don't hold back to make secrets. I'll tell them in time. Does he think I manipulate? Some, I do to keep him away if he gets too close. But he is teaching me to say STOP, instead of hiding and being tricky.

I watch and listen. James is consistent. I would catch him if he weren't.

About a year after we began, I had a dream in which I was late for class. Once again, I wanted to take my car, but I couldn't find it. I looked everywhere and lost my bearings, searching all over for my car. I never found it. It got to be too late; the class had already started. No matter how hard I tried, I couldn't remember the name of the class or where it was. Finally, I asked someone for help. I was taken to a remedial class, where the students were just learning the alphabet. I knew that attending the class I was looking for, which this wasn't, was important to get ready for finals. Now I would have to miss the exams. I was irritated and disappointed.

When I woke up, I laughed. What could be more explicit? Where I thought I had to go—where I certainly wanted to go—wasn't where I needed to go. I had to start at the beginning to learn the alphabet, the basics, before I could do anything else. James told me that the basics meant learning to tolerate my pain.

In time, I decided that I had to give up my professional ambitions. They made me crazy, thinking about what I wanted to do and constantly feeling too distracted to do any of them. One day, I decided that it really didn't matter if I lived to see the end of this ordeal, that I would stop fretting over my demise and just do the work. I put my ambitions and plans on the shelf. Giving them up and giving up my desire to know the outcome was a great relief. Taking old plans off the shelf, years later, one at a time, was the best evidence that I was getting better.

Somehow, I committed myself to continuing down the path I was on, leading somewhere I could not even begin to imagine, with one incredible difficulty after another and no end in sight. I spaced out and grew numb to the point that I couldn't understand James's words: automatic and unconscious roadblocks to avoid the pain that James said I had to learn to tolerate. I was stubborn; he was persistent. I had no idea if I would literally live long enough to see the end of the misery I was in. Shama made it clear, more than once, that it didn't matter, that doing this work was the most important thing I had to do, even if it didn't get finished.

BLESSINGS

Having greatly diminished my ambitions left me feeling adrift. I could acknowledge the huge energy drain therapy created, but I wasn't reconciled yet to the necessity. I felt mired in a mysterious, compelling mess, as if in some important way I couldn't do anything.

I thought about this a lot. One day, I also thought about the Jewish practice of saying one hundred blessings a day. The standard Jewish blessings of gratitude follow a formula: thank you, God, for creating bread, or a rainbow, or the fruit of the vine; or thank you God, for allowing this day to happen, or something else to happen.

I could say blessings. If I could do nothing else, I could say blessings.

I decided to keep a little notebook of the blessings I created. My rules were simple: any thing or state of being or event could be the subject of a blessing. Repeating myself was always allowed. While it wasn't necessary to have a different name for God for each blessing, it was interesting to try.

My first three entries were these:

Blessed be the Beneficent One who creates terror.
Blessed be the Glorious One who creates pain.
Blessed be the Holy One who creates healing.

For a while I blessed everything I could think of, profound or silly. I blessed longing, grief, and ordeals. I blessed the genius who invented traffic lights, pollution, and spiders. I blessed the almost silent sound of lapping water on a calm day.

The recitation of my blessings became a blessing, as I invariably remembered, if only for the briefest second, that I, too, had been created by something much greater than myself.

James always seemed hopeful, although I couldn't understand why. (I blessed his hopefulness and my faithlessness.) I decided to ride on his faith that the work we were doing would eventually produce the healing I thought I was seeking, as I had none of my own. He seemed to have some idea where we were going, a hypothesis about why I behaved the way I did with him, why I said the things I said. I did not ask, and he didn't tell me about his ideas until much later, when I finally confirmed his ideas by telling him myself.

A good therapist tries very hard not to lead his client to conclusions that are not the client's own. All the times I recall being over stimulated were more a body sense than clear pictures of a person or people doing something specific. James never said it was this or that. I thought about incest, but didn't talk about it. For one thing, who was the perpetrator? My father didn't seem a likely candidate. There was an incident with an uncle, but was it incest? Everything was rather too vague to say. The images and memories seemed insufficient to explain the level of fear I felt almost all of the time. I used all of my energy to hold myself together.

I kept meditating to keep pursuing the spiritual path I wanted to be on. I recited my blessings, at least once in the morning and once in the evening if not more often. I wrote in my journal daily to try to understand what was happening. I was so anxious during therapy sessions that I often missed a great deal of what transpired. I took to writing immediately afterwards, in addition to writing in the morning, to try to capture it all.

MEDITATION INTERRUPTED

From time to time after we came home from Palo Alto I had tried to reestablish a consistent meditation practice. As usual it hadn't occurred to me to ask for anyone's guidance or help. After I started to work with James, it seemed important to be meditating more, even if only to calm myself a little.

One day as I meditated, I imagined my chest opening up. Inside was a large pool of raw sewage. Babies floated in it, face down.

Over many years, I occasionally had dreamt about dead babies. There were many of them, about which I wrote:

Some stayed innocent and pure. Some cowered in dark places, ragged and filthy. The pure ones don't remember what happened because they never knew. They were full of light and curiosity and hope. As I got older, the pure ones decreased in number, one by one going into the darkness and silence. They were no match for monster eyes and dragon's tongue. In time, I thought all the babies were dead because they were all so still and so quiet.

Shortly after this image appeared I wrote:

I think about radiant Light. The Light reaches my face, but the noxious pool is still covered by my chest. I had opened my chest enough to see, but I guess not enough to let the Light in.

From this I learn that as long as I keep my heart closed and keep the pain and the stench to myself the Light will never reach. And as long as this place remains dark, the babies will float in it, drowning, choking, helpless, dying, dead.

Oh God! Can I stand such an opening?

I stopped meditating. For a long time, every time I would try, the image of the babies floating in the sewage would reappear, terrifying and horrible. I knew that I had to open myself to them, but I didn't think I could tolerate doing so.

CRITIC

The critical part of me had the most difficulty with the disruption that therapy had caused in the status quo of my life. I had learned to be very self-critical early in my life, surely by the time I was ten. Once, years before my current therapy, I had written:

I would do everything right. No one would ever be more demanding than Critic. That part of me tried to keep me doing everything right so no one would find out how bad I was. I tried to do this by controlling the entire world. I learned from everyone and outdid them all.

I was skilled at turning my considerable rage against myself. I second-guessed everything I did and said, and generally found myself wanting. I had one perfect image of myself that I found acceptable, and was hypervigilant about any deviation from it.

I had used shame for self-control for most of my life. It was a strategy that worked wonders most of the time. Now, all of my scolding was insufficient to keep images and memories and feelings from bubbling up to the surface and releasing their toxic fumes into the world. I was at a loss as to how to slow down the memories. Shama wasn't at any loss at all about what had to happen next. I wrote:

For the longest time, I met Shama at the top of a mountain. Today, Shama told me it was time to go down the mountain. "No," I said, "I am not ready." No matter, I got kicked off all the same. All I can see is a jumble of rocks, sharp rocks, in all directions. Shama never said the descent would be easy or even that I would make it. S/he only said it was time to go. The critical part of me is furious.

Shama embraces Critic without words. Critic collapses in fear and distress. Shama embraces her with love and comfort. Critic thinks she is at a cliff edge. She is dizzy with the height. She thinks to throw herself down. She thinks she is walking off a cliff anyway. She is a Wild Woman turned in upon herself. With words and thought she cannibalizes herself. Critic is feverish and dizzy, but she is no longer biting or stumbling. I cannot go on without her, she of sharp eye and sharp tongue. She sees some of the dangers I miss. She knows the rules of safety.

She speaks up, not only with warnings but instructions. I cannot go on without her.

Shama insisted. S/he held and comforted, demanded and supported me, whether I was cooperative or not. Other Guides showed up. Two were like matrons. They never said anything but surrounded me if I was feeling self-destructive. One was in the image of a young boy who saw beauty where I only saw desolation and ugliness. Sometimes, when I was in a particularly foul mood I sensed being completely surrounded by them all, as if they made a container in which I could thrash and flail safely.

Some Guides acted as a repository of faith and hope when I experienced myself as having none at all. One time I wrote:

There are silent Others standing half in the shadows, not judging, just waiting; waiting for me to give up thrashing about; waiting for me to surrender; waiting for me to yield to the terror I feel. The Others will not interfere. They will wait as long as is necessary. They will wait from this lifetime into the next. They will wait forever. They wait to be my escorts when I am ready to leave the caves in which I bury myself. They are waiting to bathe me in the River, a holy mikvah [a pool Jews use for purification] of natural waters. There are sins as well as shame to wash away. These are the Ones who will stop me from self-destruction. They will wait until I make the choice, fully, to come with them. They know all I will need to learn about living without terror and with an open heart.

I think I alone have to do this choosing. But I am not alone. Shama is smiling. S/he knows that what is happening is right. S/he holds me. S/he will not do my work for me. S/he has no need. S/he is not the one who is scared.

Betty and Carolyn had taught me how to summon Shama, but I hadn't called for the other Guides in any way. I did not know they were there to be called. But when they seemed present, when I sensed their incredible patience and compassion, then I trusted them completely to be truthful, even when I was rebellious.

FRIENDS

From my doctoral student days, I'd become very close friends with Nili and Catha, my carpool mates, who were also students of Betty Bosdell and Carolyn Conger. Each became an enormously important ally as I fell deeper into my morass. Nili loved adolescents. She especially helped me stay grounded when I despaired about my own adolescents, repeatedly reminding me that they were likely to outgrow their distressing behavior. Catha was a long-time meditator. She and I had long conversations as I tried to understand faith and the place of The Holy One in the midst of my pandemonium. The three of us opened a very small private practice together in 1983.

In 1987, just before I began working with James, Nili and her husband Hector moved to northern California, a move Nili really wanted and Hector didn't. After a few years, in 1989, he returned to the Chicago area to work as an emergency room doctor at Resurrection Hospital. In early spring after he returned, Nili joined him to look for a house. Then, just before Passover, just as the house hunting was completed, he developed a brain aneurysm and within a few days was gone. It was a terrible time for her. Nili's children flew in from California. Russell and I brought them food. I contacted Rabbi Morris Fishman, who had been our once-a-month rabbi years before, the one rabbi Nili knew, so he could help with the funeral. I tried to put aside my own shakiness to help in whatever ways I could.

After her life settled down a bit, Nili decided to remain in California. At the end of summer, I went to spend a week with her, trying to be available to her in her grief as she so often had been for me. We talked nonstop most of the week. She told me how disoriented she was with Hector suddenly gone and with her plans all awry and how difficult his death was for his teenage daughter and medical-student son. I talked about how Russell had always been my protector, but now he was taking too good care of me. I joked that both Russell and I were codependents, each trying to do for the other way more than was really necessary, only now he was outdoing me. I wished he would not be so protective.

One afternoon she had something she had to do, and I stayed behind at her home. I thought about all of the pain in the lives of so many people I knew, and I thought about my own. In a minute, I was dipping into thinking about the impossibility of tolerating or escaping from the pain that was always there when I paused. It was an easy next step to thinking about suicide.

Trying to fend off despair, I found some paper and a pen and started to write, not planning what came next. I wrote:

I have in me a deep, deep well of pain that bubbles up when I am insufficiently distracted. There is no end to the pain. There is no end to the grief.

I started years ago, at the top of the Mountain, where Shama was to be found. There are so many paths on the side of the Mountain, but not all of them lead up or down. The Valley and the City, my destinations, are still far off.

Where am I going? Why do I make this journey at all? Because it has been commanded? Because it is incumbent on each of us to gather what holy sparks we can to return them to their holy Source? Are these reasons enough? Who has commanded these things? And how am I to do this mystical task?

I fight against the Light. In that heavenly glow I see only the sharpness of the rocks I must traverse. The Valley and the City seem only a mirage in the golden God-light.

Where is my yearning? Where is my longing? Hidden in caves, protected by monsters, caves whose walls I broke with my bare hands. The golden God-light poured in, flooding the pools of grief; illuminating, in the reflections of a monster heart, the huddled forms of innocence and longing, exhausted by fear and abandonment.

Caves and mountains and rocks, the Valley and the City; and the River, which nourishes both, which comes of course, from the deep caves and springs on the side of the mountain. I forgot entirely that the Valley would be nothing without the River. I forgot completely that the waters come from the snow and the rain and the subtle springs of the Mountains. Did I think the River came, in full flow from nowhere? Could the nourishment of the Valley and the City exist without the rich, flowing waters?

And where do these waters come from but the melting ice of my heart, the rain of tears of my grief, the seepage from the tears of my shame.

And where do the energies come [from] *to enrich these waters, but from the thunder behind my silence, the lightning behind my stillness, the crash of the avalanche waiting in my cells and bones, in a mighty whoop for joy poised at the end of every nerve.*

So that is the holy mystery: so that is how the life-giving waters become wet and rich.

A paradox: The Valley and the City are beyond a certain kind of suffering. Yet, neither would exist without the River of suffering.

I don't know if I will get there. I can't get there, because I am there already.

There is nothing more to do but sing praises to the Mountain and the River and the Valley and the City. There is nothing to do except notice that today I am stumbling in the rock field; today I am napping in the tall grass; today I am negotiating in the City square; today I have lost my way in the back streets; today I am drowning in a half-opened cave. There is nothing to do except see that today I am here and here and here. I sing songs of gladness that here is where I am.

For a few minutes I stopped fighting to hold back my feelings and my life. I stopped fretting and despairing about getting out of my pain, and I just sat there, letting it wash through me in words I didn't plan, in metaphors I didn't fully understand, surrendering until the tears came and were transformed into joy.

There was a dream around the same time: I was standing in what had been a large cage-like structure, except the top and most of the walls have fallen down. Two crows perched on the remaining upright wall, calling and cawing.

"Look," they said, "most of the walls are down. There is nothing stopping you from stepping out."

That was true, of course. To feel imprisoned by the pains of the past is a kind of illusion. I did step out occasionally. That is when I could see the Others, Shama, the Mountain, the Valley, and River, and all. But for me to step outside and not go back was a major decision, made and unmade many, many times. First, I had to really know every little corner of my cage and see it for the decrepit place it really was and see that staying would never create the safety or serenity I wanted.

COMPLETE MEMORIES

In October 1989, almost two years after I started to work with James, we were in the middle of a session in which I was being as obstructionist as I knew how, doing my best to keep him away. He asked me something, and I fogged out or stopped breathing—all manner of diversionary tactics. There was a knock on the door, and his secretary said there was an urgent phone call. This was the first time a session had been interrupted.

When he came back a few minutes later, a story spilled from my mouth about an incident with my Bernard Street uncle, whose marriage I apparently saved by keeping quiet. I have no idea what shifted in me to inspire me to tell this tale.

Afterwards I wrote:

The details. The threats (I'll hurt you if you tell), the lies (this feels good, when in fact it hurt), the sensations. This feels like somebody else's dream. I don't have any feelings about this. It was someone else, not me.

James said it was important to say my story. James said if this is never to happen again I have to stop being a victim, and I am not seven any more and I'm big enough and strong enough to make him stop, but I have to tell my uncle to stop.

The critical part of me doesn't like this. She warned and warned, although I didn't understand what she was warning about. She is scolding and scolding. Critic is beside herself with fear and worry. I am beside myself with fear and worry.

Somehow I am not dying. I am coming to life. I don't understand this.

A seven-year-old part of me says," don't touch me, don't touch me." I tell her that she and I are going to have to say that out loud, no whispers, or telepathy or begging.

I took a long walk with Russell that night. I told him some of what had come spilling out of my mouth. I told Russell that I hardly believed what I was saying, that it must be someone else's story. It was unbelievable that it was mine. I felt a mile away, hearing my own voice as if from a distance. I was almost too anxious and upset to tolerate being in my own skin.

Russell listened carefully.

"I wondered from time to time if you had been molested or abused," he said thoughtfully. He never said, "Surely you're making this up," although I wondered if I was. Russell's acceptance was precious.

There was a second memory when I saw James next. I remembered that my uncle and I were in the Bernard Street building, but I can't say for sure whether it was his apartment or mine. It seemed that we were the only two people there at that moment. I remembered that something he wanted to happen didn't, with a part of him for which I had no name. He got angry and finally went off without a word as if I were no longer there. I remembered that I was alone for a while. I remembered that I didn't say anything to anyone.

I wrote:

James said when I get washed with the wish to die, that is me reliving my young self's attempt to deaden herself so she would not have to experience her fear and her pain and bewilderment and anger and all the feelings that happened too fast and too many and were awful and she had no idea how to make my uncle stop, and besides she couldn't think anyway and felt kind of sick and held her breath and did what she was told and was a good girl and didn't squirm or anything or make any noises at all and everything felt so strange.

Later I wrote:

My body is creepy with too much energy on my skin. The back of my head and neck feel bad, tight, charged. Shame. Shame is like Vaseline, thick and sticky, but sickening, not soothing.

I want to be able to say my story out loud with outrage and anger instead of this reeling shame and fear I feel. I want to be numb again so I don't have to feel all of this stuff.

On another day, shortly after, I wrote:

I feel exhausted and weak, like I am sick. I am sick. There is poison in my body and mind, and rot in my soul. What else explains my knowing so much and still wanting to die? What else besides the poisons of fear and confusion and anger and betrayal could work so insidiously to finish off a murder when the assassin is long gone?

Empty holes in the accounting of my life are getting filled in. The mysteries of my life are beginning to make sense.

I realized that the memory explained some things: the horrible feeling I would get sometimes when Russell touched me in particular places; the sensation of wanting to be out of my skin; my general aversion to being touched by anyone. At night, after telling the two stories, my whole body hurt, especially all the places my uncle had touched; I felt nauseated.

I didn't tell my parents about anything. I couldn't figure out how to do it in such a way that my mother could hear it and not get so upset that I ended up having to take care of her. I expected my father to dismiss the whole story out of hand.

The aftermath of this eruption of recollection was an even greater intensity of pain and anger. Despite James's efforts to teach me to say my anger out loud, the only expression that felt safe was to aim it at myself. Although James and previous therapists had tried to teach me to protest, I didn't believe that I could say, "stop," and survive.

The only thing I knew to do with my rage was to deaden myself against it. Shortly after reclaiming my memory of my uncle, I wrote of awful images in the detached, cold manner I had perfected decades before:

I think of rubbing my skin with broken glass.
I think of razor blades. I think of small knives.
I wonder why I think of such things.
I wonder if I would feel anything.
(I do not experiment to find out.)
I am not quite busy enough.
I don't want to do anything.
I resent any intrusion on my time.
I am bored. Without enough to do, I am depressed.
All is quiet inside. So what.
My head is full of stuff. What stuff?
I don't think of anything.
I know what I am not. I do not know what I am.
I am lonely. I don't want to talk to anyone.
I cannot tell the truth. I do not know what the truth is.
Is this a tantrum? Is this self-pity?
I am not suicidal but I think of razor blades on my skin.

I imagine the Mountain and the Valley I can see from there. This time is different. This time it is deep into night, a starry night. I can easily make out the glint of the River and a light or two from the City. I can see, in the star-lit darkness, the greater darkness of the mountains on the other side. In all of my images of the Valley over many years, I do not remember it so dark.

I know I am very arrogant and have little faith. I said, "Shama, I am doing poorly with my hopelessness. Are you still available for me? I am battered. Will you go without me if I cannot change or change fast enough? Will I ever stop thinking of broken glass and razor blades? Are you there for me?"

Shama whispered, "Yes."

I asked why it is so dark.

"Because you can't see the light, yet."

It is dark so I must move slowly and carefully. I mustn't move too quickly lest I panic and pick up sharp objects.
Yes, S/he is with me. Yes, it is self-pity.
S/he does not scold about that.

Writing about cutting was both frightening and compelling—a fine foil against letting myself know how incredibly angry I was. I liked checking into the images of the Mountain and River because whatever came up was a better clue to my true state of mind than any pondering could produce. This was the first time I realized that such carrying on was really a tantrum, a silent substitute for acknowledging my anger.

MIKVAH: A POOL OF PURIFICATION

After the first rush of incest memories, I decided to go to the mikvah, the Jewish ritual bath. The idea of the mikvah goes back thousands of years. It can be performed in a lake or a river or any pool of natural waters. The original intention of a ritual immersion in a mikvah was to cleanse the participants of impurities that rendered them ritually unclean and thereby disqualified to enter the great Temple in Jerusalem. That Temple has not stood for almost two thousand years, and during that time, other uses have evolved.

I am not an Orthodox Jewish woman who uses the mikvah each month after her menstrual period is over. I had read of other non-Orthodox women using this ritual, although not for the purpose I had in mind. These first explicit memories left me feeling soiled and dirty down to my bones. I needed something to cleanse myself far more than a long, hot shower could accomplish.

I found a phone number to call to talk to someone who could answer my questions and tell me what I had to do. The woman I spoke to told me that women came to the mikvah for all kinds of reasons beyond the usual ones and that no one would ask me why I was there. She said it was incumbent to remain celibate for seven days after menstruation stopped until after the immersion ritual in the mikvah. I could manage that easily, and Russell was willing. There were other requirements, such as sleeping with the bed sheets arranged in a way that would keep us from touching each other. That was too difficult, as I relied on Russell's touch to help me stay grounded. The important thing, the woman told me, was to do what I could. Again, she assured me that no one would ask.

I decided to try it. The woman arranged to have someone there who would also not ask questions, but would just be available to answer any questions and to give support if I needed it. The day I was to go, I saw James. He knew nothing about the ritual, but helped me open myself a little so I could take in the experience as much as possible.

The mikvah I went to was located in a very public place on a busy street but hidden by bushes and the total lack of any identification on the building. According to Jewish law the waters of the mikvah must be natural, from a stream or lake or, in this case, rain water, which was gathered in a cistern on the roof of the building. I punched in the code to unlock the door, went in, and was shown to a washroom with two doors. One of the doors opened into the public lobby, and the other, opened into the interior space where the mikvah pool was located. I was given a towel and soap, and told to take as long as I liked. I washed myself very slowly. I stood in the shower long after the soap and shampoo had washed away, crying with unfamiliar tears. I remembered that the Guides had told me that it was tears that would cleanse the soiled parts of my soul. Tears were natural waters, too.

When I was finally ready, I walked out of the second door into the interior. An older female attendant sat there to look me over, as she did for all the women, to make sure there wasn't a stray hair or piece of lint on my naked body. Then she took a large sheet and held it over her face, to preserve my privacy. She only looked when it was necessary to make sure the ritual was being done properly. I walked down the stairs and entered the pool. The water was warm and pleasant. I told her I was ready.

The words of the blessing were engraved on the wall of the mikvah, but I had trouble reading them through my tears. The attendant was puzzled that I was crying, but I assured her that I was all right, just sad. I think going to the mikvah for the Orthodox women is a more joyous occasion. She helped me say the words and then watched the prescribed three immersions to make sure I went under all the way.

I did feel cleaner afterwards. I wrote:

The world seems different somehow, like the coloring has changed, something subtle but persistent. I have a little less of my life missing. Yes, that describes the difference. Life isn't any different. There is more of me experiencing it.

I went again on two other occasions. It was a kind of shining for my soul.

MY MOTHER'S DEATH

Several months later, in early December 1989, my mother suddenly developed pneumonia in addition to her increasingly debilitating cancer. One night, it seemed certain that she would die. My sister and brother, my father, and my husband and I gathered around her bed. Her younger sister, Sarah, flew in from Connecticut. My mother refused to eat or drink. The nurses and doctors held out very little hope that she would last until the next day.

She had tiny tumors all over her brain, cancer that hadn't been touched by all of the chemotherapy she had had over the previous three years. That night, between disease and lack of food, she was quite psychotic. She hallucinated beings who were watching her. From her description, they sometimes sounded a lot like my Guides, but I didn't try to tell her. She kept saying she had something very important to tell us, but none of us could decipher what it was. She saw colors everywhere. She told me to ask Jeremy, the artist among my children, to draw the colors. I asked her which ones they were.

"Have him draw the colors," she said.

She was more fascinated than frightened by the visions she saw. Her face was relaxed. There was none of the wariness and worry on her face that seemed to be there most of the time. She wasn't worried about anything. Even the fact that we couldn't make out what she was trying to say with such urgency didn't seem to perturb her. She was wonderfully self-absorbed and not concerned with the rest of us.

As I stood by her bed and watched and listened, it was a great relief to me that my state of mind was, in this moment, of absolutely no concern to her. She didn't need to fix me. I couldn't possibly fix her, and that didn't seem to matter to her either. I loved her, then, more openly than I could have imagined possible.

It was a rough night, and she didn't die. The psychosis and hallucinations passed, but she continued to get progressively worse. My father was willing to try anything to make her get better. My mother's doctor suggested some heroic measures, such as feeding her with a tube inserted into her stomach, and trying some physical therapy to improve her muscle tone. She didn't improve. I thought the doctors and my father were torturing her.

My mother was sent home, very weak, and completely unable to care for herself. My father demanded that his children all drop everything and come and help him take care of her. He didn't in any way take our own lives, our families, and our commitments into account. He bullied and scolded us, and we all said no.

I had no energy for him or her. They were both dangerous to me, wanting me to be the sweet, compliant daughter who would not upset them, at a time that I was reminiscing myself into shreds. The disparity was unbearable. In the weeks that followed, I stayed away as much as I could.

And yet, my mother was dying. I tried to find ways to reach her before it was too late. Some of the difficulty was mine. I still had a very hard time telling either of my parents what was true, or asking for what I wanted, such as some alone time with my mother. I went to my rabbi in Naperville and asked him what it meant, to honor one's father and mother. In Jewish fashion, I expected a book list of things to read on the subject. All he said was to be honest with them. He pointed out that the commandment is not to "love" one's parents, only to honor them, with honesty. I had no idea how to do that safely.

One day, my mother and I were alone in her apartment. She was lying in a hospital bed that took up most of the living room, and I was standing nearby. I thought the moment had come when I could say something honest to her. I had nothing prepared, no last thing I wanted to be sure to say. I don't recall if I had anything particular in mind as I began to speak in a tone of voice that said this was something important.

All I can remember saying is "I want to talk to you."

Her brow furrowed, and she looked a little alarmed. The expression on her face seemed to say, don't hurt me. She didn't say anything for a few moments.

Then she asked, "What about?"

Someone rang the doorbell and that was the end of the conversation. It was the last chance I had. What I took away from it was the look on her face, the look that reminded me that all of her suffering was my fault.

The last time I saw her she was in a coma in the hospital. I sat too many hours with her and my father. He was unpredictable. That day, he was subdued with concern. In his presence I slipped into a trance, keeping myself harmless and invulnerable. We went to the hospital cafeteria for lunch. I ate without tasting or knowing if I was full or not.

My mother lay still but breathing. I wanted at least two minutes to say good-bye, but I didn't disturb either of them with what I wanted. My father talked about physical therapy and helping her eat again.

What broke the trance was remembering that I had an appointment with James that afternoon. When he saw me, he said I looked worse than he had ever seen me. My body was there, but I was nowhere to be found. Being lost had its virtues: nothing hurt.

Later that day, I told Russell that I couldn't go back to the hospital, even though I knew that I would never see my mother again. Even today, I can feel the constriction in my chest and the pressure in my head, which are the remnants of how I shut myself down against what an impossible situation we were in. My mother and I both wanted so much from each other. Neither one of us was able to deliver.

I struggled with my own dying at the same time. Partly, I knew perfectly well that my mother was dying of a disease about which I could do absolutely nothing. But I also believed that it had always been and remained my responsibility to keep her alive, and I was failing totally.

James talked to me a lot about how my dying would solve nothing. I talked to myself as well. I wrote:

My mother is dying. I can't let her take me with her. I will follow her in my own time. I can't let her death be my final undoing.

James said the decision to stay alive is mine. And so is the decision to quit flirting with death, the decision to stop deadening my life with terrifying ideas of self destruction, the decision to not honor my parents with my inert soul walking around in an unnaturally lively body, the decision to stop letting my parents whittle away at my sanity, the decision to stop letting them kill me little by little, look by look, the decision to not die or pretend to die, to not suffer my own death endlessly, again and again, over and over, the decision to do more than remain upright, the decision to learn how to live fully no matter how difficult that might be, the decision to learn how to open my heart fully when I choose. These decisions are mine. I have to decide fully.

Suicide will not make any difference. They will hurt and die anyway, at their own time, no matter what I do. My attempts to save them are hopeless, utterly hopeless.

In order to be alive, I have to give up the hope that anything I ever do will be enough or the right thing to get either of them to act right with me. Nothing I do will ever work. And most especially it will not work to keep my mother alive.

She died a week later. Russell and I went to the Fox Valley Mall that morning, to buy winter boots for him at Sears. When we came home, Sonia told me that my father had called to say that my mother was gone. For almost an hour I put away purchases and puttered around the house. Finally, the news penetrated.

There were phone calls to friends and to cancel my clients, who had been forewarned that this was coming. There was going to the funeral home and picking out a casket, and then there was the funeral. Rabbi Lorge, the rabbi I had grown up with at Temple Beth Israel at the other end of our block on Bernard Street, died perhaps hours after my mother did, but his funeral was first and hers second. Many people from their Temple went to both.

Over two hundred people came to my mother's funeral. I had no idea she meant so much to so many people. A group of my friends, who were all mental-health professionals in recovery from incest, sat directly behind me. Nili flew in from California. It mattered to me greatly to be surrounded by people who knew what was truly going on in my life, people I trusted.

There was shiva, the seven-day mourning ritual in the Jewish tradition. Some of it we did at my father's house and some at mine. I made it to all of my therapy appointments.

A part of me, the keeper of despair and plans for suicide, decided that now was the time for me to die. This was a side of me no one knew about but me. It was the side of me that was always ready to check out. Why push dying now? Because I'd completely failed to save my mother. Now that she was dead, I'd lost all opportunity to be the daughter she wanted. It all seemed very clear. All of my arguments about not dying, about coming to life were just so much chit chat when I was in this frame of mind.

I told my clinical consultant, Jeannie, who asked me to make a contract to stay alive for another couple of months. It didn't really matter to me when I died, so I said, sure. In those months James focused entirely on my despair.

I described myself this way:
I started out defeated and hopeless; and beneath that I was bitter and betrayed; and under that I longed to open my heart and trust and be ok.

It was so crucial to feel in control.

When I am not in control, I wrote, *I think I have to die to keep things right. I can't let too much feeling come because then I can't stay in control, and I don't know what to do. That's when the crazies come.*

KADDISH

For eleven months after my mother died, I followed the Jewish ritual of saying Kaddish, the Jewish memorial prayer, which is entirely a praise poem for God. I wrote:

I say Kaddish for my mother to remind me that there is glory as well as grief. I say Kaddish for my mother to remind me to stay alive now that she is dead. In one of David's psalms [30] he reminds me that while there is mourning in the night, there will be joy in the morning.

But what do I do with the night that does not end, the darkness impervious to the dawn?

I read Kaddish and wait.

I read Kaddish and wait for the earth to turn another degree.

I read Kaddish and practice having faith that because the day eventually emerged at other times when the night was too long, perhaps it will again.

I read Kaddish for me.

I do not, today at least, read Kaddish to mourn my mother.

I read Kaddish to remember what I lost long before her body died.

I read Kaddish to remember all the times I died.

I read Kaddish to remember that if my body dies now, there will be no more praising HaShem [God], no more tikkun [repair of the world]; at the moment, praise and tikkun seem more compelling reasons to stay alive than all the promises I've made so far.

I read Kaddish to remember that if I die there will be no enactment of the plans that are waiting for daylight to emerge from this night, which is lasting too long.

So, in the end, there is nothing to do but read Kaddish and praise the Holy One for creating pain and mourning and unbearable loss and sadness and death and the choice to live.

In the months that followed my mother's death, my inner life became more turbulent. It was as if I was toppled in an avalanche and was desperately trying to find something to grab onto.

Every Sabbath evening, I attended synagogue so I could say Kaddish properly, in community. One Friday night, as Russell and I rose to say the

Mourner's Kaddish at the end of services, I started to cry. I immediately figured that anyone who noticed would think I was still in mourning. But grief wasn't all that was on my mind. Holding the prayer book close to my face as I silently sobbed, I thought a simple prayer: Help! Within the one minute it takes to recite the Kaddish, I finally acknowledged that I really couldn't manage all on my own the great changes that were flowing into my life.

SOFTENING

Sometime during those months, when the pressure diminished, I got curious about the possibility that there might be more to know about than just my view of things. I softened a little. One day, driving home from James's office, I stopped to buy some flowers. I was startled to see how vivid the colors were and how delightful all the different varieties were. I began to realize that the part of me that held most of my hopelessness and despair was also the part that was most attuned to beauty. I was more than I thought. For the first time, I wrote about wonder and amazement:

Beauty is what I am good at. I am not sure what I mean except that it is true. Somehow I know that I will sit next to the young Guide and see only beauty when I get over seeing only darkness. That's amazing. Is it possible that life out there is beautiful after all, despite of, in the midst of, surrounded by and flourishing in all of humankind's pain and misery? How is this possible? Is this the God-Light, which is always there? Is that what the young Guide sees when he sees what I think are monstrous parts of myself?

This life is too mysterious, I wrote. *I wonder if the mystery is bearable.*

FATHER WITHOUT MOTHER

The crisis of my mother's death passed and new ones took its place. My father wanted more and more of me. He asked me one day to take over my mother's former role as hostess at parties they loved to give.

He wants me to be his wife, I thought. I said, "No."

He wanted all of his children to help take care of him the way my mother used to take care of him. My sister, Judi, lived nearby. He told her to make dinner for him several times a week. She was much closer to him than I, but she quickly regretted saying yes, even once, and stopped. His sister lived upstairs and was given the same command. She took longer, but she backed out, too.

My mother had been his buffer. She had devoted herself to his happiness and protected him from the consequences of his selfishness and bullying. Now there was no buffer. He scolded his adult grandchildren for the way they dressed or how they wore their hair. He scolded my brother and sister and me for not being attentive enough. We all became mute at these moments. None of us knew how to tell him to stop. With my mother gone, he managed to antagonize all of us.

Sometimes he demanded attention like a two-year-old. Sometimes he behaved as if nothing much had ever changed. He was unpredictable from time to time, even from minute to minute. I felt trapped into visiting him, and put it off as often as I could. I had no energy to sympathize with him. He never asked me, or my siblings, how we were handling our mother's death.

One time when he called I decided that I would try being honest instead of evasive, which didn't help much any more. I told him I was canceling out on a scheduled little party.

"I'm too uncomfortable being with you in a small group," I said. "There are important differences between us, and that is a problem for me."

"It's not a problem for me," he replied.

"That is the problem."

"Why can't you put it aside?" he asked.

"I can't."

"Your distress must have been hidden for a long time."

"Yes," I said, "and I can't keep it hidden any more."

"Well, how long will this take?" he said, "I'm not a young man any more."

I said, "I don't know."

"Who will I talk to? I don't have a wife any more."

I said, "I don't know." I didn't help him out. I didn't snap at him and say I don't give a damn who you talk to, but it won't be me. I spent the rest of the day exhausted and depressed, angrier than I knew. I backed off that one time, but couldn't entirely break the connection yet.

When my father leaned on my sister and brother, they turned him down too.

He confided his difficulties to my mother-in-law. Mollie lived close to my parents—about a half-mile away—ever since my family had moved to the neighborhood, first on Bernard Street and later when my parents moved to Spaulding Avenue. Mollie frequently walked past the Spaulding building on her way home from the synagogue she attended. She rang the bell and visited with my parents or my aunt for a few minutes if they were home. They had many interests in common, music and theater especially, and had all become friends over the years.

Mollie had seen my father in action often enough to understand when I described to her some of my difficulties with him. She was a great ally for me, precisely because she knew him so well and because I knew she loved me.

Mollie told me about her conversations with my father. She said she listened carefully for any recognition on his part that he might be part of the problem. The first small hint that might be so came four years later, shortly before he died, when he wondered out loud to her if he might be doing something that caused or contributed to the rift between us.

My father was acting out, picking fights with people, harassing waitresses or other service people, angrily increasing his demands. I was acting in, trying to close myself off from him, even as I was working with James to open myself. Each time my father and I met, under any circumstances, became an ordeal. As my father asked for more from me, I sensed something else was coming. I became more and more uneasy, anxious, dreading something I couldn't identify.

SOMETHING COMING

Three months after my mother died, I once again resorted to mighty metaphors to say what I couldn't say directly even to myself. I wrote:

Primitive energy. I do not like the forces that are just beginning to gather for a blizzard. A butterfly flew across the Mongolian reaches many months ago, and now the first ice crystals are forming at some impossible height in the upper atmosphere. And now, somewhere else, magma is pushing its way up through the crevices of some ancient land, venting as steam sometimes, rocking the earth sometimes.

Arrogance sits on a foundation of inadequacy. The arrogant are condemned to try to keep the earth still, the winds from blowing, and the ice from forming. But even the arrogant cannot control every butterfly wing. It is quite inevitable. In time the winds will form despite my best efforts. The Gulf Stream will shift just enough to push the winds of the south into the perfect place to bring down the winds of the north. The steaming volcanoes a thousand miles away will aid the ice- making conspiracy high above my head. The day will come soon when all will be ready. The winds will begin, and the snow will begin. It is the way of great winds and earthquakes that there is great damage and death.

I asked my Guides if I would weather this storm. The answer was maybe, if I did what needed to be done: ride the storm; stay grounded and ride the storm.

My father's lips are bitter butterfly wings. In my legs are the molten mountains seeping to the surface. In my sweat is the steam feeding the ice crystals forming high, far, far away in the stratosphere of my head. The Gulf Stream of my blood shifts a tiny bit. Harmony will have to wait for another day. There are distant shrieks and yells of a mighty wind practicing in the cirrus clouds, impossibly high. The winds that might rip me to shreds are forming even as my inhalation and exhalation stir the air around me, like a butterfly's breath.

I will learn to stay grounded and ride the storm. I don't know how I will learn this. If I don't, I will be ripped apart, my skin will split, and my pain will erupt from every opening, burning, searing, and doing great damage to the world around me.

It doesn't matter if I live. It matters how I die. I will not be murdered.

What I meant by my discourse on chaos theory was simply that my anxiety was building along with a sense of anticipation, but for what I could neither guess nor say. I was frightened and tried to bluff myself with bravado and to calm myself with fancy words. Knowing that a storm is coming doesn't really blunt the blow.

The next day, about an hour before I was to leave for an Al-Anon meeting, I sat in a chair next to a window in my bedroom, writing out a dialogue with Shama about the storm I imagined. An image came, clear and distinct, of a five-year-old me running into my daddy's arms after he came home from work. After a moment, he began to tickle me between my legs. In the memory, I was a little startled. I started to squirm a little, and noticed that he both seemed far away or distracted and held me tighter. I didn't like what he was doing. Even more, I didn't like the strange sense that he was both there and not there. He put me down and walked away without looking at me.

The storm had begun. The adult in me made ugly sense of what my father was doing in a way that the five-year-old couldn't have understood.

I want to die, right now. I thought. *If my mother knew, she would die. I can't stand this.*

I called Russell and he came home from work. I stayed alive.

I called James. He said that the alternative to dying was feeling what I felt. He said that my father's feelings were too intense and my feelings were too intense back then. I couldn't handle them then. I didn't think I could handle them now, either.

The storm is here, I wrote later that day.

The winds are beginning to whip up the snow. Riding the storm means going about my business. Riding the storm is feeling what I feel. Being numb is getting covered with snow. Saying, I hate you, is coming in from the cold. Suicide is like the snow piling up around me, encasing me, freezing me.

James said I am in charge. I have to remember that.

After the first clear memory of my father molesting me, the pretense that we were all part of one big happy family was completely blown apart by an incoming storm of memories. I wrote:

James said every time I am with someone who has hurt me badly and there is not an acknowledgment of what happened and I attempt to behave as if nothing happened, I poison myself. When I stay away, I feel like I have to kill myself in retribution for breaking the most important family rules and threatening to disrupt the family's sanity. Mine or theirs. James said dealing with self-destructive thought is easier than dealing with my family, because I can control my own behavior, but I cannot control theirs.

There it is. Clear. Concise. True.

The message about the impossibility of controlling my parents' behavior was easy to hear and easy to write down. I can't remember when I fully believed it, but it was years later. I didn't have to believe it to realize, if only vaguely at first, that real freedom would come when I could give up trying to control them.

CUTTING OFF CONTACT

For the Fourth of July weekend, the summer after my mother died, my sister and brother and their families, along with my father and my family, were to get together. I was nauseated and painfully tense with anticipation of the ordeal of being with my father. I mentioned this to Jeannie during a consultation session.

"You don't have to go," she said.

Five words: *You don't have to go.*

In fact, I could do more than not go on this occasion. I could decide when, if ever, I saw him again. I might be quick to make such a suggestion to one of my own clients, but it had never occurred to me that I could really say no to my father, that I could stop trying to manage his unhappiness at not getting what he wanted from me.

With Russell sitting right next to me, I called my father and said we would not be joining him as planned. And, I added, I thought it would be best for me to not see or talk to him at all for a while.

"How long?" he asked.

"I don't know, but not for a long time," I told him.

He promptly wondered out loud if he would die soon. I didn't respond.

"I have a weak heart," he said, suggesting that if he died it would be my fault.

He was rarely so explicit. Hearing the words, out loud, was the opposite of the crazy making he did so often. I don't remember any longer just what I said, but I refused to budge. The conversation was brief. When he hung up, I was enormously relieved.

He didn't give up trying to have me his way. He called often. I never answered the phone. If Russell answered, he firmly refused to let my father talk to me. Russell, who was normally very even tempered, was angry, too. His anger was unbelievably comforting.

Despite remaining firm in my resolve to not communicate with him, I fretted regularly about having failed my father, as well as my mother. I thought about suicide most days of the week. I stopped myself with remembering that killing myself would give my parents the final victory.

The calls diminished but never stopped entirely. Three months later, on Yom Kippur, the holiest day on the Jewish calendar, a day of asking for forgiveness from each other and from The Holy One, my father called early in the morning before we left for services. He demanded to speak to me. He told Russell that it was a holiday and it was right for a father to talk to his daughter at such a time, although he had never called on the Holidays before. Russell said "no" and "no" again as my father tried to force him to make me come to the phone. My husband finally hung up.

We drove to synagogue. I was incensed. I vented a bit with a friend. The congregation was gathering. I couldn't imagine being so angry and trying to contain myself in public, so I went home and sat on the couch, almost motionless until Russell came home after services.

In the autumn and winter months that followed, James and I worked to reduce the despair and to get me to tolerate more and more, so I would not be so frightened of myself. I wrote out a conversation with Shama:

"Shama, I am so frightened by all the feelings and the memories— more so by the feelings."

"Feel them anyway. They will nurture you."

"How can all these terrible feelings nurture me? They make me want to die."

"No, you don't want to die. You want to come alive. You said that you wanted to grow up and not be left behind, and that is exactly what is happening. This time you will live. You will not be murdered again in your soul. You will not kill your spirit or your body."

"Shama, you can't protect me from the chaos of the world, can you?"

"No. I can only be your guide about what you do with the chaos."

"Shama, I feel strange."

"You feel and that seems strange. It is not strange. It is living."

"I don't like this."

"That is not so. You do like it. It is just very different from what you think is normal."

After a six-month hiatus, I resumed talking to and occasionally seeing my father. I worked hard to find a way to tolerate setting limits with him.

THE BIG ROOM

I also worked to tolerate more feeling in my life. Anger pushed to emerge. Shame pushed me back into silence. Memories emerged in bits and pieces. When something dreadful came to mind, my back would tighten and my breath became slow and shallow. Moving forward felt literally like I was physically pushing myself.

One image that came to mind was of someone playing with the point of a knife over my bare chest, pressing just enough to occasionally draw a little blood. It seemed to be my uncle. I was terrified at the malice and cruelty I saw on his face.

Years later, I saw the film, *Schindler's List*. In one scene the commandant of the concentration camp looks over a young Jewish woman deciding out loud whether or not to rape her, his eyes glittering, the smallest smile on his face as he deliberated whether to enjoy himself or to abide by the idea that Jewish women were just animals, not suitable even for sex. As he slowly walks around her, seemingly seeing through the thin slip she wears, she stands completely still, barely breathing, her gaze a hundred miles away.

My uncle had looked at me that way, sipping my terror as if it were fine, ancient scotch and growing intoxicated by my fear. I was immobilized by fear, my gaze taking in nothing at all except the look on his face, that moment frozen in place without context, without beginning or end.

In November 1990, the year my mother died, I attended a conference on sacred stories. It was a huge event at a large hotel outside of Washington, D.C., with about sixteen hundred attendees. The poet, Robert Bly, did story telling presentations. Wendy Doniger, a Sanskrit scholar from the University of Chicago, talked about the difference between dreams and myths and how we use myths in our daily lives. The highlight was hearing the poet and writer, Maya Angelou, a big, outrageous, amazingly lively woman. I loved it all.

Between sessions, images and sensations began to emerge, like toxic chemicals leaking from old rusted storage containers. There was an image of a big empty room with one very large, old wooden worktable under a bright work light. People. Men in shirtsleeves and dark pants. Flash bulbs and floodlights. Beer and knives. I was there, doing what, I didn't want to think about. I could barely contain the leakage until I got home.

I saw James the day after I came home. I could hear the flatness in my voice as I told him about the big room and what I thought had happened there. I told him about my uncle taking me there, about being taunted and stripped. I told about being pushed and prodded and poked and penetrated and passed around from one to another, floodlights and cameras going all the while. I told about the drinking and the fights and the knives. I told how every time I moved in any way they said, "She wants it. She likes it." If I was very still, they were disappointed and sometimes angry.

Once, at least once, there was another girl there. I stood naked, watching as they yelled at her to stop crying. Every time she cried they cut her, not deep but enough to hurt, and yelled at her to stop crying again. I watched, terrified into absolute stillness. Some of me got stuck there, never knowing if I would be murdered in the next minute or the next.

In time, there were many stories of the big room. Much of what went on there was planned, but some seemed spontaneous, especially when the men were drunk.

There were never very many details. I am fairly certain that the building was associated with the place my uncle worked in a location that is currently near or under Interstate 94, as it makes its way from downtown Chicago through the north side neighborhoods and eventually on to Wisconsin. I remembered how filthy the washroom was and the fact that I was never allowed to close the door. (I had near-nightmares for years about needing to use the washroom, but having to do so in a very exposed place. The nightmares stopped after the memory came.) But I have no idea what was on the walls, paint or brick or wood, or what color they were. There was a smaller side room with a big frosted window, the kind with wire going through it so it couldn't be easily broken. That room was a pale green that turned my stomach whenever I saw it afterwards, a particular mint green.

I remembered that the table was hard and rough and that the floor was probably concrete. The room always felt cold, although I can't say with certainty that the season was cold.

I remembered light rain on the windshield of a car I was in when my uncle sent me home with a stranger who took me up to his apartment on a street lined with two-flats and mature trees. Light rain on the windshield made me nauseous from that time on, until I remembered where the nausea came from.

I have never had a sense of the smells of the place or the sounds beyond what was said to me directly. I used every skill I had to avoid paying any attention to what was going on.

When I finished telling James my first recollection of the big room, I asked him what it was like listening to me. He looked upset. He said it was like listening to death. He said I spoke of atrocious things but with no feeling at all.

Later, I wrote a dialogue between this flattened part and me:

"To die now means that they win."

"They did win, already. They took everything."

"The men did not take your soul or spirit."

"Yes they did. It's gone."

"Remember Maya Angelou. Some people in her life tried to take away everything, too. But the people near her loved her and taught her to love life."

"I didn't have anyone to teach me to love life. I just want to die. James wants me to feel. They said not to make a noise. They said to be still. James said I will never be in that room again. I heard him say that what happened there was atrocious. I don't know what to think. When I think I get strange feelings in my head. I don't want to be here."

It was a dangerous time.

PRACTICING

My greatest skill was being very quiet and very still: frozen. I never had to think about if or when to play statue—doing so was as easy as water turning to ice at thirty-one degrees. After my mother died and before my father died, my work in therapy was all about deciding to move and deciding to make noise, making noise and moving, doing it. Each session with James was an opportunity to practice.

Once I wrote:

I said, "I don't want to do anything…"

James continued my sentence, saying, "…that would make you feel anything."

I said, "Why, why would I want to feel? Why bother?"

He said to just say, "Why!" He said, "You just want to be frozen and let them do what they want."

I said," To be frozen and let them have my body and leave me alone."

He said, "That is the myth, if you froze enough they would leave you alone."

But they didn't, of course. They were always coming up with ideas I could not anticipate.

In the end I cried. He gave me his hand to hold and I began to melt.

I wanted to stay frozen and I wanted to melt. I was scared. I began to be hopeful. I was melting. I wrote:

There is a pond
   Made to hold the rain.
This morning
   Before the sun emerged
The water was
   Covered with ice.

I am confused.
How do I hold the rain?
How do I stop the floods?
How do I darken the sun

Or bring it forth?
How do I make ice
    Or melt it?

By now almost all the ice is gone.
By now the geese are swimming.
By now only a thin patch hugs a shadowy shore.

Tonight the sun will go again.
Tonight the ice will form
    And thicken in the dark.
The water will forget the geese.
Will the ice always melt?
Will patches always hug the shadowy shore?
Where will the ice go in summer?
Are there shadows deep enough to hold it?

GOALS

When I began to work with James, I told him that I wanted to open my heart, that I wanted a fuller life.

"If all I can have is the half-life I have now, then I don't want any of it," I said.

What I didn't say to myself or to him was that I wanted a full life without changing very much. James knew that. Any experienced therapist knows that about people beginning therapy, including me. His goals for me were to have a full life and deep, real change.

Almost immediately after I started with him, my goal became to stop the pain and terror. James said I had to learn to tolerate my pain.

I wanted to avoid thinking or talking about sexuality or pleasure. James added learning to tolerate pleasure to learning to tolerating pain.

In time, I recognized that all along my goal had been to change myself enough so I could continue being a good daughter and save my parents without making myself sick and crazy. James's goal was to help me learn to save myself, because I couldn't save them.

My goal, always, was to hide and keep hiding, without appearing to do so. James found me again and again and told me so.

My goal, so I said the first time we worked together, was to tell the truth. James told me much later that he knew I wasn't going to. I wanted to change but not really; I wanted to cooperate but often didn't. I both told the truth and lied about wanting to know my own story and to stop the pandemonium. His goal was to help me find the truth and to tell it, first to myself and then out loud: my truth, not the story my parents wanted to hear.

Three years into our work, I realized that what I wanted was for James to fix me, adjust a few things here and there, and send me out into the world ready to love and not offend. He did none of the above.

Once, I asked James if my recovery would kill me, literally. He said, "maybe." In time, I came to say it didn't matter. I wrote:

My survival skills are killing me. Hiding is a defense. Getting crazy is a defense. Gagging is a defense. Spacing out is a defense. Suicide is a defense. I am terrified to let them go, lest I die. I will die if I don't let them go.

I began to understand that if the pain was really ever going to stop, I was going to have to risk whatever it took to get well.

THE PARTY, 1991

In 1991, as December approached, I couldn't tolerate the idea of trying to put on a happy face at the annual family party. It was probably a sign of progress that I didn't think I could fake the big happy family routine that we all did so well. For the first time in my life (not including the two years I was in California and unavailable) I decided to not attend and to say something to everyone about why not.

I still have the original of the letter I wrote and edited in blue ink on a torn piece of typing paper that had once been used for something else. My handwriting was large and vigorous. Phrases were scribbled out and new ones added until it said what I wanted it to. I'm sure Russell read each version before the final copy was made and mailed to my father, my siblings (who already knew what was going on), my aunt, and my cousins. I told my children what I was doing.

The letter said: *I have decided not to come to the family party this year, and Russell won't come either. Over the past few years, I have been remembering terrible things that various members of my family did to me as I was growing up. I don't want to spend time with my family right now, with all of this stuff on my mind. I don't feel like pretending I'm having a good time when I am not.*

Russell and I spent Christmas Eve in a motel in a far northern suburb. We saw a movie and had dinner someplace. It was basically a miserable night. I'm sure, even if I didn't fully acknowledge it at the time, that I wanted to get my family's attention, I wanted to tell them that something dreadful had happened and most important, I wanted them to care.

When I spoke to my children the next day, they all reported that the party went on without any mention of the fact that Russell and I were missing. Apparently, I'd gotten no one's attention. I was very disappointed, but looking back, their lack of response was probably predictable. The truth of my life and experience had been missing, unacknowledged by anyone from my Bernard Street family (except my brother and sister) for almost fifty years. Nothing I did in December 1991 or before or after ever broke through the family trance.

EXPRESSING MORE

Each time James and I met, we worked a little more on experiencing and expressing what I felt with my body and my voice. Often James would ask me to let out a sound, a cry. Sometimes, I would recall what happened in the big room with my Bernard Street uncle and his buddies, and my whole body would ache but I couldn't make any sound at all. I was puzzled about how I could get the message from my legs and arms and torso to my mouth. I was a telegraph line with the wires cut. I was beginning to understand that if I wanted passion and joy I needed all of the lines connected.

Once, in an effort to encourage me to open my mouth and make a sound, James reached over and lightly placed his finger on my chin and then took his hand away. As my lips parted, my throat closed. I could barely breathe. My lungs hurt as if I were suffocating. My heart missed a few beats.

When I finally settled down, startled and unnerved by what my body had just been doing, I asked James what happened. He said something vague, a speculation about something filling my mouth at some time in the past. After a while, an old memory came to mind, of lying on the dining room chairs of my grandparents' apartment on a very dark and stormy night. Now there were more details. My arms had been pinned down at my side as someone straddled me and shoved something into my mouth and into my throat. I hadn't made a sound, except for gagging when I was two, and I couldn't make one in James's office.

Other memories, a torrent of memories, returned.

I never remembered crying or complaining or making any other sounds.

I remembered being silenced by my father, when I was very young. I wrote:

Sometimes when I got angry with my father he might put his hand or a pillow over my face. His voice would be gentle perhaps, but his hand was not. I could not breathe. Was he trying to kill me? Or kill the rage in himself? Or both. Life in danger. No more angry faces. Daddy didn't like that. He made it hard to breathe. Sometimes I didn't breathe at all. Sometimes I tried to make me die so I wouldn't be angry and he would stop the hurtful things he did and stop the looks and stop the hands over my face.

Another time I wrote:

I remember times with my father, his fingers all over me, stroking me, stroking my cheek. Soft his touch, soft his voice. Not soft the warning about complaining. Not soft the hand over my face. Not soft his hand on his big self or the look on his face. The juice. The smell. The silence afterwards. Me, watching. He, forgetting I was there. I was so quiet.

There were many memories of silencing myself and stilling myself in the big room and other places.

I spoke to Shama often, for guidance and comfort. S/he was as demanding a Guide as my earthly teachers were.

I wrote:

I asked Shama when this memory flood was going to stop. I said, "I got it. I got the picture. The men met fairly often, and many bad things happened. Do I have to remember all of them?"

"Until you learn to feel."

"This feels like being abused all over again."

"The abuse is over. Now it is you who abuse yourself by holding on."

"What am I to do? I don't know how to let go; I've been holding on for so long, a lifetime. When I just think about these memories I feel so completely helpless. My genitals feel raw and painful most of the day. I itch all over. My body is screaming in pain, and my voice is silent. Shama, your demands make me feel trapped."

"You were trapped."

"I don't know what to do."

"Do with James what you couldn't do then. I will not leave you."

"I am afraid it will be too much for me."

"It will not be too much."

"Shama, they got turned on by my embarrassment and my pain."

"I know. It is over. You died once for them. You don't have to do it again."

"Shama, with all these memories, I am not all here. I am disconnected even from my husband."

"It is not the memories that disconnect you. It is you trying to die. Come alive. You are not alone now. We will help you handle the pain."

"Shama, I will fail the people I love."

"No you will not. You are only failing yourself."

Shama was right, as always. As more memories came, I grew angrier and less frightened of being angry.

One day I wrote:

I feel like I have crossed a major hurdle. Somehow I realized that the plank across the abyss was plenty broad and strong enough. I will not fall in. My memories are awful, but I am not afraid of them any more. I have moments of doubt, but that is all. I am coming alive. No memory or feeling, at this point, is going to kill me or make me crazy.

My memories frightened me less and less. I learned to tolerate feeling more and more, but I still couldn't get the sounds out of my mouth, the sounds of rage and anguish. I cried more, but still the tears rarely came.

CRYING

I rarely cried. The very thought of really crying, sobbing, was frightening to contemplate. Three years into our work, James told me I was like a rabbit, prepared only to be quiet and hide, hyperalert.

I wrote of his comment:

Crying out doesn't help. Crying gets something in my mouth. Can't breathe. Crying out never makes it better, often worse. I would rather be dead than protest.

I always listened to music in the car going and returning from my sessions. Usually I tuned into WFMT, the Chicago area classical station. Sometimes coming home I played tapes of Lorena McKennitt, a clear soprano whose taste for melodies in minor keys perfectly matched my mood. Sometimes I would cry listening to her or others like her. Sometimes, I cried hard enough to have to pull over and park for a while. I rarely cried like that in any one's presence.

Four years into our work, James wondered out loud if there was something the matter with my eyes. There was no anatomical problem.

I wrote:

Too much holding back crying makes me feel crazy, suicidal. I deaden myself so I won't cry.

A year later I wrote:

I imagine I will cry so hard I will wash away all of my outer layers and be revealed horribly ugly and deformed, too awful to look at. And in a moment of insight, I followed with: *I imagine I will cry so hard I will wash away all of my outer layers and be surrounded by light that will soften my wounds.*

Almost a year later, I had a meeting with Jeannie, which turned into more of a therapy session than a case consultation. She confronted me to acknowledge how angry I was with her for not rescuing me from a hole I had dug for myself. As I was preparing to leave, clearly upset and not sure what to do, she reached out and held me. I started to cry. Then, unexpectedly, I sobbed from a depth that startled me.

Later, I wrote:

I thought I would die or go crazy. But I did neither. How did Jeannie know the moment? She held me and held me. I cried and cried. She made a container. As much as I could I poured myself into it. I was puzzled by her, but chose not to think, just to be. I said, later, "It is a dangerous place." She said, "It is a power place." I said "that is what makes it dangerous, but there were no dangers today."

Around that time there was another insight about crying with tears and with an unusual acceptance I wrote:

Shama, what a wonder it is that the spot where we stand is glowing with light even as the rain falls. Rain for the River. There would be no River without the rain. Rain in the mountains, rain running down the boulders and high passes. Rain breaking up into rivulets. Rain dripping from everything. Even my eyes. Even my eyes. Tears seeping deep into the soil, deep, deep into the soil, all the way down to that dark, silent place where the River flows for a while, a long, long while, until it finds its way out of its secret places, just as my tears find their way out of their secret places, to run down my face, to run down the banks to join the rest, to join the River that makes its way to the Valley that makes its way to the Sea. How I long for the Sea!

And yet, and yet, I understand that longing alone will not do it. No wishing and standing at the edge forever, praying for deliverance, will do it.

The waiting, paralyzed with fear, is a kind of doing, and I remember what you said, Shama, that it is not what I do. Lighting up with your love is not doing. What happens after I step off the edge will not be a doing either. I understand that, Shama. I understand so much. I understand that the rain on my cheeks is cold and wet. That is not a doing either, that coldness, that wetness.

Somehow, Shama, it seems that crying is not a doing either, even as it is I who am doing it. It is being. It is being wet with grief and fear, soaked with sadness as deep as the underground River. Or is this the place where the River leaves its dark path and comes out, out into the open? Or is this the place where I unlock the box in my heart where my hope was hidden, just as the River was hidden? Not lost, the rain at the upper regions of the mountain; no, those holy waters are not lost when they go underground, just as my hope and my love were not lost in the box in my heart. Not lost; no, not lost.

But having lived so long away from the source of the holy waters, so long in the shadows of the mountains but away from the top, so long away from knowing that the waters were not lost, I forgot.

I forgot. Every now and then I would recall. Every now and then you would remind me, but I was in such pain from stumbling around among the boulders in the shadows of the source of the holy waters, that I forgot again and again that the waters were not lost, they were only underground.

And here, Shama, and here and here, Shama, the River is breaking through the surface, which is not as solid and impenetrable as it seems. This River of tears burst forth in a dozen different places, my lamentations pushing aside the rubble, clearing a space.

And now, Shama, I see that these tears are carriers of light even as your love is. My hope grows, just like a River grows as all the rivers join together. Rivers of hope. Rivers of grief. Rivers of love.

I do not understand, Shama, how hope and love and grief are rivers. I do understand, Shama, that I do not need to understand everything. I understand that some puzzles can be left unsolved to float downstream in the rushing waters, and that the puzzles will reach the Sea as surely as everything else. As surely as everything else, Shama. Everything. Including me, Shama. Not too soon, Shama, I will not have to die too soon. I will not have to die of longing and terror mixed into an impossible glue. No, I will not have to die in order to loosen the glue. I only have to step off the edge with you by my side, Shama. I only have to remember somehow that you are there and that your love will be all the protection I need.

NOTICING CHANGE

I began to notice new possibilities for my life. One wintry day I wrote:

I feel different. I am becoming different. It is at a time like this that I can remember that there is more to me than my terror. At first the sense of spiritual movement and light makes me doubt that the other stuff is real, all that darkness. I wonder if I have been living in darkness only because I put my hands up to my eyes and was too stubborn to take them down. Then I realize that the misery is real <u>and</u> the light is real. I think I need to learn how to have them both. Perhaps there is hope that I will not only recover but can grow something beautiful in the damaged places.

I started to learn that one of the ways I kept myself trapped was in struggling with wrong questions. Some had no answers at all. These were all the shame questions, such as what do I have to do to be good enough? Some were procedural, such as what do I have to do to stay in control while letting myself go? Some were an addict's questions, such as how can I hold onto suicide as a distraction and lead a full life? All of these were wrong questions, because there is no satisfactory answer to any of them.

At one of Carolyn Conger's retreats, several years after my mother died, I realized the impossibility of the questions I had tormented myself with.

I wrote about what some of the right questions might be:
When the drum beats, how do you dance in the mud?
When the rains fall, how do you dance in the sand?
When the flute sings, how do you dance in a swamp?
When the sun shines, how do you dance in a pond?

I realized I could always dance, anywhere. I came to realize that wonder, not understanding, was the antidote to despair.

LAUGHTER

In between the deaths of my mother and father, during the tumult and trials of the great outpouring of memories, a lighter version of life was beginning to fill some of the vacated spaces.

In September 1992, Russell and I attended a weekend retreat in Milwaukee with Rabbi Gershon Winkler and his wife, Lachme. He talked about the need for each individual to find the joy of the Sabbath, which resides in each of us all the time. I wondered how I could find that joy when my heart was breaking, but even without knowing how, I did.

I wrote:

Reb Gershon is so funny—so much laughter with him. So much taking lightly what I have been taught to take so seriously. He echoed Tom W. [an Alcoholics Anonymous speaker whose tape I listened to until it wore out], *that God is up there having a good time, inviting all of us to do so as well, if we want to. So much pleasure with so much richness. Nothing at all frightening. No challenges to face the fears that terrorize me. Just an invitation to richness and pleasure, an invitation to laugh and sing and dance, all of which I did. And a reminder again and again that our charge is to do what we can, not to finish the job of creation.*

I am a little unnerved by my experience of myself at this place with these people. The focus of the weekend was on joy, not on pain. It is strange to put the pain aside.

In June of the following year, my husband and I went to a "Music for People" workshop in New Hampshire for a week of learning music improvisation with cellist David Darling. The group had professional musicians and amateurs, a jazz harpist, a young genius on drums, singers, flutists (including me), two French horn players (one of whom was Russell), a violinist, and many others. We were encouraged to pick instruments we didn't know how to play and to try something new. For a week in New Hampshire, we sang and danced and played with strings and flutes and drums. We sang or played alone and in improvisation groups where we listened to each other and played in response to what we heard. We performed for each other and then went off to rehearse playing together, making music without attention to technique or a composer's instruction. It was a week with nothing but music, a week in which it was impossible to make a real mistake and in which all activity was play. I was too excited to sleep. Even so, I couldn't keep up with the people who jammed half the night. I had more fun than I could recall at any time in my life—another good sign.

There were signs upon signs that the ice around my heart was softening and melting, that I was coming to life. I came out of hiding more and more and not just in therapy. As I let myself be seen and heard, my relationships with almost everyone deepened in ways I'd only experienced rarely before. Sometimes, I was more forthright and explicit about what was on my mind. In return, the people I spoke to seemed to listen with interest and hear what I said, as opposed to merely defending their own ideas. I got feedback during this time that I was more present and more real. I could feel the truth of what they said, and I felt glad.

THE DARK TIME OF THE MOON

IN THE MIDDLE

The middle of a journey of transformation, whether through therapy or spiritual practice or some combination, is moon time, the dark time of the new moon. For me, this was the time when I'd gone too far to turn back yet not far enough to know exactly where the destination was or if I would get there. From this middle place, there were increasing glimpses of a destination, but it seemed indistinct and very far off.

The path seemed treacherous in the dark. I was like someone taking a blindfolded walk across a minefield. I, who trusted neither myself nor anyone else, had a great need to trust and follow the guides I had chosen to lead me through. Their certainty that my task was possible provided the guide rope I held onto. As the new moon eventually began to show itself, I discovered that the blindfold was an illusion, as were many of the mines. To the rope provided by my guides was added my own growing skill and confidence.

What was changing this time was the entire paradigm of my life, all of the foundations for the beliefs, known and hidden, upon which my life was based. The steel girders, which supported the structure of myself, were a victim's helplessness and powerlessness, fear that the entire world was dangerous and untrustworthy, and shame—most of all the shame of believing that I was irredeemably broken and soiled. All of my victim beliefs were not true. My greatest mistake was to believe that my version of reality was in fact Ultimate Reality.

I was like Pharaoh, whose heart was hardened by his own certainty and arrogance, who steadfastly missed the miracles of the God of Moses. In the face of information contrary to what I knew to be true, I tried harder to maintain what I believed. Unlike Pharaoh, I was at least edging towards surrender, towards giving up my insistence that the world was the way I thought it was, and towards giving up insisting that I should and could be in charge of everything.

As the crescent of my own moon began to illuminate the darkness, those beliefs began to disintegrate. The change was disorienting and disturbing. I wrote:

Shama, this path I am on is so unspeakably hard and painful. My faith and my courage falter and leave me all the time. Each mountain I must scale seems taller and more rugged, each minefield more treacherous. Getting to the treasure is fraught with consequences and no guarantees. I have not had enough experience with tolerating either pain or pleasure to say that it is worth the trouble. I cannot stay here. I am terrified of moving on. How do I muster the willingness to proceed?

What I saw, as my path began to lighten, seemed familiar, yet foreign. Common language seemed to take on new meanings. I was uncertain about what to do and how to behave.

The Jewish exodus story starts in the land of *Mitzrayim* (Egypt), which means the narrow place. I had started my exodus from a place that seemed narrow to the point of strangling life itself. As the light of awareness brightened, I could see that there were much wider choices than I had thought, but at my deepest levels I think I didn't believe the changes I saw before me. I had read about this new "promised" land in books and stories by others who had made the same sort of journey. Approaching my own "promised" land was another matter.

TESHUVAH, *OR RETURN*

In the midst of moon time, I began to understand that my inner work was like the Jewish concept of *teshuvah*, which means to return from sin or to repent or to turn back to God and holiness, which is our promised inheritance.

In Hebrew, the word for sin, *chet*, means a lack or a diminution, implying that sin diminishes the sinner. Sin is what I return from and about which I do *teshuvah*. When I use the word "sin," I mean all of the ways of mistaken thinking, believing, and behaving that keep me separate from God consciousness—pride and shame being the root of them all. "Your iniquities have been a barrier between you and your God," says Isaiah (59:2).

Deep psychotherapy, which is what I did with James and my earlier therapists, is a kind of ongoing *teshuvah* and a way of learning to recognize that what was learned is not embedded in my genes and therefore could be changed. *Teshuvah* adds the spiritual element to what might appear to be only psychological. Psychological change becomes a kind of *teshuvah* when a person, like myself, expands her awareness, not only of the fullness of life, but of the Source of Life as well.

In the Jewish Way, *teshuvah* is a two-way process, which people initiate and in which the Source of All actively participates. There is a famous story: "A king's son was at a distance of a hundred days journey from his father. Said his friends to him, 'Return to your father.' He said to them, 'I cannot.' His father sent to him and said, 'Go as far as you are able, and I shall come the rest of the way to you.' Thus, the Holy One, blessed be He, said to Israel (Mal. 3:7): 'Return unto Me, and I will return unto you.'" (Goldin, 1975, p. xxi)

The work of *teshuvah* may seem overwhelming, but we never do it alone. Part of what made therapy possible for me was coming to understand that I could not recover on my own, as I'd once attempted to manage my abuse alone. My therapists were all Godlike in a way, reaching out to me, meeting me where I was, and walking with me as far as they were able and I was willing to let them at the time. However, I had steadfastly, if mostly unconsciously, refused to allow myself to go very far, intent on being one woman against the world.

I came into therapy with James at a time when it was increasingly clear that all the chewing gum and rubber bands in the world couldn't hold together a damaged foundation. Perhaps that was the first step in killing pride. The second was to allow myself to trust him, one tiny bit at a time, to help me.

The Days of Awe, or High Holidays, are the major time on the Jewish calendar when sins are acknowledged and the community strives for *teshuvah*. As I worked with James, I began to realize how my mistaken beliefs could be understood as sins, in the sense of keeping myself closed and separate. Once, as the Days of Awe approached, I was confused about what to do with this new awareness. I wrote:

How do I approach sin when I am only learning how very dead I've been? The idea of sin leaves me bewildered, implying choices I did not know I had. Or, did I? How do sins get weighed when done out of terror? When I think about it, it is terror most of all that has created my insensitivity and blindness, terror I did not even let myself know was there. Is it enough to say I did the best I could? I often could not imagine the possibility of a God. It took so long to learn to ask for help because I was so sure there would never be any forthcoming. How could I have done better? How could I have rejoiced more in the gifts I've been given when I was too scared to notice?

SPIRITUAL PATH EXPANDED

My sense of consciously being on a spiritual path had begun in the 1970s, when I learned to meditate, and it intensified at the Gestalt Institute where I was drawn to the instructors who incorporated spiritual teaching with Gestalt training. Betty Bosdell, my teacher and mentor during my doctoral program and friend before and after, taught about the spiritual dimension of psychotherapy. Carolyn Conger taught a universal kind of spirituality.

From the time I began my work with James at the end of 1987 through the moon time—the moonless walk at midnight through the wilderness—I thought I'd abandoned my spiritual journey entirely. I struggled some with the matter of how God could possibly have regard for me when I had so little for myself. I mostly didn't have the energy to think about God at all.

I mentioned abandoning my spiritual path one evening at the beginning of a Conger retreat, as I gazed out of the large picture window of our meeting room into the dark January night. Carolyn leaned over toward me and said, "No, you haven't." I couldn't make any sense of what she said at the time and made no reply.

Now, I know that the very fact that I wasn't indifferent to my spiritual life, the fact that I showed up at Lake Geneva in the middle of every January, was proof enough that my spiritual path was active. At that time, I was like a hiker on a wooded path strewn with tall boulders and gnarly roots, so twisty and irregular that I couldn't see beyond trying to figure out where to put my foot next. The path was difficult, but I was definitely on it.

I may have meditated only a few minutes a week, but I never entirely stopped. At my mother-in-law's suggestion, I read Abraham Joshua Heschel and let his amazement and wonder stir my own, at least a little. Reading Heschel and other Jewish writers reminded me of what other people had found possible and what I might find possible someday, too.

I did not know then about the kabbalistic idea of *kleipot*, which are the shards of primordial vessels broken by the intensity of Divine light that distract us all from full presence to life and to God. Today, I would describe my spiritual path as having been blocked by an avalanche of *kleipot*, which had been there from before I could remember. Throughout my life there were occasional intimations and glimpses of what might be beyond this apparent pile of rubbish, but our efforts during the first four or five years I worked with James were the first concerted attempts to clean them up.

I didn't understand then that even paying attention to the glimpses—the reading I did, the conversations I had with my mother-in-law, Mollie, and some of my friends, and the return each winter to Carolyn's retreat—were spiritual practices.

Rabbi Israel Baal Shem Tov, the eighteenth-century mystic and founder of the Hasidic movement, taught: "If...you will...think of the Supernal World, you will instantaneously be in the upper worlds. For a person is where his thought is. Thus if you had not been in that upper world, you would not have thought of it at all." (Schochet, 1998, p. 55) Even to lament having wandered far from my spiritual path was to bring myself back to it immediately.

In moon time I came to realize that to remove the most obstructive obstacles on both my path to psychological wholeness and my spiritual path involved three things: killing pride, acceptance, and choosing life.

KILLING PRIDE REVISITED

After my brief "conversation" with Death in the mid-1980s, I learned that shame and its flipside, grandiosity, were the kinds of pride I had to kill. Shame meant that I thought I was irreparably flawed at the very core of my being, so much so that even the loving, compassionate Divinity of my tradition was helpless to fix or forgive me. In my shameful grandiosity, I held a perverse belief that somehow the laws of the universe had been altered to create impossible standards just for me and no one else, and that it was possible and necessary for me to meet them.

This sense of irreparable uniqueness persisted despite the fact that almost every client I ever worked with shared the same mistaken belief, which clearly suggested that I wasn't unique in this way at all. Most of my clients, especially those who stayed and did the work, recovered from what was distressing them, which suggested that I might, too.

I believed that my shameful flaws, my strong feelings, my selfishness, my every imperfection, and my inability to be endlessly cheerful and selfless, had to be kept out of sight, preferably from myself as well as everyone else. My anger was one of those flaws. Growing up, if I got angry with my father, he would get mad at my anger and convince me that I was responsible for what had upset me in the first place. If I got angry with my mother, she would act as if I'd wounded her. Either way, I was wrong. It was best to never get angry.

It is also impossible never to get angry: we are all born fully equipped for that emotion, which healthy infants demonstrate immediately. I diverted my anger into being spiteful, sneaky and mean when I thought I could get away with it.

My rages brought no relief. They planted another shame-seed, another sprout in a thicket of rhododendron-like growth, with tangled roots and branches in which I could get stuck and lost forever.

Of my three children, Jonathan was the most sensitive to the shame secrets I was trying to hide. When he was in preschool, he would sometimes say he wanted to kill himself. I doubt that he actually knew what the words meant. I could feel the horror of his words contort my face and body. I could see him watching how upset I got.

I never talked about suicide to anyone, not even Russell, but I imagined I had contaminated Jonathan in some mysterious way.

The next to the last time Jonathan talked about suicide, when he was fifteen or sixteen, I knew enough about how I operated and how manipulative he was to say that if I thought for one moment that he was serious, I would call 911 first and ask questions later.

The last time the subject came up from him, I calmly asked him what kind of a funeral he wanted. By then, my shame thicket was much, much smaller.

My grandiosity was expressed perfectly when I wrote:

After meditation I wanted to see Shama, but in the image I was enormous, much bigger than the mountaintop.

S/he said, "You cannot approach me that size." Then Shama covered the mountaintop with a dark, translucent cover.

I did not know what to do.

"Get smaller," s/he said. "I cannot be with you or talk to you when you are so large."

It took a while, but finally I was small enough. I said I was afraid because I didn't know what was happening.

"What is happening is that you are beginning to grow and change. You don't need to know how things will come out. I can comfort you, but not when you are too big. You are fine, and there is a difference between fine and comfortable. I am not worried about you or the outcome, even if you are uncomfortable."

To destroy shame is a tricky matter. To merely lop off a branch does little to attack the roots, which are devilishly difficult to find. It was as if the tips of the roots were buried and tangled with the spirals of my DNA.

As I began to realize how buried the roots were, I wondered how much of me would have to be destroyed to eliminate shame. I wrote:

I'm worried about being too open and vulnerable, light. Would I be too light and float away? Would I be too open and get overwhelmed?

Who am I without my shame? The answer is, I am no different than with my shame. When I am fully me, without the distortion of shame, the question answers itself.

I guessed at this truth long before I believed it.

KILLING PRIDE THE JEWISH WAY

The Jewish path is concerned with two completely interrelated things: increasing God-consciousness and increasing one's fullest presence in life. While I'd read a lot of Jewish philosophy in an unstructured, haphazard sort of way, I didn't really begin to understand the importance of these things until I was in moon time, that intermediate, indeterminate place that wasn't the past but wasn't fully the present yet. It was then that my heart began to understand some of the fundamental Jewish concepts that my mind thought it knew, which is to say, that these ideas were now deeper and informed my life experience and were not just the surface knowledge that came from my intellect alone.

Perhaps I needed to actually be much more whole before the concept of wholeness was really meaningful. Perhaps I needed to actually be present to life, instead of trying to avoid it, to understand what being present actually means. Perhaps I had to stop hiding and waiting for God to find me, in order to find God waiting for me.

MYSTICISM AND MY MISTAKES

The Jewish mystical tradition has some major tenets that proved to be important in helping me correct some of my mistaken ideas.

The first and most fundamental concept is that God permeates every aspect of creation. "...for I fill both heaven and earth—declares the Lord." (Jeremiah 23:24) That statement, in and of itself, is a powerful antidote to pride, either in its shameful or grandiose forms. God's omnipresence means that the Divine is present in every shameful moment and event for perpetrators and victims, for hiders and seekers alike. It means that lack of awareness of the Divine is not equivalent to the absence of the Divine.

I realized this after a meditation many years ago, when I was working on my doctorate and was not in therapy. I wrote:

The Spirit of the Divine appears on the porch of an old house, a poor house. The Spirit of the Divine appears in ways known only to itself in the shadows and omissions of this old house. It shows in the shadows. It shows in the worn banister and old wooden steps. Is there a spot so poor or so dark that the light does not glow there? Is there a direction one must go to find the light? Is there a direction in which one can go and not find the light?

Periodically, even in the midst of the most agonizing part of my work, this awareness would reappear in my writing, only to get lost again for a while.

For me, this Jewish understanding that "everything is God" means that the laws of the universe apply indiscriminately to everyone. There is no one who is outside the "everything" that is God and therefore set aside for special punishment or special anything, no one who is so fatally flawed that connecting with The Source of All is impossible.

Another important idea is that "the task of the soul is to know itself. The ultimate goal of the soul is to be revealed through the qualities of enlightenment (*mochin gadlut*), and to be free from the deep obstacles that plague it." (A. Davis and N. Gefen, working paper, 2001). If this is the task of the soul, then, by definition, each soul must be capable of this self-knowledge. For me, it is less important that I know exactly what it means for my soul to fully know itself than it is to know that it is valuable and worthwhile for me and my clients to work on that self-knowledge to the fullest extent we are able.

This concept, which is shared by every wisdom tradition I know about, is also the foundation for the faith in the possibilities for change that I brought to my work as a therapist, even when I doubted it for myself.

As my therapy with James began to reach the end stage, I wrote about my understanding of this idea:

I think sometimes of the utter insignificance of my life in the universe and that complete insignificance turns around instantly. "For dust you are, and to dust you shall return," (Gen. 3:19) and "The universe was made for my sake alone." (Mishna Sanhedrin 4:5)

I am my universe. In this particular corner, I am all that matters. This is the only life I have at this time. It is mine to either hide from or live in. There is no avoiding suffering. Hiding to avoid suffering only increases it. I can imagine the ascent from hiding to being fully present to my grief, to the possibility of transcendence.

The great sin underlying all else, from which I must be cleansed in the great purgatory of knowing my suffering deeply and intimately, is my lack of faith that I am capable of transcendence.

The Jewish mystics taught that we are cocreators in partnership with God. We have a powerful ability to influence the world and ourselves, especially with our attitudes: joy begets joy; anger begets more anger. The great Jewish medieval philosopher, Maimonides, describes the many ways people make transformational change (*teshuvah*) impossible. He lists everything from indifference to minor stretching of the law, from selfishness to perpetrating heinous crimes. Yet, he completes the list by reminding us that a true intention to change can trump everything else.

In my own healing and that of my clients, it has been a persistent mystery why one person chooses to change, chooses to do whatever it takes for as long as it takes to really do *teshuvah*, to completely turn his or her life around; and another, with seemingly the same resources, or even more, does not. Perhaps in some there is a primordial faith that such complete change is possible, even if this possibility is not at all obvious.

It has been my experience that when there is a heartfelt intention to open to the Holy One, the Holy One is right there. Many of my clients and friends (almost none of whom were Jewish) observed the same thing. This is not a grand kind of enlightenment. I have not become a saint. But these experiences have been important and impressive all the same.

To effort and intention must be added willingness and trust.

A few weeks before my mother died, I wrote:

I said to God, do you have room in your heart for me. In the next moment, I imagined my heart. I expected to see the shit-cave, the horrible image that had come earlier. But instead, all I saw was a small diamond light. It is still here.

Open my mouth, HaShem, to sing your praises. I do not know what else I can do, but I can do that.

CHESED

The Jewish mystics assert that the fundamental energy of all creation is *chesed*, which means lovingkindness and compassion. There is no place without this quality, just as there is no place without the Holy One. One's knowledge and awareness of *chesed* begin with self-compassion, for without self-compassion there can be no true compassion for anything or anyone else.

My first taste of self-compassion was around the time I changed my name, about five months after I left the hospital.

Over twelve years later, at the beginning of my work with James, I wrote:
I feel nauseous. I swallowed so much gunk as a kid. There is nothing at all to be done but love this wounded child of myself. Love her and love her and love her until her sobs subside and the pain melts away. She is sick, filled with poison. It has to come out. All the junk has to come out so she can be clean and pure again. All that poison gave her demons in her belly and demons in her mind.

Toward the end of my therapy, I wrote:
Myself, my heart, is open and ready to give. I have plenty to share. There is no danger at all of being robbed of all I have, because I have more than enough to share.

As I have learned so very painfully, love and compassion cannot be manufactured or shipped in from anywhere. I think they must reside in our hearts, acknowledged or not. If we look elsewhere then we are doomed to never find them. When my self-compassion is high I have an open heart that is in no danger of being drained. When I am full of self-compassion, my spitefulness and bitterness vanish.

Hopelessness was bred in the same moment as shame. It was this sense of being irredeemable that created the barrier that separated me from the Holy One. Both shame and hopelessness were products of being in thrall to my suffering. In my distraction I made the mistake of imagining myself outside of the realm of the holy and of *chesed*.

VOLUNTARY AND INVOLUNTARY SUFFERING

I was blameless for the malicious harm that came my way and the immediate terror and pain that it caused. I didn't think about or plan the strategies I used to try to protect myself. If something seemed to work once, that was enough to keep it up. If it didn't work another time, I tried harder.

Nothing I did really made the terror or the pain stop. Nothing stopped the abuse. All of my perpetrators had their own agendas, which didn't include what I wanted.

There came a time when the abuse stopped. I never recalled any incest with my father after I was about five. The trips to the big room ended when I was about sixteen, perhaps around the time I pulled away from my uncle on his couch.

The abuse stopped, but I was so attached to how I protected myself that none of the strategies stopped. That produced consequences that Rabbi Jonathan Omer-Man calls voluntary suffering.

I was very upset and angry when I heard Omer-Man talk about involuntary and voluntary suffering at a meditation retreat in the summer of 2001.

What does he mean by "voluntary?" I thought indignantly. *Does he think that I brought all the miseries of my life upon myself?*

I'd spent far too many years trying to learn just the opposite.

After I calmed down, I realized he was right.

If someone cut me with a knife, the pain was immediate and dissipated as the wound healed. Living in fear of the next cut was a decision, however unconscious it was. Deadening my feelings all the time was a decision. Shaming myself all the time was a decision. Obsessing about suicide was a decision.

Jeannie, my clinical consultant, often pointed out that there was always a decision point before I moved into protective mode. I had to learn when that was so I could make another choice.

There is a subtle but profound shift when the abuse is over. At this point, the defenses begin to generate negative consequences of their own. For me these were ongoing fear and anxiety, shame, passive (or not so passive) aggression and manipulation, lack of contact and intimacy despite a great longing for both, and a great deal of constriction from life.

When the trauma is over, it is necessary to eliminate the habitual mounting of extreme defenses in the face of minor trouble and to correct the mistaken beliefs that traumatic survival strategies produce. *Teshuvah* is a powerful tool for these tasks.

HEARTBREAK

More often than not, the way to *teshuvah* is a broken heart. There were many reasons for my heart to break. First was the original heartbreak of betrayal, especially by people who allegedly loved me or who said their abuse was occurring in the name of their love for me—people who were supposed to protect me.

Then there was the heartbreak that emerged with the awareness that my pride and shame were, in fact, voluntary sufferings, even if their origins were not voluntary. There was the heartbreak of recognizing that my attempts to make things better for either myself or for the ones I loved by contorting myself with pride were not good for anyone. There was the heartbreak of realizing that my heart had been closed and sealed in an effort to protect myself from hurts that were no longer coming from the outside. There was the heartbreak of realizing that I'd become my own perpetrator, maintaining the abuse in the form of fear and self-punishment and self-loathing, long after the outer perpetrators had vanished.

There was also the heartbreak of coming to recognize the full magnitude of what was lost originally and continued to be lost so long as I didn't allow my heart to break. If I could allow my heart to break, I could stop trying to find what was lost and simply grieve. There was the loss of illusion, the facade, the pretense that my life circumstances were excellent when they were not, which was coupled with the delusion that what was flawed was me. There was the persistent heartbreak of not allowing my heart to break.

My self-protection strategies—shame, fearful mistrust, and self-destructive distractions—created what I am calling sin, because of their ability to keep me from deep contact either with other people or with The Holy One. Allowing my heart to break allowed this sinfulness to be healed.

I think the first time I realized the healing power of a broken heart was during the year I said Kaddish for my mother, especially the day I said Kaddish during services and cried and called for help.

Rabbi David Teutsch describes the healing qualities of a broken heart this way:

"Repentance, like deepened spirituality, emerges from inner brokenness. I can put on a brave front, denying that I have done wrong, and evading my own inner knowledge of transgression and loneliness, doubt and failure. But in doing so I have failed to tap the insight and recognize the brokenness that can bring me to humility. Only from the place of humility can I sense the redemptive power in the Transcendent Unity that brings release and healing." (*Kol HaNeshamah Mahzor*, 1999, p. 760)

I was beginning to understand this shortly after my father died, when I wrote:

Holy One, loving you feels like such a burden. As I struggle to open my heart, I find so much pain. At each step you ask more and more of me. I know, at least I think I know, that each step is mine. Each step is the one I must take next. You do not show me any other. None of them comes simply or easily. I know, even as I don't know how, that each step truly brings me closer to you. Is it true that my grief is my greatest gift to you, as I have heard? I want to ask you, what about joy? What about joy, HaShem? But I know that my grief is only a measure of how I keep from you, that my grief is the gateway to my joy, that my grief is for lost joy, for lost pleasure, for lost love. I know, even as I don't know how, that when I learn to trust you enough to grieve fully, when I trust you enough to let my heart break entirely, that break will not be destruction but a great opening to your light.

My recovery sped up after my father's death, when dealing with him was no longer an ongoing source of confusion and stress. About a year and a half later, I wrote:

I said, "I am sick."
James inquired, "What kind of sick?"
I said, "I don't know."

I love how he takes his life seriously. I love how he takes me seriously. Microbes, viruses, bacteria, parasites, poisons. I am sick at heart. I am sick with grief. I am impatient with the suffering of the world. I am impatient with my own suffering. I do not know how to love it, this suffering, as part of loving life itself.

My heart is broken. The weight of possibilities that never happened and never will presses down, breaking open the capsules of grief and anger I had tucked safely away, near my heart, tucked away lest they betray me with their impossible demands and bring bodily death.

So, I did not die after all. Nor am I likely to die this day. The enemy is gone. A strange and lonely wind took their place. And in the quiet of a snowy dusk, with nothing more to stop it, the weight of sorrow cracks the capsules of my heart. Of course I am sick. This is grief both fresh and rather putrefied from too much time in cold, damp places. A physician might say I've caught a virus, and so I have. A plague of hope. An epidemic of love that softened my heart.

I am not complaining. The breaking of my heart is a good thing. This pain is a sign of cleaning and mending. I did teshuvah. *I turned away from my self-inflicted suffering, acknowledged my true suffering, grieved my losses, and opened my heart. In order to do those things I learned to tolerate myself and my story and to trust first of all myself and then the people who helped me and loved me and the Source of All who, in fact, had never abandoned me, but had been shut out.*

ACCEPTANCE

Not long after my hospitalization, I had a dream in which there appeared a sign that said, "Have What You Have." I quickly recognized that the sign was about acceptance in every area of my life. Acceptance begins with acknowledgment that things are the way they are, and so, my story is what it is. Gaining acceptance has turned out to be a slow, ongoing process.

Years ago, I heard a story about a martial arts master who had a small bird standing in his open hand. The master was so sensitive that he could feel the bird begin to bend its legs, preparing to push down so it could launch itself. When the bird bent its legs, the master dropped his hand subtly but enough to match the bird's movement. In so doing, he prevented the bird from lifting off. It was effectively stuck, unable to fly away.

When people walk, they must push down with one foot to propel themselves forward. When the ground is even and stable, walking can proceed almost effortlessly. If the ground is soft, uneven, or unstable, the effort becomes difficult.

Whatever my story is, it is unavoidably the ground of my life. What happened first largely determines what comes next. Before I reclaimed my story, my ignorance prevented me from knowing what kind of ground I was stepping off of or even how to do so. I grew up not knowing where or how the ground was, whether its surface was irregular or very unstable. I ended up feeling as immobilized as the bird was.

When James worked with me to get grounded, asking me to stand with slightly bent knees and feel my feet or legs, I often became frightened of what feelings might come up. Many times, I sank into a psychological quicksand of uncertainty about what to do next. Instead of trusting the experience of my body I would practically stop breathing and would watch his face intently, at least for a moment, to try to read what he wanted from me.

For me these prey-like responses were a result of being humiliated and having my words twisted if what I said to my parents implied that I was less than totally compliant with their intention that we be happy all the time. Speaking up about anything that might imply otherwise only meant that my parents would tell me that I didn't feel what I felt or think what I thought, and then they would scold me for being so wrongheaded.

After the incident when I got angry about my parents' response to my wanting to move out, I never told my father anything important again, until after my mother's death. I learned to protect myself from further crazy-making by avoiding my parents as much as I could, while maintaining the pretense that we were a happy family. But, by the time I knew to avoid them, it was too late. I frequently doubted what I said or did, and I was often too terrified to give my real opinion about anything beyond the completely trivial. The confusion was often too intense to manage, so I numbed out and shut down, automatically and thoroughly. That only made it less possible to try to find my ground.

Underneath my confusion about what was true was a profound sense of helplessness, which was one of the girders of the structure of myself. In my public life, in my profession, and in my community I was seen as competent and effective, even assertive when I needed to be, and sociable, even gregarious. I tried to avoid any kind of situation where I would have to take a strong stand about something I cared deeply about or even stand up for myself, lest someone act like my father. I kept my vulnerable places way out of sight, but I knew they were there.

Letting myself know just how helpless I felt growing up and how helpless I could feel in the right circumstances throughout my adult life was an invitation to despair. Well into middle age, I didn't really understand that I could come out of my self-imposed trance, especially with my parents, and stand up to them. In the months after my mother died, that began to change.

I remember vividly the last time my father pulled me toward him for a hug. Russell and I were entering his apartment for a visit.

When I hesitated to hug him he said, "Good daughters give their fathers a big hug and a kiss." He aimed his mouth toward mine.

I finally recognized his manipulation, implying that I was a bad daughter if I didn't comply. Even more importantly, I finally recognized that I was primed to automatically do what he wanted. I finally understood that my response didn't have to be automatic. I finally said, "No."

My father was taken aback. We walked into his foyer and took off our coats before he had a chance to say anything. The hugs were forgotten for the time being. I never let him hug me again.

As an adult, I was only as helpless as I thought I was.

JEWISH TEACHINGS ON ACCEPTANCE

The Jewish wisdom tradition has in it two seemingly contradictory teachings about acceptance: that the world is exactly as it should be and that it is unfinished and broken.

First of all, the Divine is omnipresent and infuses everything. That being the case, every moment is perfect in its way, a reflection or embodiment of the Divine and a manifestation of the Source of Unity of All Existence. Experiencing this underlying perfection of the moment is one of the ways we experience *mochin gadlut*, or God-consciousness.

The second teaching is that human beings are co-creators of this world and that we must do what we can to complete what the Divine Source began and to repair what is broken or incomplete.

The Jewish mystics elaborated on this by describing a process of ongoing creation which depends on the upward flow of positive, holy energy from us, which stimulates more holy energy from above, which in turn stimulates more holy energy from us, and so on, and on, and on, in a continuous loop. This is the great principle of *tikkun olam*, our responsibility to work with God to heal and repair the world.

Avram Davis gave a very good example of this paradox when he said in a lecture, "Our impulse to want to release the light for those who are in dark, hard places, is what draws God to those places, despite God, in fact, being in all places at all times."

As I looked back at my recovery, I noticed the movement away from fighting and struggling with myself about who I was and where I came from. As I gradually replaced self-hatred with self-compassion, I naturally began to have more compassion for other people, more empathy, and correspondingly more interest in being of service to others. As I turned away from shame and struggle, I had more positive, compassionate, and loving energy to use in my life. As I spread my compassion outward, more came toward me, not unlike the kabbalistic image of the circular flow of Divine energy, from above to below and back, repeatedly.

I have noticed this same circular flow in the stories of all of my trauma clients who stayed with the work long enough.

SELF-ACCEPTANCE

Despite all of the therapy after the hospitalization, years later when I began to work with James, my confusion about self-acceptance hadn't changed much. I wrote:

Don't think so much of yourself. It's wrong to be self-absorbed. Yet I can hardly stop myself when I am so agitated. I must not, yet I must. It makes me nuts. I must be nuts. It's all trivial. Everyone suffered as I did. And some suffered so much more than I. Who am I to make such a fuss? At least I had parents who wanted me. I don't know if they wanted me. They wanted a child, but I don't know about me.

My work with James moved quickly to a deeper level than I'd worked at before, perhaps because the earlier therapy had prepared me.

Looking back today, it's easy to see that because I never allowed myself to have even a glimpse of the most upsetting parts of my story and my tremendous shame, those things remained to poison every aspect of my life. As I started therapy with James, they flared up repeatedly. Each time, I immediately grew depressed and suicidal.

Despite the prior improvements in my moods and my ability to stand up for myself, my deepest anxiety and fear had barely been touched. Being so anxious most of the time seemed to mean that I was still crazy. I knew that too much energy was going into keeping that craziness hidden. I knew how to talk about good self-esteem, but when pressed, I seemed to have very little. There were still aspects of myself that I held in contempt and wished I could just excise.

As my deeper, hidden story began to emerge, my attitude about my feelings alternated between embarrassment, denial, and fear. After my mother's death and the growing awareness that my father had molested me, I achieved a begrudging, defensive sort of acceptance. At that time I wrote:

I am still picking around the ruins of the cave, crouching in corners, peering around fallen boulders. Everything looks ordinary. The light stops at night and returns in the morning.

No more hiding. No more hiding that my father is vicious as well as a fool. No hiding my contempt for him or trying to hide my shame under my contempt. There is no compassion for anyone here.

Then again, I like sitting here in this restaurant where I am writing, sharing my thoughts with pasta sauce, smelling the oregano I just put on the spaghetti, drinking coffee.

My details matter as much as anyone's.

For a time, I resisted the idea that what I was working on with James was as all encompassing, as it seemed to be. I wrote:

I told Russell that at one time I thought of this therapy as a sidetrack away from the main road of my life. But now I see that recovery of my life is the road. It has been going on for a very long time. Therapy is an especially intense, difficult part of the path. But there is no fixing this problem and getting on with my life. This is it. I am not just marking time.

The work became smoother every time I became more patient with myself and the process of recovery.

About four years into our work, James said that he thought that my fear and paranoia were so deeply imbedded that we were not likely ever to root them out entirely.

Shortly afterwards I wrote:

When James told me that he believed that there were elements in my personality, like paranoia, that may be intractable, that I would just have to learn to live with, mostly I heard that with relief. Somehow the idea of not pushing so hard to do what did not feel possible anyway, felt like changing the focus to acceptance.

Later, when our work was almost at an end, I wrote about the same subject:

The fact is that under stress my first line of defense was and will remain the oldest. Maybe being finished with therapy means that some aspects of my story have healed as much as they are going to, and under the right circumstances they will be painful for a while, like old injuries that ache when the weather turns wet and windy.

WHAT IS MINE IS MINE

I had to learn that my story and my responses to it were mine, that they belonged to me as surely as my skin. I needed to learn that there is no judgment here, only the fact that I am who I am, my history is what it is, and my decisions about what to do with my story, as it happened, are themselves part of my story. As I learned these things, my attitude changed to considering my story as another gift.

Another thing I had to learn was that even though I often said I had no idea what my destination was, that wasn't quite correct. I held on to a fantasy that when all my inner work was done, my life would be as if my story had never happened, as if I'd miraculously grown up in the most supportive, nurturing environment. I hoped I would have no scars. I also held onto a wish that having suffered so much, recovery would mean the end to all future suffering.

Intellectually, I knew that I would never be without scars or remnants of earlier damage. That didn't stop my initial disappointment when, in the middle period of my therapy, I took a long break. I knew that there was more that could be done, but I was exhausted. However, I was also newly patient with myself. I realized that I didn't need to know if or when I might return. In so doing, I honored my need to stop and used the time away to work on accepting the things that might never change, although I was disappointed that I was not fully healed.

Six months into what turned out to be a pause, my disappointment changed into acceptance. I wrote:

I am a little sad, resigned, and compassionate as I write this. What I've learned since I more or less left James is that the kind of newborn perfection I sought is not to be. My task is to have what I have, not to strive for what cannot be. I have very few open or even half open wounds left. I have multitudes of scars. And that is that.

I feel settled and content that all is right, somehow. I do not need to see the destination, or even know what it is, to know I am on the right road.

PASSION AND PLEASURE

Acceptance is about more than just patience and self-compassion for all of the negative thoughts, experiences, and emotions in one's life. It is also about the positive—about pleasure and joy, passion and energy. Wholeness means acknowledging and possessing all the aspects of one's self, including the most difficult and unwanted. With some trauma survivors, very positive traits may be viewed as difficult and unwanted. For me, that included my sexuality, my passion, and my intensity.

One day, in the middle of working with James, he said he thought it would be a good idea to address sexuality. I would never have suggested it myself. I spent the drive home thinking about how I would kill myself. I wrote:

It comes back to the 'S' word. I couldn't and can't stay present and listen to him talk about it, or even think about it. To acknowledge my sexuality at all in any way, except with Russell, is to invite abuse. James said he would not touch me in any way that could be construed as sexual nor would he ever ask me to touch him in any such way. And then, he said it is possible to feel my sexuality and my boundaries and feel both safe and guiltless!!! When I am even vaguely in touch with my sexuality, I fog out or get numb or something.

James said the only choices I had as a young person were to act out or to deaden myself. He said I was very unusual in that I didn't become promiscuous. He spoke about the subtleness of my parents' crazy making— their words about how dangerous sexual feeling and behavior were, coupled with being taught to submit without protest to my father. Being taught to submit without protest made me an easy mark for my uncle. I was trained to give myself without thought or question to anyone who wanted me.

James was absolutely true to his word; I still didn't trust him.

A few months later, I wrote about my extreme difficulty in appearing sexual and saying no:

I said to James that if I behave in any way that can be construed as sexual, that is an open invitation that I cannot refuse, because my body's "yes" is stronger than my verbal "no." Any "yes," except with my husband, creates a risk of rape. I said the only way I can say no is to be very still.

I was very adept at staying away from discussing sex. In all the therapy I did with Phyllis, whenever the subject of sex came up, I always said everything was fine and refused to pursue the matter any further. Addressing sexuality was terrifying; accepting it was unimaginable. Yet I was being urged to do so by more than James.

Of a conversation I had with Shama, I wrote:

"Sex. The word makes me so uneasy, confused, terrified. Shama, what do I do? It seems important to go on. Shama, I'm afraid it will kill me. I'm so scared. I'm too scared to cry."

S/he answered: "Don't be afraid of dying. You will not die of fright, even if you think you will. Nothing bad will happen."

"I want to be of service. I want to contribute to beauty and healing."

"Terror limits you."

"I don't want inner limits. I want soaring."

"You will not soar without the energy between your legs. You are missing too much energy. The earth is the route to heaven. Stomping, pounding the earth with your feet. That is how you will soar. Not any other way.

"Face the terror," S/he said. "Die if you must. Die stomping the earth. Die fornicating with the earth. Do not worry about headaches or illness. Do not worry about finishing the task, whether this body will finish the task. Do not think of dying. Think of stomping on the earth. Do not think of killing yourself. Learn the earth dances. It is time to be dancing. Leg dances. Pelvis dances. Sexual dances. Yes, joyful sexual dances. Orgy dances.

"Do not think, I can't do this. You are right that you have no choice. Your only choice is to continue. Stopping now only puts the task off until later. It will wait for you. It will not go away.

"You wanted to hear from me," S/he said. "This is what I have to tell you. The outer ones are all still here. They and I will not leave you."

"Shama," I asked, "I can do this, can't I?"

"Yes, or you would not be required to do so."

"Am I special or different?"

"No," S/he said, "no more special than anyone else. Different. Your task is harder than most. Don't waste time wondering about this."

Even in the early stages of claiming my sexuality for the first time, I somehow knew that beyond the fear was something worth striving for. I wrote:

This is the secret: that joy and pleasure are a natural outcome, some of the time, when I am fully in touch with myself. I can love only when I am in touch with my whole self. I can grieve only from all of me together.

It is not only the sexuality of two people coupling that gets shoved aside when physical sex becomes dangerous and hidden; there is also the aggression and passion that go with physical sex. Aggression frightened me as much as sex did.

I had a dream about being sexually aggressive and vicious, a perpetrator. I was too embarrassed to even write about it in my journal. James told me about how perpetrators get wounded in the wounding. If they can recognize that, then they can heal; if they cannot, they don't heal. I wrote:

I felt that [referring to the comment about perpetrators] *keenly. I was sorry for the attitude I brought to sex in the dream, remorseful.*

And I was not sorry. I relished the power. I relished the power! I must not forget how good it felt. Nor may I forget the remorse!

To fully feel my sexuality was to invite abuse. To fully feel my aggression was to seem like being one of the perpetrators. I wrote:

This is intolerable, so I don't allow myself to feel.

James insisted on working on increasing my tolerance for feeling everything and anything the entire time we worked together. Feeling and being comfortable with my sexuality came very slowly.

The presence of curiosity in my writing, and a bit of humor, was the signal that I was taking in the idea of other possibilities than the ones I knew. I wrote, after describing some comments James had made:

I want to cry. I want to giggle. He said it is not that I am not sexual. He said I was way over stimulated and spent all my energy trying to hold myself back. My, my. What if I did not hold myself back? My, my.

Sexuality wasn't the only appetite I kept under control. I rigorously minded all of my appetites.

As my distress and defensiveness went down, all of my appetites went up. Once I wrote:

I am hungry. What happened was unexpected. A surprise. I did what I did and nothing bad happened. I am still guarded, but the guards are in some disarray, not quite knowing what to do when the attack not only doesn't come, but seems unlikely to ever come.

I like this aliveness. I like getting bolder, more fearless. I like being hungry.

JEWISH PASSION

The Jewish wisdom tradition is infused with passion and desire. Many of the ecstatic mystics went about their practices with great intensity and with a great intention (*kavannah*) to know the Divine in a powerful, intimate way. That way is called *devekut*, which is often translated by the English word, "cleave." Jewish mystics didn't merge or evaporate or melt into the Godhead, but understood themselves to be doing something very muscular and energetic.

In the Jewish tradition, this sexual passion can be seen especially in the Song of Songs in the Hebrew Bible, and in the *Zohar*, the great Jewish medieval mystical text.

The *Zohar* not only describes human sexual union as a metaphor for the coming together of the worlds above and the worlds below, it goes on to say that the act of a husband bringing pleasure to his wife, literally, is necessary to unify all worlds. The text makes clear that the sexual union is to be joyful and happy for the unification to take place.

A story is told that among the rabbis who redacted the final version of the Hebrew Bible, there was great argument about the inclusion of the Song of Songs, specifically because of its voluptuous sexual imagery. Rabbi Akiva, the most exalted master of his generation (and many others), insisted that it be included because the Song best expresses the passion Jews bring to their quest for God consciousness.

The depth of love we can have for another or for the Divine, and perhaps the depth of love that can be received, are contingent on the fullness of the expression of that love in all the realms of our lives. Another way to put this is that only by being in touch with all aspects of our experience of love and passion, which includes sexuality, intention, aggression, longing, and desire, can we most fully have what is in front of us to have.

It is here, that the message to "Have What You Have" moves beyond only focusing on accepting what is difficult or disturbing. I finally learned that my sexuality, my passion, and my intensity were gifts of birth, as were my talents and the color of my hair. I could cover up and ignore them or I could struggle and fight with them, but I couldn't make them not belong to me.

I understood this first about the negative feelings such as shame or anger or fear, as I wrote:

I thought, I am afraid to look foolish. Shama said to be foolish.
The gift is to have what I have.
Have what you have. Have the fear. Have the shame. Have the foolishness. Have it.

Later, I could bring the same attitude to my sexuality and other positive attributes.

Near the end of therapy, I wrote:

I am learning that I need to surrender to the pain so that I can also surrender to my passion. To have it all, I must have it all. There is no recovery. There is no cure. There is no solution. There is only tolerating and embracing life more and more and more. There is only giving up trying to make life be as I wish rather than having it just as it is. "Only." Indeed!

WANTING AND NEEDING

Tolerating life as it actually is was the last element in developing full acceptance. I had to learn, and am still refining, the distinction between what I want and what I need. What I learned first was that when I could allow myself to fully have what I already had; I needed very little else.

I also had wants, which often involved other people. As a child, I learned that to have what I wanted came at someone else's expense, creating multiple opportunities for shame. With the help of a group of friends, all mental health professionals with incest in their backgrounds, I learned to have my "wants" and to become skillful at discerning what was likely and possible. I learned to ask for what I wanted, knowing that if I got it no one else would have to do without.

I had several dreams, which told the story of what I was learning. Of one, I wrote:

I dreamt about being in a large open-air market, with friends with whom I share this experience. I am particularly happy and happy to be here (what an astonishing thing for me to say!). I go up to one stall. There is a big bowl of melon, cut up and combined with a limejuice marinade. It looks absolutely delicious. I don't see any bowls or utensils or anything with which to eat it. So, finally, I dip my hands in, bowl-like, and eat and enjoy a drippy feast of fruit. A dream of literally plunging into the juiciness of my life, mess and all!

Then I go over to another stall, where the owner seems to be out of what I want (an old recurring theme). When I ask, he says he can easily get more for me. I can have what I want, although I may have to ask.

About a year later, I wrote of two other dreams:

A healer I am working with suggests I pack my bags, or just a back pack, and go out and wander for a few months; take little luggage, and a long time, and just wander. I start to think about what I have and remember that <u>I have what is necessary</u>.

Another dream: I am at a meeting, but this is not where I am meant to be—my destination is elsewhere. It is getting late, and I start to leave. Several times, I pause to check to see if I have my keys, my directions, or whatever it is I need. Each time I see that <u>I have everything</u>.

I only thought I was lacking what was necessary when I was trying to have what someone else thought I needed, rather than what already belonged to me.

We are not only all capable of learning what we need for God-consciousness. Each of us, because of our unique combinations of biology and personal history, also has a unique approach to God. This is reflected in the Jewish adage that to save a life is to save a world.

After I stopped therapy, I wrote:

Every detail of my life is a part of who I am. As there are an infinite number of ways to approach God, it is my task to approach in the way that is particularly mine. For me, no other way will be quite right. This is hardly the first time that I've encountered the idea of the precious uniqueness of each of us. It is the first time that idea has penetrated so deeply for me. It is more than acceptance. It is more like rejoicing that I am exactly who I am with all the givens of my life, all the details of my history, and all the choices I have made and not made. I think the more I know and have and rejoice in precisely who I am, the more I can discern the way that is my particular way to God. And, the more certain I get about my particular way, the less fearful and the more happy I become.

The great eighteenth-century Hassidic mystics teach that joy is the natural outcome of spiritual work and a sign that the work is being done properly and well. Managed care and insurance companies are not interested in joy as a goal. But, because recovery from trauma is both a spiritual and psychological journey, joy and serenity are always on my list of goals. Deep acceptance corrects the mistaken struggle to have the world be how I would prefer rather than how it is, in all of its outrageous, wild majesty. Deep acceptance is a royal road to joy.

CHOOSING LIFE

The Jewish Way is about being alive, literally and fully. Deuteronomy 30:19 states:

"I call heaven and earth to witness against you this day: I have put before you life and death, blessing and curse. Choose life—if you and your offspring would live."

In the middle of therapy with James, what I've called the moon time, I had to learn that I was in charge of choosing to face death or face life, choosing to be in this life or merely go through the motions of pretending to be in this life. I often played with suicide as a way of distracting myself. While I never actually did anything that might end my physical life, the possibility was always there. For a long time, I wasn't willing to give up the possibility. I wrote:

Choices. So much of my learning is about how I am making choices to remain a victim, to hang onto old defenses that were making my life more difficult. It is very arduous to understand this and make changes. Focusing on my confusion, making myself confused, focusing on pain and distress, despair and suicide, were all ways to avoid being in the world, even as they were once legitimate responses to the world.

I found ordinary life frightening. I had grown up believing in my bones that I was dangerous to the people I loved the most, and they were dangerous to me. To be simply in the world confronted that mistaken belief every day.

Instead of ignoring Russell when he said he loved me, or when he promised to not leave, instead of getting into an internal shame rant about how he was just lying or making nice, I began to try on the possibility that he was telling the truth. After we had been married over thirty years, I finally decided to believe him instead of believing that I was unlovable.

I noticed more and more that I had choices about whether I brought on darkness or light or whether I accepted the love around me or shut it out. I could choose to notice that when I expressed something besides placating platitudes to the people I cared about none of them reacted with the disgu and crazy making that I assumed was just the way of the world.

I also noticed that choosing to be fully alive was the embodiment of having what I had. Deep acceptance helped enormously to kill pride. Almost every day, I found opportunities to reconsider my beliefs. Once in the moon time I wrote:

I said to James, it seems that I am just now discovering how hard this is, which doesn't make sense after all the years I've already worked at this recovery. But it made sense to him (for which I was so grateful) that now I am coming to <u>feel</u> just how hard it all really is.

He said, "You have come so far in these years."

I said, "I've been off the planet as much as I could arrange, and now I am here and I am not happy. I am just beginning to get it that you won't hurt me."

He said, "You've had lots of good reason to be cautious, very cautious."

James kept pushing me. I kept asking him to and then dug in my heels. I wrote:

Again and again and again [this went on, actually, almost the entire time I worked with him] *James talks about me getting into a power struggle with him. He says I keep my focus squarely on him, to know what to think, feel, and do. True. True. True. Too true. I want to rant and scream: how do I know what is right? what I am supposed to do! James won't say. I won't listen if he does.*

I hadn't learned yet the part about killing pride that involves giving up trying to control the world.

We went back and forth, every time. James kept at me, and I, little by little, let myself be pushed.

I also wrote:

How do I talk about this?

How can I find the words when my experience is between the words?

I am headed directly for the space between, between now and then, between then and now; that horrible place which is nowhere, between struggling and not-struggling; that place where the laws of the universe end and all things become possible.

My heart is bursting with longing to get there. But there is no "there" to get to. I understand that in the midst of this time and place where all things are static and I am dying, right here, in between the inhalation and the exhalation, my inhalation and my exhalation, is my moment of change. Change to embrace life. Change to embrace the terror. Change to embrace the passion and the shame and the horror and the joy. Change to get giddy with energy. Change enough to fall down in amazement.

Between my breaths I see darkness.

I exhale and pause and slide off the end of the earth.

I inhale and grab at the end.

I want dying. I want living.

Meaning. I scramble after meaning. I miss the point, I think.

I am so afraid of getting crazy. Again. I cannot live and stay crazy, too.

I understand that my life is poised right there, right in between the light and the dark.

I want to die.

I am dying. And in so doing I am coming alive this time. This time I make no meaning, sobbing and writing and writing and righting.

I was coming to life, but I clung to suicide, at least the thought of it, as if it were a kind of perverse lifeline. More to the point, it was a way of ultimately being in control. Jeannie, my consultant, told me, from time to time, that if I really wanted to fully come to life, as I said I did, the day would come when I would have to give up suicide as an option, permanently.

I understood that this was more than just a no-suicide contract. I rarely had ever been an actual danger to myself, and was less and less so as I progressed. But I thought about suicide a lot. I distracted myself with deciding whether to actually do it this time or that, tempering the intensity of my feelings with reminders that there were always knives around. Jeannie never pushed very hard about this, understanding that suicide is not so easy to give up. She didn't let the idea slide, either.

The winter of 1993–1994, the fourth winter after my mother died, was exceptionally cold. In early March 1994, Jeannie and a friend and colleague of hers held a women's workshop at the George Williams Campus on Lake Geneva, the same place we continued to meet with Carolyn Conger the second weekend of each January. Even in March, the lake was still frozen enough to walk on.

Jeannie invited everyone to bring some object that she was willing to part with, for a give-away ceremony. I had a small, yellow-handled paring knife that I found outside years before. I took it home and stuck the blade into a potted plant, saving it for the day I would use it to kill myself. It sat in the pot, a reminder that I would not have to look far for a knife if I ever wanted one—a reminder that I could always use it.

I decided I was ready to part with the knife.

I went to the workshop with Eileen, who had been a fellow doctoral student and disciple of Betty Bosdell. She knew much of my story, and I trusted her. She and Jeannie were the two people who knew what I was about that weekend.

When the ceremony began, I realized that not only was I supposed to give the knife away, but someone else was supposed to take it to use it in some new way. I was horrified. I imagined the knife was dangerous because of all of the deadly intent I put into it. I was willing to give it away but not to have anyone take it. What I decided, instead, was to take it out to a hole in the ice, which I'd seen earlier that day, and drop it into the lake. Eileen and Jeannie came with me.

Later, I wrote about the experience:

The deed was done on the frozen surface of the sounding waters, under the stars, in the stars. Last night in the dark, in the wind, we found the hole, marked off with a sawhorse. It had frozen over again. We threw things at it, things that were too small. Jeannie went back to get something bigger. When Jeannie came back we three stood out on the lake, on ripples of ice, solid ice, ephemeral ice. Eileen put the knife in an old sock. We all put rocks and stones in the sock. I tied the sock with dark ribbon. We finally broke the ice. Eileen said, come to this side, it will be easier. I walked to her side. The package of death slipped easily into the water, like a man into a woman who is welcoming him in.

The next morning Eileen and I walked out onto the Lake, this strange Lake who sounded her acceptance last night after she took my knife, who shifted herself around in the night and the cold and the wind. This morning, under the milky sun, the Lake was quiet except for the clacking of runners from the ice-boats. Eileen and I walked out into the puddles and ripples and cracks that were like details of a Lake Goddess's winter coat. My boots leaked and my socks got wet. I walked mindfully, wondering about drowning, knowing this Goddess could swallow me up, knowing that she accepted my offering last night and had shifted and sounded in acknowledgment. We walked further and further into the middle. There is no other way to walk on the Lake's coat except mindfully. The wind blew hard in my face and later on my back. Halfway out, I was filled with terror at being so present. Back on solid ground I know very well how to step forward and leave me behind. But not on the belly of the Lake.

Eileen and I parted in the middle. I needed to come back. She needed to go on, all the way to the other side.

On the Lake I could see bubbles dropping deep, deep into the ice. I could see cracks and pathways made as the Goddess shifted around. I found feathers and leaves that she gathered, examined, and released. She held me.

It is so new, yes, it is so new for me to be held.

In the days, immediately afterwards, I thought about suicide a lot. Sometimes I was angry that I had given up something so precious and wanted it back. Then, I would imagine a Goddess sitting like a Buddha at the bottom of the Lake, holding onto my knife, with a thin smile on her lips, as if to say, I am not giving it back.

I dreamt that I was driving on a dark night, very close to home, but that I couldn't recognize where I was.

"Yes," I thought, "I am very close to home. I am not lost, I am sure of that."

Two weeks later, I was beginning to appreciate the impact of giving up the option of suicide. I wrote:

Two weeks ago today, after Sabbath had begun, after the sun was down, the moon was dark with its monthly mourning, and the stars were lit with their wintry brilliance, I made a death offering. I offered a deadly knife, ritually prepared, as I was ritually prepared. The knife was kosher, having lived in the dirt of a planter for many years. I did not wash it. I brought the knife to Wisconsin wrapped in the fur of an unknown creature. I put it in a box decorated with symbol upon symbol upon symbol, whose meanings I will never know. The fur-wrapped knife in the box was my offering to the give-away table.

What I know is that at the beginning of Sabbath, two weeks ago, I removed the knife from the box, Jeannie, Eileen, and I walked out onto the ice, and I made my offering of a death-knife, which the Lake Goddess holds even now, she of great depths and an icy belly. She alone in that place could take the knife in a gesture that looked like coitus, which it was because new life came from my offering. The Lake had been making noises, loud rumbles and groans. There was only a small splash when she accepted the knife. Only a small sound, but the offering was made and accepted all the same. And now I am here, at home, Sabbath candles glowing like stars in my darkened room. The new life in me stirs and grows accustomed to this place.

A month later, I wrote:

I imagine the Lake Goddess, hand firmly holding my little yellow knife, laughing with pleasure. It comes to me that she holds the knife so I can have pleasure. I had to give up dying in order to be here. And here I am.

MY FATHER'S DEATH

Two months later, Russell and I took a vacation to the East Coast, to see some friends and just play a bit. When we got back, my father called to say he had been to the doctor, who told him that perhaps he had a mild pneumonia. Given a choice to go home or to the hospital, my father elected to go home. The next day, he was hospitalized. He felt all right, except he seemed to be having increasing difficulty breathing.

As the days passed, he slowly got worse, and the reason why remained a mystery.

Six days before he died, I wrote:

My father seems to have pneumonia. He was opened up by his illness. My sister said his mortality is staring him in the face. I am glad for him. He wants to know how to heal the great rift between us. I am farther away from him than ever. My father may have to die, now or later, without me. His longing may be insufficient to bring what is dead back to life.

Five days before he died, when the doctor was still holding out hope, I wrote:

Is it congestive heart failure? I think of my heart, massively congested with too much feeling. I am tangled in guilt and longing: longing to be free of him and guilt for the longing.

I called the hospital three days before he died, when he could still talk. My father immediately asked when I was coming.

I wrote: *He grabs for my love and thereby pushes it away. He allows no opportunity for my own generosity to emerge. He is like an infant, in this respect, so that must be where some of his woundedness began. I prayed last night and this morning for an end of my hatred. When I woke up I understood, at least for now, that my hatred covers the pain of his betrayal. My father, in his broken, infantile clumsiness, betrays me almost every time I see him. That is why seeing him is so dangerous—it is so painful and I do not know well enough how to manage the pain. I have also scared myself plenty with my own infantile beliefs that my rage alone would kill him and the unholy union of wishing and guilt that goes with that. At least I am not suicidal.*

How pathetic and tragic and crazy.

Two days before he died, I wrote:

Do I need him to die so that I may heal? His illness is like acid on the open wound of my love for him. Is it true that there can be no real healing while the wounding keeps taking place? I have no idea.

The day before he died, he suffered cardiac arrest but was revived. When I saw him next, his mouth was full of respirator equipment, as he was no longer able to breathe on his own. His eyes implored me. I told him that we had both done what we could. He closed his eyes and seemed relieved. Even that day, with the medical staff scrambling to try to understand what was happening, the doctor held out some small hope. When we left the hospital that night, my father looked at us and gave us the thumbs up sign.

By the time I made it back the next day, my father was comatose and entirely on life support. My sister and brother and Russell and I sat and watched his fingers and hands turn colors, like the sky in the minutes right after the sun has set. Finally, I went to the nurses' station and asked what was supposed to happen next. They said, "We were just waiting to hear from you when to remove the life support." Sol, Judi, Russell, and I had discussed this possibility and had agreed to stop heroic measures when the time came.

"Do it now," I said.

Eleven days after his phone call, my father was dead of respiratory failure, due to unknown causes. There was no autopsy. My siblings were devastated; I was surprised and sad, but not devastated.

I wrote:

My father gave me all kinds of gifts, some of which I may come to cherish. Being with him when he died was one of them. How good it would have been to be able to really be with him alive. I think it will be a long, long time before I miss him. We missed each other so much.

I haven't missed him yet.

The next day, my brother and sister and Russell and I went to his apartment to start the process of closing his affairs. As we approached the building, two neighbor boys saw us and somehow figured out who we were.

"Where is Mr. Fisher?" they asked. "We haven't seen him for a while."

When I told them that he died, they ran into their house and returned with their parents, who cried when they confirmed what the boys had told them. My father took walks in the neighborhood every day, and he knew many of his neighbors. He was remembered with great affection, which was so at odds with my own feelings. I knew he could be charming and gregarious, especially with people who were not too close.

The funeral was a big affair, with far more people attending than I expected. After the burial, after we had each put in our shovel of dirt, after I said Kaddish and did the things that had to be done in community, I pulled Russell aside. We walked through the cemetery, and I cried and called out to all the dead around me, that my father would never hurt me again.

Sometime after I had started to work with James, but well before my mother died, I asked my father what his childhood had been like. He paused a moment at my question and then said he really couldn't remember anything before he turned twelve. Sometime not long after my father died, Russell and I took my father's sister out for dinner and spent the evening visiting with her. Actually, I was using all of my considerable interrogation skills to try to find out more about this man we had so recently buried. My aunt was seven years older than her brother, about the same as the distance between my brother and me.

At some point, I asked her straight out what his early childhood was like. As I recall that evening, she, too, paused and then said she really couldn't remember anything. After all, she was so much older. She must have been too busy with her own activities. And what did it matter, anyway?

Apparently I wasn't the only family member with a memory problem.

Not long after my father's death, as the period of great release of memories ended, when I no longer had to spend so much energy trying to figure out how to endure my father's continuing crazy making, I became more curious than condemning about myself. This was a notable improvement over the constant battle about whether it was all right to feel as I did. I wrote:

Is not the gift the very thing I fear? So much to fear. I am so used to being afraid. I am alarmed. I don't want to show myself. I want to hide. I want no one to see the shame I still keep behind the sparkles of my public face. As if I am the only one. As if I am special in this shame. As if no one else has shame like mine. It is mine, and that is the gift, is it not? I don't understand this. Yet it seems true that my fear is my gift. Mysteries are always a gift, and this is a great mystery: how my fear can be a gift? how my shame can be a gift? I think if my shame is a gift, then my brokenness is a gift. I don't need to struggle so hard or at all. If my bones were broken and never set right and I will be gimpy all my life, then I can stop trying to walk straight.

A few weeks after my father died, during a routine examination, my doctor found a lump on my breast. She thought it was probably a benign fatty tumor, but she and the surgeon thought it best to remove it and do a biopsy. It was to be a simple business, strictly outpatient under local anesthetic. I told the surgeon that there was some nasty business in my history involving knives and my breasts. He offered general anesthetic, but I wanted to try to just use the local. I hoped that talking to him would help some, which it did.

Before the surgery I also decided to do an Eye Movement Desensitization and Reprocessing (EMDR) session with my business partner, Peg. Several years before, Peg and I learned this powerful technique for dealing with traumatic memories. Hoping I would be able to reduce or eliminate the potency of at least some of my traumatic memories, I asked Peg if she would do an EMDR session for me with the focus on the incident of the girl who cried and was continually cut. We did it in James's office, with me holding on to him with every bit of strength I had.

In an arduous, terrifying session, it became clear that I never thought I would survive that time in the big room. With much more vivid details this time I could recall how I stood naked off to the side, all the men's attention on torturing the other girl, taunting her, playing with her confusion, making little nicks and cuts when she started to cry, she mystified about what they wanted and how to make them stop, I frozen with fear that they were going to murder her, that they were going to cut me, not knowing if I would live or die. In some ways, I had remained frozen in the terror of not knowing ever since.

This time I didn't stay stuck in that most horrible moment but began to remember that the incident ended. I never knew what happened to the other girl or even her name. When it was over I got dressed and my uncle brought me home. I went up the back stairs and into my kitchen, where my mother was getting dinner ready. My arrival was totally unremarkable to my family— no one commented on it, or wondered where I'd been. Perhaps they thought they knew. I was neither early nor late. I think I just went to my room. The EMDR session ended with Peg reinforcing the fact that I survived and that the old trauma would never happen again. I was astonished that I really did survive.

I was exhausted but deeply relieved. None of us said much as we walked out into an intense rain and went home.

The surgery went as planned without general anesthetic or emotional repercussions. The mass was an uninteresting fatty tumor. The next week, we went to California for a long weekend. I saw my teacher, Carolyn, who I usually only saw in the winter. I told her my father was dead, and that I felt freedom the likes of which I could not have imagined. She agreed that my life was mine, to do with as I saw fit, not in the service of my parents or anyone else. She said I did not have to do anything.

What an idea!

My father had left no will and no written instructions. As the eldest, it mattered to me that I claim the executorship. Sol and Judi had no objections at all; they were probably glad they didn't have to do the work.

The first few times my sister, my brother, Russell, and I went into my father's apartment were odd, knowing that he was gone. We wandered around without a plan, opening drawers and closets, wondering what to do with what we found, all of us feeling like naughty children going where we knew we were not supposed to go. At first, we all felt a little like thieves when we decided to take something home. All of us also felt like explorers, wondering what we would find that would help us understand him and our mother better.

My father had stashed little caches of money all over the place, especially $2 bills. Every time we found one, we called it lunch money. The total was perhaps several hundred dollars. When we were all together for long days of sorting and deciding, we often took the lunch money and went out to someplace interesting to eat, well aware that it was our father's treat.

Sol didn't want any of my father's clothes. Nobody had the energy to sort them and research worthy places to send them. My father's illness and death had been very sudden, so he had a pile of laundry in a hamper. I didn't even want to handle it, as if it were contaminated. We threw it all out. On another less upsetting day, we put all of his shoes and suitcases out by the garbage, but not in it, so they were clearly visible. As we expected, within the hour, someone pulled up in a small pickup truck and took it all away, probably to sell.

My sister and I rescued the houseplants—the surviving remains of my mother's extensive collection of plants—and took them home. I think in a small way it seemed as if I was rescuing her.

We generally worked at the apartment on weekends. All of us quickly discovered that we couldn't work alone without starting to feel overwhelmed with emotions within the hour, so we learned to work at least in pairs.

I got a pile of death certificates and started closing accounts. I went to the post office to get my father's mail forwarded to me, so I would be sure to catch any bills. I not only got his bills, but almost immediately started getting solicitation and sales calls, and mail welcoming him to Naperville. Sometimes I got angry enough to call people, who had left phone messages or sent mail, to tell them that he was dead. They often told me that they had no way to know and were so sorry to have troubled me. I was chagrined at their embarrassment and stopped making the phone calls.

My father had a safety deposit box at the LaSalle Bank in downtown Chicago. I was very curious to know what was in it. One day I made the trip downtown, proffered the death certificate, and was admitted to the vault. I found a few scraps of paper, a rubber band, and perhaps a paper clip. I don't recall the contents clearly. They were garbage, totally trivial. I have no idea why he kept paying for a basically empty safety deposit box well out of his neighborhood. Of all the things we found in his apartment, none illuminated his life any more than the empty box did.

After about five months, the apartment was ready to rent. Everything that wasn't distributed, given away, or thrown out migrated back to my basement, where some of it remains to this day. These are things like my parents' collection of opera recordings and photographs of their European vacations. Nobody in the family wants to take them, but when I suggest that I'm ready to throw them out, I hear from various family members to please wait. My mother's baby grand piano has resided in a number of places since my father died. Her grandchildren especially don't want it to leave the family, but none of them has the room for it.

MY SISTER AND BROTHER

My sister and brother and Russell and I grew closer together in the weeks and months that followed my father's death as we helped each other out emptying the apartment and settling his bills. We were soft and generous with each other, avoiding disputes over who got what. Russell, who had never been as entangled with my father as the rest of us, was the great stabilizer.

My siblings and I got to know each other better as we worked together. Our parents had distorted all of our lives. Being in our parents' presence via their belongings was invariably upsetting, but we were able to talk about what was troubling us.

In long conversations, Judi told me she figured out very early in her life that she had to keep her distance from our parents. Our father's capacity for spacing out scared her. Somehow she decided that our mother was just "talking bull shit," so Judi didn't pay attention to what my mother said. She was much better at setting limits with them than I and much better at being sneaky. She told me that as she grew up she noticed that I was trying very hard to be a good girl, but there was something very wrong about what went on between my parents and me.

If I collapsed in on myself, Judi acted out, but usually she was very careful not to get caught. If I unconsciously kept deep secrets about what was going on in me, she consciously kept equally deep secrets about what she was doing.

There were intimate conversations with my brother, too. He had reached this point in our family's life deeply burdened by our father's loud and adamant assertion of his power and superiority, and the terrible arguments that took place in the years Sol still lived at home after I married. Because of the frequency with which Sol second-guessed everything he said, I could tell that my brother heard the same sort of twisting, distorting talk from our father that I experienced. He was also still in the thrall of our mother's helplessness.

It was enormously helpful to all of us siblings to talk about our experiences growing up, noticing the great similarities, acknowledging the damage, and knowing that neither of our parents would ever again contradict our understanding of what happened to us.

MY PARENTS ARE GONE

For me, all of the work of settling my father's estate was about ending my parents' physical presence in my life; secondarily, it was about getting the apartment ready for a tenant.

When we were almost done I wrote:

My parents have vanished, evaporated into the air, as will their phone number. Tomorrow, someone will push some buttons on a computer keyboard, and 267-2506, the number that belonged to them for forty-five years, more or less, will suddenly no longer be theirs, or by extension, mine.

I want to cry. I, who do not cry, want to cry and wail that I am lost. There is nobody left to care for me.

How foolish these words are and how untrue. And yet the thought of my loving husband and friends offers little solace, little comfort at all.

My parents did a poor job of caring for me, but they made a display of it [being good parents] sometimes, when it didn't cost them too much. And, I wanted so much, yes, so much. I understand that I fashioned my life around that longing and the hopelessness of my cause.

But, and what a qualifier this is, I seem to be wrong, or incomplete, or misguided or something, the word for which I cannot find or maybe don't even know. The glue that held my understanding of myself is softening and loosening. Sometimes I feel like I have lost my bearings, moments when the next obvious thing to do is not so obvious, when obligations have drifted off, as have the demands and requests for my time and the grabbing of the world, and I am just left with me.

By Thanksgiving, Ron, a cousin who was Jeremy's age, moved into my parents' apartment with his small family. In the eight years they lived there, I came to the building only three or four times. Ron agreed to be the "man" around the building, shoveling the walk, mowing the tiny lawn, letting us know what bigger maintenance needed to be done, and keeping an eye on my aunt. In exchange for letting me be an absentee landlord I was happy to charge a reduced rent.

As I was discarding old possessions of my father's, I was discarding some of my own. I wrote:

My pain and suffering have been precious to me, cracked and mended crockery, but mine as much or more than any other possessions. This is how I knew myself, by the thoughts of dying on splendid days, by how I scared myself, by how I suffered to deny my suffering. I am losing all of this, slowly, so slowly, but losing it all the same, like ashes lifting out of a fire circle where the fire is long gone out.

I grieved for what I was losing; and, I began to get the idea that pain could be transformed. I wrote of my pain as a raw treasure waiting to be made into something beautiful, something delightful, even as it contained the energy necessary for creativity:

Pain lies like nuggets of gold in shallow waters. I do not have to look hard to find it. It shines in the sunlight. It stands out even when spring sends down torrents of icy water turning all the rocks and stones black.

What kind of treasure comes from this horde? Is there joy to be found also in this mountain of gold I have collected?

Once I saw several ancient Korean crowns made with hundreds of tiny disks of gold, each one attached with gold wire to the crowning castle base, each one a shining sun, each one dangling and playing as the Emperor walked, as the Empress turned and bent to say a word.

I have picked up my horde from my section of the river. I have not found it all, yet. The water keeps moving stones and leaves, and the telltale color comes to light.

I have also picked up my pen, my needle and thread, tools of my creativity. The gold of painful experience is worth nothing if it simply sits on the treasure house floor. Now is time to make it into something beautiful.

Pain and suffering were not all that became transformed. The mistaken belief that I was eternally a victim was shifting under me. With that shift was the realization that I had some responsibility for my suffering.

Almost a year after my father died I wrote:

Grumble, grumble, grumble. I hate all of the wisdom, and the responsibility that comes with it. It is very hard to sit in a pit of shame slime and suffer to my heart's content when I know full well that the pit is shallow and easy to get out of, and I can at any time.

The payoff of victimhood is lack of responsibility. But I have not been a victim for many, many years. It is time to give it up and take charge of my own happiness. The antagonists in my life are gone. The only one aggravating me is me. The only one who can save me is me.

A STORY

Many years ago I read a tale about a spiritual teacher, perhaps a Tibetan lama, who had a reputation for being an exceedingly harsh master. A young man came to be a disciple of this master. He was put to work cleaning latrines for many years, without further instruction, until the master decided he had been humbled enough to receive spiritual teaching. Although the teacher was a great taskmaster he was sought out because he was also known for his great wisdom.

Another young man came, also wanting to be a disciple. He fully expected that he would be treated to years of menial labor. Instead, the master welcomed him, set him up in a comfortable room, provided him with holy books, parchment, quills and ink, and a fine desk to write upon, and began his instruction immediately. I expect that the master could discern the second student's humility very quickly when they first met. It would have shown in the student's demeanor, his words, his tone of voice.

Despite the obvious differences between the second disciple and me, I have often thought of our similarities. In many ways, since I left my parents' home, I have been given everything I needed and my instruction began immediately. My husband's patience and stability grounded me as I embarked on my learning. In the rawness of their youngest years, my children pushed my tolerance, and in a way they kept suicide at bay. The teachers I needed appeared when I needed them, just as many traditions say will happen. No matter how brief or deep my relationship to them, each showed me where I needed to go next. I was blessed with freedom from want. My family was blessed with good enough health. All the pieces were in place for me to study and learn, as was so for the second Tibetan disciple. It was only up to me to do what I could.

NOT THE END

CHANGING PARADIGMS

I was fifty-one the year that my father died. I had spent most of the previous twenty years trying to identify and correct the many mistakes I made growing up. I spent my entire adult life trying to leave my parents' home.

After my father died, and the minor matter of the fatty tumor was taken care of, I noticed an immediate and obvious change: I didn't feel as helpless and desperate as I had before. For the first time since I started seeing James, I didn't need to see him as often. This marked the ending of moon time and the beginning of the lightening of the skies that signals the dawn's coming. The image may be trite, but it seemed literally true that my life seemed brighter and clearer.

I told James that my biggest regret about my father's death was that I never got to the point where I could be in a room with him and feel safe or comfortable. James said he didn't think it was possible. I was taken aback by his conviction.

I didn't spend much time thinking about the opportunities that may have been missed when my father was alive. He was gone, and I never had to be in a room with him again. Even though his voice and attitudes lived on in me, bumping and rubbing against old wounds from time to time, the pain wasn't at all like having the wounds reopened, or even just the threat of them being reopened, when I was in his presence. With his permanent absence I could begin to look around and take in the rest of the world much more than before.

A few months after he died I wrote:

I have lost my bearings a little. I don't quite know where I am. My past used to be my beacon, the light, which colored all I did and thought and felt, a strange light which deepened the darkness around me. It is no longer a beacon, but a candle lost in the glare of mid-day. Mostly I do not even notice whether it is lit or not, there is so much else that catches my attention. I am dazzled and distracted and sometimes confused.

I grew bolder and expressed myself more than ever before, sometimes in unexpected ways. An example was the first time I ever told Russell about being angry with him in uncensored language.

Russell and I had an unspoken and largely unconscious but binding contract that was probably in place before we were married, a sort of mutual protection pact. It was based on my belief that my anger was deadly and Russell's belief that he couldn't tolerate anyone being angry with him. We had a very civil relationship; annoyances were smoothed over before anyone could get into trouble. We almost never got angry at each other, at least not out loud.

About six or seven months after my father died, Russell decided to deal with a high cholesterol count with a strict, very low fat diet, which I adopted as well. Russell was either very disciplined or rigid, depending on one's point of view. About a year after starting the diet, we took a day off and went to the Field Museum of Natural History in Chicago. Lunch was a dismal business: the only thing in the restaurant that was acceptable was a salad of iceberg lettuce, a scattering of grated carrots and perhaps one cherry tomato. Russell decided to, in effect, skip lunch rather than compromise his diet. I decided I would rather do without the alleged health benefits of the diet than go hungry.

During the time we were on the diet, I became increasingly afraid that Russell's inflexibility about what he would eat would end up more damaging to his health than the cholesterol, and I was angry that he wouldn't see things my way. As we wandered through the ancient Egyptian exhibits and displays of purloined mummies on the lowest level of the museum, my anger, triggered by the salad incident, turned into words. The more I talked to him about it, the more upset and angry I got. I was startled and frightened by my intensity.

My tirade was unprecedented in all our many years together. By the time it was over, I figured that now Russell would leave me for sure. Neither of us had much experience with this kind of honesty. Russell was more optimistic about our marriage than I; but he felt backed into a corner and confused about how to take care of himself and me at the same time. He wasn't sure what to do.

Our marriage easily survived, both of us stronger and more resilient than we knew. Slowly we gained a new way to trust ourselves and each other at a fuller level of honesty. Today, we still don't raise our voices very much, but we squabble and fuss enough to make me laugh sometimes, remembering how restrained we used to be.

I practiced letting myself know what I wanted. I tried out getting what I wanted without guilt, without shame for either wanting or having. My first big experiment with having what I wanted was a trip above the sixty-sixth parallel, the Arctic Circle, the year after my father died.

I mentioned my interest in the far north to Carolyn Conger, who suggested that we head to northwestern Canada instead of Alaska. After a year of planning, Russell and I went to Inuvik in the Canadian Northwest Territories and then to the Yukon and Alaska. For me it was a dream trip. I justified the expense of the trip by telling myself that I was spending my inheritance. I loved the idea that my father was financing my trip.

During a layover in Seattle en route home, we checked our home phone messages, which had been difficult to do in the North. One of the messages was from Jeremy, who announced that his son had been born two days earlier. We were grandparents.

Later that summer, I went off to the Split Rock Arts Program in Minnesota and got addicted to bead-weaving. I had been making dolls out of socks stuffed with laundry lint and embellished with my mother's beads, which I'd found and taken after my father died. Someone suggested that the Split Rock program might include doll making, which turned out not to be so. However, Virginia Blakelock was teaching loom weaving with beads, a class which was suitable for a complete beginner like me.

I went out of curiosity more than interest. I went partly because Carolyn had suggested that I start doing things without Russell because I was so dependent on him, and because he wasn't in the least bit interested in beads. I went only to play, which felt decadent. I put aside the guilt that came up about my selfishness, played with tiny bits of glass for a week, and was entranced, perhaps for life.

I wasn't "fixed," but I was changing. Sometimes I got angry, and sometimes I was disappointed that the end of my father wasn't the end of challenges and difficulties. All along, I wanted to get to the Promised Land right away, without the long walk; but it wasn't for nothing that my ancestors had to take forty years to cover what is actually a fairly short distance. Like them, I had to wander the wastelands, discard the distractions, and get fed repeatedly on magic and miracles before I learned to trust the reality of my new experience. I wrote:

I wanted, after so much work, for my river to flow unimpeded, headlong into the sea!

By the end of the year my father died some changes were obvious. I wrote:

There is nowhere else to go but forward. For the first time I noticed that I really have gone too far to go back.

I confuse myself, still. If I did not confuse myself, what I would see in my heart is a freedom that seems reckless. If I was really not confused, I might see that it is not reckless at all.

What was going on during the years that followed my father's death was a paradigm change: not only my mistaken beliefs were changing, but also the very foundations upon which they were established. Like any other natural process, I vacillated back and forth between old ways and new, between catching a glimpse of what might be and retreating, sometimes frightened, sometimes shy, sometimes despairing, sometimes bold, often angry and just as often grateful. I wrote:

Yesterday I read about Robert Coles asking children what they might say to God. I thought, what I would (and could) say (daily, hourly, at every moment) is Yes. Yes. And again, Yes. And then, Thank You, and then, Yes, again. Yes. In my theology that is all that needs to be said. Anything else is commentary. Everything else is a reminder to say Yes.

The mistaken beliefs that pain and suffering were part of who I was were not so much altered as washed away. They had created an unnatural dam. I wrote:

There was an earthquake in my father's death and major aftershocks after my EMDR session and surgery. The dam is mostly gone. Water must flow if it is not frozen, and I am mostly not frozen any longer. Freedom flows like water. So far some of mine has flowed into pools of peacefulness, pockets of creativity, rivulets and cascades of imagination, pleasure and pain jumping in the waters like trout.

Along with freedom came passion. At the very beginning of my work with James I told him I wanted all of my life or nothing.

In my mid-fifties I wrote:

I am nearing the end-stage of my life with a greediness for life that is unprecedented. I want everything I can lay my metaphoric hands on. I am not afraid of the price. My fears are transitory; they will not stop the quest. I don't know how much I can have, but I'll take all I can get.

Freedom and passion created playfulness. Being serious and intellectual were always ways to keep safely away from spontaneity, when I might not be in enough control of myself. After my father was gone, I no longer had to concern myself as much with safety—I could allow myself to get distracted by beauty and magic; I could play.

At the end of the summer my father died, I dreamt of a living room with a most unusual fish tank setup. It went from floor to ceiling with an imperceptible, invisible wall. The effect was as if the fish were swimming in air. It was possible to put my fingers out for them to nibble. They were large tropical fish, colorful and delightful. At one point, one of them swam across the floor and went under a chair, as if it was hiding. I noticed in the relative darkness there that the edges of the fish were luminous.

Who, I wrote, *are these large, silent swimming parts of me, delightful and beautiful, separated in their proper life-giving element by only the thinnest barrier, and a luminous part whose ability to give off light isn't noticeable until it goes into hiding.*

If I glow like that then I will be easy enough to find. I think I may not be safe. But, then I think, I am not in any danger.

There is something very magical about this.

I played with beads. I discovered quickly that even though seed beads come in very inexpensive, very small containers, everything but the smallest project takes many containers. And then there are the qualities of the glass beyond color to consider: opaque, translucent, matte, transparent, silver-lined, various shapes, each creating somewhat different effects. And then, there are the myriad ways they combine and the many ways color and stitch make texture. And, then, there is just the way beads look under a well-lit magnifying glass.

I wove beads on a loom and off loom with peyote stitch and brick stitch. I went to Split Rock three more summers to learn single-needle, right-angle weave from David Chatt. I loved how right-angle weave made textures, how the underneath beads played with the top ones. I loved handling the beads and how they glittered in the strong work light I used. I loved my growing proficiency. I, the queen of impatience, discovered that I could be patient. I loved how my beadwork didn't really matter to anyone but me.

The critical part of me would fret from time to time that I wasn't attending to other people enough, that I had no right to spend so much time just amusing myself; but that belief was changing, too.

Once, I dreamt about a child who runs away from me. I thought I had to tell him that he had to stop playing and do something more serious and purposeful. But he knew that his purpose was playing, so he ran off to play somewhere else where he would be uninterrupted.

DANCING ENDS AND MEDITATION INCREASES

When we returned years before to Naperville from Palo Alto, I promised myself I would never have to take a dance class again for all kinds of reasons. As much as I enjoyed dancing, it was rare that I could keep Miss McRae's critical energy entirely contained and not let it damage my pleasure in movement. Some kinds of movement, especially in jazz class, were upsetting because they were so sexually suggestive. The fact was that the pleasure of dancing had rarely compensated for the effort it took to keep my emotional life steady at the same time. In 1981, I was thirty-eight and getting old for a dancer. Besides, I was going to be busy with the doctoral program that I was just entering.

After we returned to Illinois and after briefly teaching modern dance in a lovely little studio over the Lantern bar in downtown Naperville, I settled on teaching yoga. I called my class Yonah's Yoga. I said it was kosher because it was ritually butchered, which is to say that it had only a loose connection to classical yoga, with a healthy dose of modern dance, tai'chi, and pure invention.

I also taught my yoga group everything I learned from Carolyn that I understood well enough to pass along. We played with making energy balls. We did guided imagery for healing. We did all kinds of meditations. There was always meditation. For some years, those few minutes I meditated with my yoga group were almost the only meditation I did, except for a few days with Carolyn in January. My meditation practice was a very thin thread, indeed, but a thread that didn't break.

In 1990, inspired by Carolyn's retreat, my friend and colleague, Virginia, began a drop-in meditation group on Friday evenings in her office in a big, expanded house on Jefferson Street in downtown Naperville. On the first floor there were boutiques, gift shops, and a restaurant that specialized in dainty sandwiches on crustless bread, salads, and lovely, rich desserts. Small offices filled the second floor. Spirituality filled Virginia's office. Russell and

I went almost every week. Several other people came regularly; others came and went.

With Virginia's group my meditation spread out and strengthened. By the middle of the nineties, I was meditating most days, if not all.

DEPRESSION AND GOD

The Rabbi Israel Baal Shem Tov, the great eighteenth-century Jewish mystic, was an insightful psychologist as well as mystic. He wrote, "This is a major principle in the service of the Creator...avoid depression as much as possible." (*Tzava'at Harivash*, 1998, p. 37)

    I was all too well acquainted with how depression creates marvelous self-absorption. Worse yet, depression so easily leads to despair, that impossible state where none of the light or love in the world can penetrate.

    The Baal Shem Tov also taught that one was to serve God with joy. Had I known that in the fall of 1974, when I was hospitalized, my total joylessness would have only been one more piece of evidence that I was failing as a human being. That I know it now is the great miracle of my life.

THE VASHTI GROUP

In the spring of 1997, Marilyn Scott, then the minister of the Naperville Church of the Brethren, sent out an invitation to all the female clergy in town to come to a meeting to discuss creating a women's worship service especially for disaffected women. Our congregation had a male rabbi who offered me the opportunity to attend. We met at least several times a month in Marilyn's church on west Jefferson Street. Within a short time, the group membership settled to three Church of the Brethren ministers, one Unitarian minister, a former nun who was still active in her church, and me.

We called ourselves the Vashti Group after the queen in the Biblical book of Esther who refuses to be made into a plaything by her king. She was a woman who stood up for herself.

Although we met for a couple of years, we never produced the service that had been the dream of the originator of the group. Instead, we had wonderful conversations about the nature of worship, the nature of human relationship to God, and the universality of our traditions, as well as their singularities. In time, I realized that I didn't care much whether we ever produced an event, but I cared deeply about the conversations we had. Every topic was interesting to me; what I heard almost always left me thoughtful.

I remember leaving the church one very clear, early spring evening, the full moon high in the sky, the air cold and refreshing. I was almost in tears. I loved talking about spirituality and worship with other people who cared about those things as much as I did. I'd never had an ongoing opportunity to do so like this one. But, I lamented later to Russell, where are the Jews having this conversation?

JEWISH MEDITATION

For many years, Russell and I had been getting catalogues from the Omega Institute, a center for spiritual and personal growth in upstate New York. In 1997, we noticed that they were scheduling a full week in August as a spirituality week, including David and Shoshana Cooper teaching Jewish meditation. Six other teachers from other traditions, including Catholic, Buddhist, and Native American, also taught that week.

Less than a year before, I received David Cooper's book, *The Heart of Stillness*, as a gift for joining a book club. In it, he wrote about his decades-long meditation practice and discussed the process of spiritual growth, its attendant problems, and likely outcomes. I was particularly struck with the similarities between meditation practice and the kind of deep psychotherapy I was doing with James and that I was practicing with my own clients. These were the kinds of details I had hoped to find as a young woman, but the books had yet to be written. When I discovered Cooper, I quickly bought his other books and read them all.

Cooper also wrote extensively about silent meditation. I'd never experienced extended meditative silence before and found the idea very intriguing. After I saw his name on the Omega roster, Russell and I decided to go.

Each day started with a silent sitting practice, open to everyone on campus, in a very simple, beautiful meditation building on top of a hill on the Omega grounds.

With the Coopers we learned and practiced a lot about meditation. Each morning, we alternated between a simple chant and ten minutes of silence, for each of about a dozen parts of the traditional Jewish morning service. We practiced the very esoteric, complex Abulafian chants, based on combining all of the vowels, one at a time, with each of the Hebrew letters of the *tetragrammaton* (the four letter, unpronounceable Name of God). There were many questions and many useful answers. However, we didn't spend any nonmeditation time in silence, which was a disappointment.

One afternoon we paced the great lawn in the middle of the Omega campus, talking out loud to God, in the manner described by Reb Nachman of Bratzlov. I cried much of the time walking back and forth on the grass and asked God to care for my deceased parents, as I clearly couldn't.

We were there for six days and five nights. By the last day, I finally relaxed. I thought that was a very long time to calm down given that I was meditating so much.

I mentioned this to James when I returned. He asked if I'd ever considered medication. I replied that no one ever asked me. I rarely acknowledged out loud to him or anyone else how anxious I felt. In the past that would have been equivalent to announcing that I really was crazy. This time I made an appointment with a psychiatrist who agreed that I was a good candidate for anxiety medication. The first drug she recommended was an old reliable remedy that took several weeks to get established in my body. We experimented with gradually increasing the dosage until we found the right one. With the proper dosage I felt calmer than I could ever remember. The difference was so pronounced at first, that I felt as if someone had their hands resting on my shoulders, literally holding down the anxious energy. It was wonderful.

Back in Naperville after studying with the Coopers, my meditation practice deepened and expanded. Establishing a strong, daily meditation practice was an important sign that I really was healing.

Once, at Carolyn's retreat, when I was full of images of dead babies, I said I no longer had a spiritual practice. Now, I understood that her contradiction then was to teach me that the dark time wasn't an end or a failure but a passage.

Russell and I both came home from New York with a fuller understanding of the meditative process and were eager to have more. Not long after our return, we got a flier announcing a Jewish meditation conference in Los Angeles in late December. We quickly signed up.

The workshop at Omega had about forty-five participants. The conference in Los Angeles had ten times as many attendees. The presenters included most of the major Jewish meditation teachers in the United States, including the Coopers. I'd already read Ron Kamenetz's book, *The Jew in the Lotus*, about an incredible meeting in 1990, between the Dalai Lama and a group of Jewish leaders, some of whom were at the Los Angeles conference. In his next book, *Stalking Elijah*, Kamenetz interviewed many of the meditation teachers who were at the conference. Just to be in the high school auditorium with them and the other four hundred fifty people was exciting.

The plain cheese on white bread that passed for lunch was poor, but the spiritual fare was rich and completely nourishing.

In the months that followed, I decided the time had come to teach Jewish meditation. I had been meditating on and off for over twenty years. My meditation practice was the strongest it had ever been, especially now that my perfectionist voice had settled down. I'd been teaching meditation and relaxation techniques for over fifteen years. With good teachers, I now understood Jewish mysticism well enough to introduce others to the subject. I also was interested in teaching more and doing counseling less.

In addition to meditating more, Russell and I also added to our Jewish spiritual practice. We began to take on the observance of more of the *mitzvot* (commandments) as a spiritual discipline. I stopped working for money on the Sabbath, and we became more scrupulous about keeping kosher. My friend Susan and I decided to study Hebrew together. Even my rudimentary Hebrew skills gave me a deeper understanding of Jewish ideas.

By the spring of 1998, all of the summer programs had sent out their schedules for the coming season. I signed on for another bead-weaving class at Split Rock, and Russell and I registered for a week in July at Elat Chayyim, a Jewish Retreat Center about sixty miles east of Omega, in the Berkshire Mountains of Massachusetts. The main attraction that week was the presence of Rabbi Zalman Schacter-Shalomi and his wife, Eve Ilsen, teaching about the Song of Songs. I'd heard him speak on several other occasions and had read some of his work. He is considered by many to be one of the most important Jewish spiritual teachers of our time. He is also the founder of the Jewish Renewal movement, a kind of neo-Hasidic movement fond of fervor and ecstasy. His teaching tries to imbue modern Judaism with that fervor but, it seemed to me, often at the expense of something deeper and more grounded. Or perhaps, I'd had enough intensity and wanted a quieter path. Schacter-Shalomi's and his wife's teachings were interesting, but did not touch me.

Another teacher that week was Rabbi David Wolfe-Blank, an Orthodox rabbi who had migrated into Schacter-Shalomi's circle. He came to Elat Chayyim to teach kabbalistic meditation. It was the word, "meditation," that attracted me to his workshop; we knew nothing at all about him. It was a very mixed experience.

Although at least a hundred and fifty people went to hear Schacter-Shalomi in the morning, the afternoon attendance at Wolfe-Blank's presentation was closer to fifteen. A few of the afternoon participants had obviously been studying the more esoteric aspects of kabbalah and kabbalistic meditation. When they got into conversation with Wolfe-Blank, I couldn't understand anything they were talking about. In fact, the entire workshop was beyond me. I even skipped one afternoon, deciding that I needed a nap more than I needed to try to figure out what they were discussing.

And yet, there was something going on, something profound and important. In a way that is almost impossible to describe, Wolfe-Blank, himself, was the teaching as well as the teacher. In some regard the information and ideas he was trying to impart were far less meaningful than the way he stood, the tone of his voice, the color of the shirt he put on that morning.

Russell agreed there was something about his manner. My physicist husband is no fan of the vague and metaphoric language of mysticism, yet he said Wolfe-Blank seemed to glow.

One afternoon, Wolfe-Blank and I walked together as we returned to the main building after his class. He fretted about his lack of skill as a presenter. He was right about his lack of skill; yet, he was teaching something else that wasn't on the syllabus, something that required no group or teaching skills.

He emanated a sense of serenity and wonder, which underlay even his fretting. That serenity and wonder seemed embedded in a kind of devotion to Jewish life that permeated everything about him. He seemed to be the very embodiment of *devekut,* the Jewish mystical goal of attachment to God. I had never met anyone like him before.

On Friday night, he led the evening Sabbath services. Wolfe-Blank conducted services with a look of great happiness and contentment because Sabbath had finally arrived and there was nothing more to do than rejoice. For the first time I understood what was meant by Sabbath joy. He didn't have to stir up ecstasy by beating the drums harder or shaking the tambourines faster. He was completely captivated by the incredible beauty of the Sabbath celebration. It was as if the extra angels, who are said to join the community on Friday night, had truly come to fill the room with their portion of holy light, encouraging all of us to do the same.

When we left, I felt a total confirmation of my longing to find my spiritual place in Judaism. It was another piece in place to make me whole.

Six weeks later, David Wolfe-Blank was killed in an automobile accident, in which his wife and young daughter were badly, but not catastrophically injured. To me, he seemed like an angel whose wings had just touched me as he flew by.

The next summer, Russell and I were at a very large Jewish Renewal conference, the Aleph Kallah, in Corvallis, Oregon. A group of about fifty people, many of whom were from the congregation that Wolfe-Blank led in Seattle, gathered on the lawn for an impromptu memorial service. Some people had known him well. Some, like myself, had only barely met him. Some knew him only from correspondence. Again and again, people talked about how he worried about some variation of the "I'm not a very good presenter" story, the same one he had told me. Almost everyone who spoke told of Wolfe-Blank's profound influence, because of who he was more than because of the words he spoke. I wondered how many of us there that day had harassed ourselves about our imperfections, when what mattered to the people around us was something else entirely.

Later, I imagined asking him what I should do. I imagined him telling me to continue his work. I couldn't do that literally, because, for starters, I couldn't begin to duplicate his education. What I could do was to be as fully myself as was possible for me to be and to teach what is mine to teach.

The next spring, in 1999, we finally tasted a weekend of silence at Elat Chayyim. There, the principal teacher was Sylvia Boorstein. Boorstein is an observant, if not Orthodox Jew, and a practicing Buddhist meditator.

This time we maintained silence from Friday evening until late Sunday morning. When the retreat was over, I wanted more. Being in a group of people who were present in proximity, but not interacting with each other was wonderful. There was no question of whether I was being attentive enough to other people and their needs when the instructions were to avoid interactions with each other as much as possible.

Being around Russell, but with both of us agreeing to not talk or interact with each other, taught me that much of what we talk about was unnecessary. In silence, I was much less likely to concern myself with whether he was satisfied or content. I could let go of worrying about whether I was paying enough attention to him when I was instructed to not pay any attention to him at all.

There was a freedom in silence that I hadn't anticipated.

A few months later, in the summer of 1999, Russell and I went to the Aleph Kallah, which I have already mentioned. About nine hundred Jews of every kind and description came together to study, sing, meditate, pray, and play together. The gathering took place at an Oregon state university and took up most of the campus. There were morning prayers, yoga, short presentations (including one I did on some of the spiritual outcomes of recovering from incest), week-long workshops, evening meditation, singing, evening prayers, and drumming late into the night, thankfully some place that was inaudible from the dorm rooms we were in.

We learned ancient Spanish-Jewish melodies and chants from Cantors Richard Kaplan and Michael Ziegler each morning. I thought, *what could be better than singing all morning?* Every day, the music class grew bigger as word spread about what a good time we were having.

In the afternoon, we had another opportunity to learn more about Jewish meditation. This time the teacher was Avram Davis, one of the cofounders, along with Nan Gefen, of Chochmat HaLev Jewish Meditation Center in Berkeley, California. Avram was naturally excited about the Jewish Path, talking about it with an infectious energy. I especially loved his teaching that wherever I was on the spiritual path was a valid place to be and a place from which I could always go further. He taught that there was no inflexible one right way to open to God, but many. While not a rabbi, he was a scholar of Jewish mysticism and passionate about teaching. I ended each day feeling full and wanting even more.

CHOCHMAT HALEV

Among Avram's handouts was a brochure announcing a three-year program at Chochmat HaLev to train Jewish meditation teachers. The deadline for applications was less than two months away.

A few years earlier, I looked into becoming a rabbi, but it would have required about six years of being a student full time, more work than my doctorate, and at least one year in residence in another state. I had no interest in leading a congregation; I basically just wanted to study. Becoming a rabbi would have been too much work.

The meditation teacher's training program seemed to fit all of my requirements: access to teachers and texts without the demands of a full academic program; immersion in a subject that fascinated me; support for the teaching I was already doing; and most of all, a community of people to do this with.

I applied with trepidation. I'd been meditating off and on for over twenty years but still considered myself a beginner. My history was disturbing, to me at least. Surely they would be swamped with applicants far more qualified than I.

On the other hand, I was already doing most of what they said they would require of their students: I was studying Hebrew (albeit at a very slow pace); I participated in regular Torah study at our synagogue; I was already teaching meditation and would continue with or without the additional training.

Happily, I was accepted. My excitement was a bold sign that the direction of my life was shifting from looking backward to recover from my past toward seeking out the next step forward. From about this time, I no longer saw James on a regular basis. The healing process was largely complete, with only occasional straggling matters to clear up.

The teachers training program began with a week-long retreat in California, a few days after the turn of the millennium. For the first time in almost twenty years, I chose to miss Carolyn's retreat. Before the training program began, I spent several days visiting Nili, who lived near the retreat center, bolstering my courage to go spend a week with more than forty strangers. In a beaded bag, I carried blessings and expressions of love and confidence from my recovery friends, tangible links to people I knew were safe.

On a Sunday afternoon, Nili drove me up into the mountains, just west of where she lived in San Jose, to a Catholic retreat center where the first week of the program took place. The center was embedded in a heavily wooded area about half way up the mountain. January in northern California can be chilly and wet, but I remember getting out of Nili's car into sunshine that afternoon, nervous and eager, not unlike a child going to school for the first time.

I was certainly not new to going to school, to big endeavors, to meeting new people, and I most certainly wasn't naïve. My attitudes and beliefs about myself were new. I came to this experience fresh and unafraid in an unprecedented way— more present and far less shameful than at any time I could remember.

My nervousness calmed quickly as we spent the first few days getting acquainted. We were a mix of Jews from very Orthodox to relatively nonobservant and from very knowledgeable to some just beginning their serious Jewish studies. Some were fluent in Hebrew and others, like myself, barely literate. Some had been meditating for decades, others for only a short time. One man had converted to Judaism only the month before. Among us were several physicians, fewer therapists than I expected, a fireman, business people, four lapsed lawyers, one new rabbi, one student rabbi, and a woman studying to become a cantor. We were young adults, middle-aged, and entering our elder years. As I came to learn in time, I wasn't the only one with an incestuous history.

We all had in common an intense desire to study Jewish mysticism and meditation. Our desires to teach varied greatly, but were enough to get us into the program. Everyone was as interested in talking about God as I. Here was the group I longed for three or four years before as I walked out of the Naperville Church of the Brethren. At this retreat and at each that followed I felt like a child who had been shown the sweets table at a banquet and told I could have as much as I could carry and, when I was ready, could go back for more. I was happy.

I was happy and very busy. In February 2000, after about a year and a half of preparation, my friend, Susan, and I celebrated our belated Bat Mitzvahs, which girls normally celebrate when they are about thirteen years old. We had been studying Hebrew together for a while, visiting and laughing more than seriously studying, although we kept making some progress. One day, in the summer of 1998, I mentioned to our rabbi that we wanted an opportunity to read from the Torah.

"Oh," he said, "you want to celebrate your Bat Mitzvah. Fine!"

That wasn't at all what we meant, because in our congregation celebrating a Bat Mitzvah usually meant learning to lead most of the Saturday morning service, reading a part of the Prophetic literature, delivering a teaching, as well as reading from Torah. We were not feeling that ambitious!

I was startled by our rabbi's suggestion. However, without much thought, I replied, "Sure."

Susan had given this idea even less thought than I, but since I said yes, she did, too.

So, here we were at the end of February 2000, ready to do all we were required to do. We had joked between us that, unlike the usual thirteen-year-old Bar or Bat Mitzvah celebrant, we had no mommies to plan and produce our party. Susan was the director of our synagogue pre-school, so she invited all of her families and all of their children. The presence of so many little people and their eager energy ensured that the event would not get too serious. We both invited lots of friends and family. As was expected, some people came who were not specifically invited, simply because it was Sabbath.

Susan was sick that day, running a fever and operating on adrenaline. For me, the day was a celebration of the fact that I had seen my recovery through to unimaginable results; that I found joy in my life, not just struggle; that life was good, and not just an endurance trial.

At the end, we invited everyone into the social hall for lunch. Susan had made sure that there was macaroni and cheese and other foods that would appeal to the children. The adults got to it before some of the children had a chance. Not having enough of the old-time comfort food was the only mistake of a day that was a triumph for both of us.

I was busy with other, ordinary joys as well. Jeremy married Cheryl in a judge's chambers at the end of 1998, after the birth of their second son. Jonathan and Judy had a big, complicated Jewish wedding in April 1999. And Sonia married a Frenchman, Olivier, in November at Chicago's City Hall, in what surely was the shortest marriage ceremony I ever witnessed. For their first anniversary, Jeremy and Cheryl had a church wedding ceremony. Twenty-month old Tyler in his tiny tuxedo outlasted many of the adults on the dance floor. Sonia and Olivier had a formal Jewish wedding and celebration on a hot, muggy July day in 2000, eight months after they were legally married.

That was a lot of weddings and marriages in a short time. What mattered to me then and now is that all of the commotion was the ordinary stuff of life. It was just what was going on in my family, mostly uncontaminated by my past.

Ordinary life was a miracle. Ordinary life is a miracle.

LABYRINTH

In March 2001, Russell and I did an unstructured silent retreat at the Cenacle Retreat Center in Warrenville, Illinois. On a chilly afternoon, I walked the Cenacle's outside labyrinth, as old and new themes walked the path with me. Afterwards I wrote:

I am angry. I am thankful for the breath of life in me.

I am impatient. I am thankful for the breath of life in me.

I walked the labyrinth in rhythm to Modah ani, *the morning blessing that offers thanks for the breath of life in me, for the simple fact that I am alive.*

I sent blessings to my friends who are sick or injured. Modah ani.

I sent blessings to my children and their spouses and to my grandchildren.

I thought of the horses and the very shallow river. Now it seems clear that this was a moment of enlightenment that I was too young to understand when it happened; a moment of wonder and wholeness that I never forgot and was free to experience again.

Modah ani, *into the middle of the path. A pause, and back out again. At one point I wondered how much longer until the end.*

Where am I? Modah ani.

I thought about impatience. I thought, I have no time. I thought, I have all the time in the world. Death will come when death will come. In the meantime, my days are endless. Modah ani.

In the middle of the labyrinth I thought about being in a hurry to get on with things. Then I thought, what is there to do in a labyrinth but go in or go out! What does it matter if I go quickly or slowly or both? What does it matter if I step across the lines and the leaves? What does it matter? Modah ani.

I thought, The Source of All is never missing. It is always only a matter of paying attention. It is a matter of choosing not to be distracted. It is always a matter of choice. Modah ani.

I set before you life and death. Therefore, choose life that you may live. If I have not chosen to be present, to be in my life, then life is death, gray and silent in the sunshine and bird song. Modah ani.

The Holy One is omnipresent, never more than a blink of recognition away, ready to bestow all of God's gifts to anyone whose heart asks for them. Modah ani.

The Source of Strength is mighty, indeed, but powerless to choose for us. In arrogance and in wisdom, we choose all the same. In full awareness or unconscious or indifferent, we choose. Modah ani.

I choose to choose life. And when I slip into choosing death once again, so old and so familiar, I choose to make the life choice again. And again and again and again until my days have reached the end of the horizon and there are no choices left to make. Modah ani.

I understand that opening to The Most Trustworthy is about trust, all about trust. What I have learned is that trust, too, is a choice. What does it matter if I trust The Magnificent to be there or not? The difference is in me, not in the Holy One. How do I know this? I know this. Modah Ani.

The task is to continually make the choice, forever if need be. My days are few. My days are endless, beyond my farthest sight. I have an endless number of days until they end, endless opportunities to choose life until there is no more life to choose. Modah ani.

To trust or not to trust is a distraction. Shall I step forward? Shall I step back? Shall I step into life with its terrible beauty? Shall I back away into the gray world of death? The path remains the same whether I debate it or not. Modah ani.

The debate does not create new directions. There is only forward or backward, in or out, conscious or unconscious, present or elsewhere. That is all. For all of our elaborate complexity, the path remains as it is, simple, plain, indestructible, unalterable. MODAH ANI!

After I learned to not be afraid of myself, or my story, I learned to stop distracting myself with suffering and dying. After I recovered from the shock of committing myself to living, my life grew easier and then it became ordinary. There was and still is plenty of drama, challenges, and excitement of varying kinds. There still are tender places that smart when they are bumped; sometimes they are very painful, indeed. There was and still is plenty to learn.

My life is easy to the extent that I have corrected the mistakes I made as I tried to understand everything and control the world. Everything is easier without the shrieks and howls of mistaken shame bouncing back and forth in my brain. I am much more patient without the mistaken prodding of perfectionism. Mistaken beliefs no longer complicate my life. Some are no longer relevant: I know deeply now that I am no longer a helpless victim. And some were never true in the first place: I know now that I don't have to sacrifice my life and liveliness to save anyone else.

My life is full of mundane matters such as pointing out the full moon to Russell through the trees outside of our bedroom windows or listening to my sons and daughter talk about the challenges of their jobs and children and trying to make ends meet, or my deciding which beads to use for my next project. My friendships are deep and loving.

I don't worry much about my children and grandchildren. I know they will make choices, which will not always be what I would have made. Do we not all stumble around only doing the best we can at the moment? I don't have to save them, either.

I have stood again in the supreme silence of the far North and have known in my bones that in this wondrous world I am truly nothing. Knowing that, I can acknowledge that I have importance in my unique time and place, among the people I know.

Years ago, Carolyn Conger said I didn't have to do any thing. In that holy freedom, I can pay attention and notice the next right thing for me to do.

I'm very busy with many things. The details don't matter, whether it is beads or books, or whether I am retired, or how much time I spend singing. I still meditate almost every day. My current mantra (of course, Jewish meditation includes Hebrew mantras) translates as "Blessed Source of Compassion, Ruler of the All." Compassion is what I want in my heart. I also want never to forget that I will never be the Ruler, never be the Master. I write in my journal sometimes, but not often. Many mornings, I have nothing much to write about. I try not to struggle with very much. I take my learning when it approaches me. I teach what I've learned.

What matters the most for me is that I catch the remnants of my mistakes before they can ruin a day. What matters is that when I forget what has taken so long to learn, when I slip into the slavery of sourness or grandiosity, that I remember that true freedom is sweet and simple.

WORKS CITED

Berlin, A. and Brettler, M. Z., editors, Jewish Publication Society, translators. *The Jewish Study Bible*. New York, NY: Oxford University Press, 2004. (translation, 1985, 1999).

Davis, A. and Gefen, N. "Foundational Reminders" (working paper), Chochmat HaLev Jewish Meditation Center, Berkeley, CA, 2001.

Goldin, J. "Introduction," in S. Y. Agnon, *Days of Awe*. New York, NY: Schocken Books, 1975.

Klem, Y. *The Blessings Book*. New York, NY: Authors Choice Press, 2008.

Kol Haneshamah:Mahzor Leyamim Nora'im (Prayerbook for the Days of Awe). Elkins Park, PA: The Reconstructionist Press, 1999.

Schochet, J. I. *Tzava'at Harivash: the Testament of Rabbi Israel Baal Shem Tov*. Brooklyn, NY: Kehot Publication Society, 1998.

ACKNOWLEDGMENT OF PERMISSION TO QUOTE

From *Kol Haneshamah: Mahzor Leyamim Nora'im,*, p. 730, commentary by David Teutsch, The Reconstructionist Press, 101 Greenwood Ave., Ste. 430, Jenkintown, PA 19046, Phone: 215-885-5601, Fax: 215-885-5603, email: press@jrf.org.

From *Tzava'at Harivash: The Testament of Rabbi Israel Baal Shem Tov*, p. 55 quotation "if…you will… think of the Supernal World." Also, p. 37, "This is a major principle in the service of the Creator." Kehot Publication Society, 770 Eastern Parkway, Brooklyn, New York, 11213, Phone: 718-774-4000, Fax: 718-774-2718, email: kehot@chabad.org

ACKNOWLEDGMENTS

This book has been a lifetime in coming. The people I needed to help me take the next step invariably offered their assistance, right up to the final edits. First were my teachers who taught me the basics about living a full life: Phyllis, Ray, Betty, Carolyn, James, and Jeannie, and especially my mother-in-law Mollie, who loved me without reservation. At Chochmat HaLev Jewish Meditation Center, in Berkeley, California, Avram and Nan, and the teachers they assembled for the course on training Jewish meditation teachers, were my guides into Jewish mysticism, which enlarged my life, giving it a richness I'd only heard about in other people's stories.

Many people read various renditions of *A Long Journey to Joy* in the many years it took to produce, and provided me with essential and invaluable feedback. Joshua and Linda, in particular, were insightful in their comments and suggestions about how to make the work stronger and more readable. Other readers included my recovery sisters and other colleagues and friends. All of my readers strengthened my confidence that this project was worth doing, and if I only worked out this or that problem, it would be worth reading as well. I am profoundly grateful that they read my work so thoroughly and thoughtfully.

At the beginning, throughout, and at the end I have been and continue to be beyond grateful for the support of my life partner, Russell. I have often thought that marrying him was the single best thing I ever did. In addition to being my mainstay for over forty-five years, he has always been my first and last reader, my best editor, and the sharpest challenger of my thinking and ideas.